1981

PAR FOR THE COURSE

Par for the

A GOLFER'S

ANTHOLOGY

for the

Course

edited by Robert Cromie

THE MACMILLAN COMPANY, NEW YORK

Second Printing 1964

The Macmillan Company, New York
Collier-Macmillan Canada Ltd., Toronto, Ontario

Library of Congress catalog card number 63-16100

Printed in the United States of America

ACKNOWLEDGMENTS

The author wishes to thank the following for their kind permission to include in this anthology previously copyrighted material:

Appleton-Century, New York, for a poem entitled "The Land of Par" from *Songs of the Stalwart* by Grantland Rice. Copyright 1917 by D. Appleton & Co. "The Perfect Golfer" from *Locker Room Ballads* by John E. Baxter. Copyright 1923 by D. Appleton & Co. Pages from *Dormie One and Other Golf Stories* by Holworthy Hall. Copyright 1917 by The Century Co.

The Atlanta Journal, Atlanta, Georgia, for "The Unofficial King of Scotland" by O. B. Keeler, *The Atlanta Journal* of July 15, 1927.

A. S. Barnes & Company, Inc. (including Publications of Thomas Yoseloff), New York, for "Let Golf Play You" from *Love That Golf* by Don Herold (1952) and for an extract from *Championship Golf* by Babe Zaharias (1948).

Ernest Benn Limited, London, as successors to T. Fisher Unwin, for extracts from *My Fifty Years of Golf: Memories* by Andra Kirkaldy, as told to Clyde Foster (1921).

The Bobbs-Merrill Company, Inc., Indianapolis, Indiana, for pages from *All Things Considered* by Howard Vincent O'Brien. Copyright 1948 by The Bobbs-Merrill Company, Inc.

T. Warner Laurie, Ltd.–The Bodley Head Ltd., London, for a paragraph from *The Art of Golf* by Joshua Taylor, 1912.

Chilton Books, Philadelphia and New York, for pages from *The Autobiography of an Average Golfer* by O. B. Keeler. Copyright 1925, 1933 by O. B. Keeler.

Country Life Limited, London, for the piece "Is Golf Funny?" from *Golf Addicts on Parade* by George Houghton, published by them in 1959. An extract from *Putting* by Jack White, published in 1921.

Robert Cromie for a verse called "Sorry, Baby, But" from Postscripts, the *Saturday Evening Post*, April 11, 1959, © by Robert Cromie.

Sir Robin Darwin and Mills and Boon Ltd., London, for extracts from

v

J. B. Lippincott Company, Philadelphia and London, for two paragraphs from *Golf* by Cecil Leitch, published by J. B. Lippincott, London, 1922.

David McKay Company, Inc., New York, for an extract from *Golf* by Henry Longhurst, 1937.

The Macmillan Company, New York, for excerpts from *Modern Golf* by Harold H. Hilton. Copyright 1922 by The Macmillan Company.

Macmillan & Co. Ltd., St. Martin's Street, London, for passages from *The Happy Golfer* by Henry Leach (1914).

Reg Manning for "Golf's Siren Song" and "Woodcraft for Golfers" from his *From Tee to Cup* (Reganson, Phoenix, Arizona, 1954).

Methuen & Co. Ltd., London, for "The Complete Golfer" by Harry Vardon from *Concerning Caddies*. Extracts from *The Spirit of the Links* by Henry Leach.

Frederick Muller Ltd., London, for "The Freemasonry of Golf" by Henry Leach from *In Praise of Golf*, edited by Webster Evans and Tom Scott, published in 1950.

John Murray, London, for pages from *The Last of the Empresses* by Daniele Varé, 1947, and John Murray, London, and Houghton Mifflin Co., Boston, for the poem "Seaside Golf" by John Betjeman from his *Collected Poems*.

The New York Times Company, New York, for an extract entitled "A Remarkable Woman" from *Sports of the Times* by Arthur Daley, September 30, 1956. Copyright © by The New York Times Company.

Mr. Francis Ouimet for two extracts from his *A Game of Golf: A Book of Reminiscence*: "The Open Championship of 1913" and "A St. Andrew's Card," published originally by Houghton Mifflin Company, Boston, 1932.

Popular Publications Inc., New York, for "Gallery Shy" by William Campbell Gault from *The Argosy Book of Sports Stories*. Copyright 1954 by Popular Publications, Inc.

Prentice-Hall, Inc., Englewood Cliffs, New Jersey, for an extract from *Thirty Years of Championship Golf* by Gene Sarazen. © 1950 by Prentice-Hall, Inc. Extract from *Are Golfers Human?* by Robinson Murray. © 1951 by Prentice-Hall, Inc. "Slamming Suki Sukiyuki" by Ted Barnett from *Fun in the Rough* from *Golf Digest*, edited by Howard Gill. © 1957 by Prentice-Hall, Inc.

The Reilly & Lee Company, Chicago, for "The Lay of the Troubled Golfer" from *Collected Verse* by Edgar A. Guest. Copyright 1934 by The Reilly & Lee Company.

Mrs. Catharine Holis Rice, New York, and Mrs. Fred Butler, Honolulu (the author's widow and daughter, respectively), for the following three pieces by the late Grantland Rice, © Grantland Rice: "Keep Your Eye on the Ball," a page of verse from *Fifty Years of American Golf*, edited by H. B. Martin, Dodd, Mead & Company, New York (1936). "The Fabulous Commodore Heard," an article from *The Complete Golfer*, edited by Herbert Warren Wind, Simon & Schuster, Inc., New York (1954). Lines from "Any Golf Championship" included in *Wake Up the Echoes,* edited by Bob Cooke, Hanover House, New York (1956).

Charles Scribner's Sons, New York, for "Hole Eight" from *Nine Holes of Golf,* pp. 79–85, by Royal Cortissoz (1922).

Seeley Service & Co. Ltd., London, for an extract from "In Middle Age" by Bernard Darwin, which appeared in *Golf* and *Anthology of Sporting Prose and Verse,* edited by Eric Parker (Vol. XII), both in their Lonsdale Library.

Simon and Schuster, Inc., New York, for portions of "St. Andrews: The Cradle of Golf" from *The Gilded Age of Sport* by Herbert Warren Wind, Copyright 1950 by Herbert Warren Wind. Excerpts from *A New Way to Better Golf* by Rex Beach, Copyright 1932 and 1960 by Alex J. Morrison (Simon and Schuster, Inc., 1932).

W. A. Wilde Company, Natick, Massachusetts, for an extract from *Penguin Persons and Peppermints* by Walter P. Eaton, 1922.

Willis Kingsley Wing as agent for Mr. Graves, for three paragraphs from *Candid Caddies* by Charles Graves and Henry Longhurst, Copyright by Charles Graves, published by Gerald Duckworth & Co. Ltd., London, 1935.

P. G. Wodehouse for "Afforestation" by the late A. E. Wodehouse, published in a collection entitled *Fireside Book of Humorous Poetry,* edited by William Cole (1959) published by Simon and Schuster, Inc., New York.

P. G. Wodehouse and his New York agents, Scott Meredith Literary Agency, Inc., for "Ordeal by Golf," Copyright 1910, 1919, 1922, 1923, 1924, 1938, 1947, 1948, 1949, 1950, 1951, 1952 by P. G. Wodehouse; and Messrs. Herbert Jenkins Ltd., London, for the same piece from their edition of *Wodehouse on Golf.*

The World Publishing Company for "Anyone for Golf?" from *How Much Is That in Dollars?* by Art Buchwald, Copyright © 1961 by Art Buchwald.

Chicago Tribune for an extract from "In the Wake of the News" by Robert Cromie which appeared in their August 29, 1957, issue.

AUTHOR'S
INTRODUCTION

I remember the first time I hit a golf ball. It was at the Palmer Park course in Detroit, and my drive off No. 1 tee started out splendidly, rising with lovely power, only to swoop into the woods and vanish as the result of a slice which, it turned out, was to remain my constant companion for years. In fact, it still returns from time to time for an unwelcome visit.

That was in 1930, give or take a year, and I have been golfing ever since, with the exception of three and a half years during World War II when I was overseas as a correspondent. Even in those lost times I could have been practising, I suppose. But I lacked the wit of one of the printers for the Chicago Tribune, who, during that same war, showed up in New Guinea (an area singularly lacking in golfing facilities) complete with battle gear and golf clubs. Nor did I have the ingenuity of Patrick (Packey) Walsh, youngest of the famed Chicago family of golf professionals, who gave lessons to fellow GIs somewhere in the South Pacific with the aid of a tree branch crudely fashioned into the shape of a golf club.

But that is neither here nor there. I am presenting my own credentials as a card-carrying hacker and golf enthusiast in order to explain my interest in gathering this collection of writings about the world's most fascinating sport.

Naturally, after so long a time, I have some shining memories of my generally undistinguished links' career, some stray pennons of glory which somehow attached themselves to my game.

There was, for instance, the hole-in-one at Sportsman's Golf Club near Northbrook, resulting from a beautifully hit three-iron shot into a strong wind, which hooked in quite professional fashion onto the sixth green of the No. 2 course, then ran like a frightened ferret into the hole. I cherish a couple of eagles, too, although I've always been suspicious of the announced yardage in both cases, and I recall, as from a fading dream, the 48-38 I somehow put together on Medinah No. 3, a legendary layout respectfully known as The Monster, where Cary Middlecoff won the 1949 National Open crown.

It was during that tournament, incidentally, that Charles Einstein, then writing sports for the International News Service in Chicago, described No. 3—an ominous region of skeleton-thin fairways, beckoning water and erratic breezes, whose tangled rough borders on giant trees and boundary fences—as resembling the place where elephants go to die.

I recall, too, without particular nostalgia, a fellow most of us no longer play with, because his tricks included a jangling of coins when opponents were putting and—at least once—kicking his ball slyly from under a bush. He was not a true golfer at all. Then there was the day at Mount Prospect when Bill Sturm, a charter member of the Friday Bunch, with whom I have played for twenty-odd years (odd being the key word), waved us on—we were in two foursomes—at a short hole. Sturm immediately moved next to the pin and announced: "Cromie is hitting. We'll be safe here."

Fond as I am of Bill, I still grow surly when I remember that the ball, perfectly propelled by a seven-iron and about to drop within easy birdie distance, struck Sturm on the head, driving him momentarily to his knees, then bounced high into the air and almost into a nearby creek. I have seen balls hit boulders with less spectacular results.

There are other bright memories of the Friday Bunch: Harold Revoir, who instituted the rain-or-shine policy which many times brought us all to the course through storms so violent as to keep sensible golfers home but which often halted so that we could play. Or the time at Bonnie Dundee when the pins were frozen in the cups, and Joe Rice fell on an ice patch and almost broke a leg.

There was the aftenoon Ed Feeney and I drove many miles searching for an open course (this was rather late in the season) and finally played one so covered with snow that we lost several balls on the first fairway, "putted" with our eight irons, and quit at the end of nine because of cowardice. There also was that wonderful day when Bill Sturm took a magnificent 41 on *one* hole at White Pines by hitting 20 balls into the water. His companions, sympathetic at first, rolled on the ground in helpless mirth before he finally got across and down in two for what still stands as a Friday Bunch record.

Red Powers, it is true, threatened Sturm's mark at the second hole on No. 3, which demands a long carry over water to a slick green that sometimes seems to sidestep as the ball approaches. Red put 16 balls into Lake Kadijah before reaching the far shore, and undoubtedly would have kept swinging until dark if necessary. I once saw this same tiger hit a fairway shot which went into the air and landed *behind* him, a trick few professionals would attempt, and Red has given his name to one particular type of approach. Any chip or medium-length pitch which is topped, but nonetheless rolls to within easy distance of the cup, is known as a Powers.

The term may yet become as much a part of the golfing vocabulary as the Mulligan, since it already has spread beyond our own company. Even Red sometimes shouts happily after such a shot: "There's a real Powers!" seemingly unconscious of the fact that he is dropping his own name.

I myself have acquired an unjust fame in Friday Bunch annals for a remark made during a rainfall in a successful effort to prevent a mass return to the clubhouse. I still think the statement a sensible one, Dick Williams to the contrary, and not deserving of the mockery it received. After all there *was* a strong wind, and all I said was: "It's not really raining here. It's raining over there [pointing vaguely westward] and blowing in." What's so funny about that?

Other recollections from the postwar years center around some of the tournaments I covered before I became the book editor of the Chicago Tribune. I still can see Mildred Zaharias, the incomparable Babe, pretending to study a ball lying on top of a spectator's raincoat just over the second green at Tam

O'Shanter. The Babe must have known she was entitled to drop without penalty, but the lie was good and the Babe a born show-boat. She chipped delicately off the coat and dead to the pin.

And I still hear her curiously intent voice when I asked, as she showed up at Tam one year shortly after an operation, why she was insisting on playing in the World Championship, an event she had won yearly since its inception. She obviously was bone-weary and not herself, and I asked: "Babe, why are you doing this? Your doctor must have told you not to play so soon."

"Because I don't want nobody to win this thing but me!" was her fierce reply.

Louise Suggs, of the marvelous swing, was cut from the same mold. During the final match of the 1954 Women's Western Open tournament at Glen Flora, in Waukegan, Suggsie faltered in the late holes and surrendered what had seemed an impregnable lead (and the title) to Betty Jameson. I was chatting with Louise afterwards, trying to lure her from an evident depression, and said a painfully stupid thing: "You don't want to win 'em all, do you?" Her answer was short and professional. "Yes," she said.

Another mind-picture shows Prospero Gianvito, a one-armed player from somewhere in Ohio, smashing a drive down the middle of the No. 1 fairway at Tam, then hitting his second onto the green for an easy par. And I remember the wry remark of an army colonel, a stranger with whom I chanced to be walking: "Now I know what's the matter with my game. I've been using both hands."

Naturally my golfing souvenirs include meetings with Patty Berg, one of everyone's favorites. Patty had become so aggravated at not being able to discover how Feeney and I fared in our frequent matches (she claimed our stories failed to jibe) that she at last suggested putting up a cup to be competed for yearly by the two of us. The cup was ordered by Lois Hayhurst of the Wilson Sporting Goods Company, and we named it the Inquisitive Patty Berg Trophy, because its donor stipulated that we must keep accurate records.

This particular morning, during one of the Tam O'Shanter tournaments when she should have been thinking of nothing but her own game, Patty spotted me in the gallery as she walked from the ninth green to the tenth tee. She stopped and pointed.

"Hey, Cromie," she demanded loudly, "how did you and Feeney come out yesterday?"

But it's not only the golfers who are colorful. Golfing galleries, too, are filled with eccentrics, most of them charming. I know a downstate Illinois couple whose hobby is following the women's tour, and a Chicagoan, Harry Radix, who went to England for the sole purpose of watching Ben Hogan's play in his first British Open.

But I think my favorite galleryite would have to be a feminine spectator I watched in horrid fascination during a tournament near New York City. She was asked by one of the marshals to stop walking through the sand traps. A few moments later she waded into another one, and the marshal, justifiably annoyed, called out: "Madam! Would you *please* keep out of the traps!" The woman was equally aggrieved. "But I have golf shoes on," she snapped.

Among scenes I regret having missed were first-tee dialogues at Tam O'Shanter and at Westgate Valley, a public course south of Chicago.

At Tam, I am told, Martin Stanovich, a fine amateur with a most unorthodox spread-eagle stance and a swing that looks like money-out-the-window but keeps its owner forever in the neighborhood of par, was about to play a friendly round with a well-known professional. Stanovich wanted strokes. The professional, understandably, wished to play even. The thought horrified Martin.

"Oh, no, Frankie," he said in injured tones, "you are a P-R-O! I want two a side." He got them and won handily.

Tom Walsh, former president of the Professional Golfers Association of America, who now runs Westgate, told me about the other. One of Westgate's regulars, a man in his late sixties, played 36 holes each time he came out, which was as often as possible. One day Walsh saw another golfer, a doctor, approach the older man.

"It's really none of my business," the doctor said, "but I should warn you that it's unwise for a man your age to play 36 holes in one day."

The older man received the advice coldly. "Look," he replied, "the last two doctors who told me how to play golf are both dead."

Such avid golfers are not rare. There was one—let us call him Smith—who loved St. Andrews, near West Chicago, and whose will directed that his ashes be scattered over its rolling acres when the bad day came. The golfer died during a cold snap, however, and Joe Jemsek, owner of St. Andrews, apparently playing winter rules, sprinkled his late customer on the frozen ground. A day or so later Joe dropped in to visit his mother, who lives in a house just off one of the fairways. It was windy, and Joe accidentally left the door ajar.

"Shut the door, Joe," Mrs. Jemsek said. "Mr. Smith is blowing in."

Golf, then, is a game of memories; memories of shots made yourself (for on a given hole at a given time any fair-to-middling hacker can outgolf Palmer or Hogan or anyone else you care to name) or of shots made by someone else: Lew Worsham's low-flying wedge to the front of the 18th green at Tam in 1957, for example, that went into the cup for a $50,000 first prize, and which I watched while standing on a table in the upstairs press-room overlooking the final hole.

Perhaps that's why the literature of golf is so captivating. Can you imagine anyone remembering a complete tennis match, stroke by stroke? Of course you can't, but any real golfer can remember all of his shots and quite probably his opponent's too from first drive to last putt. Or perhaps the fascination rests in the fact that in golf your principal opponent—the course itself—is never twice the same. No matter how easy or how difficult the layout, it plays differently in the summer than in the spring; in the fall than in the summer.

There is no other contest on earth in which the game is brand new each time you play it. No two drives come to rest in exactly the same spot. The wind shifts and what was a wood-shot yesterday becomes a short-iron today. The sun bakes the earth and adds yards to your drive. The rains come and you are a short hitter again. Pins are moved or the greens are cut and nothing putts the same. Even a significant rise or fall in the temperature means (or should mean) for the average player a change to balls of higher or lower compression.

GOLFING—THE COCK OF THE GREEN

Amongst the grotesque portraits engraved by John Kay of Edinburgh, there was one entitled "The Cock o' the Green," representing an old man, whose real name was Alexander M'Kellar, engaged in playing at *golf* on Burntsfield Links, in the neighbourhood of the Scottish capital. In the curious and amusing work in which Kay's engravings have been republished with illustrative letter-press,* we find a learned and at the same time droll account of the game of Golf, introductory to an equally whimsical notice of the said Alexander M'Kellar. The article is here, with the obliging concurrence of the publisher, presented in a somewhat abridged form:—

The game of golf (Scottice, *goff*), is a pastime, although not entirely unknown in England, more peculiar to Scotland, and has long been a favourite with the citizens of Edinburgh. In the Teutonic, or German, *kolbe* signifies a club; and, in Holland, the same word, pronounced *kolf*, describes a game—of which the Dutch are very fond—in some respects akin to the Scottish pastime of *golf*.

At what period this amusement came to be practised in Scotland, is not precisely known; but from the circumstance of *football* being prohibited by a statute in 1424, in which no mention is made of *golf*, while it is specially noticed in a later enactment, 1457, the presumption is, that the game was unknown at the former period, and, consequently, that its introduction must have been about the middle of the fifteenth century.

Early in the reign of James VI. the business of club-making had become one of some importance. By "ane letter" of his majesty, dated Holyrood House, 4th April 1603, "Williame Mayne,

* Two volumes, quarto. Henry Paton, Edinburgh, 1838.

bower, burgess of Edinburgh," is made and constituted, "during all the days of his lyf-time, master fledger, bower, *club-maker,* and speir-maker, to his Hieness, alsweill for game as weir"; and in 1618 the game of golf appears to have been so generally in practice, that the manufacturing of balls was deemed worthy of special protection.

From this period the game of golf took firm hold as one of the national pastimes, practised by all ranks of the people, and occasionally countenanced by royalty itself. "Even kings themselves," says a writer in the Scots Magazine for 1792, "did not decline the princely sport; and it will not be displeasing to the Society of Edinburgh Golfers to be informed that the two last crowned heads that ever visited this country, used to practise the golf in the Links of Leith, now occupied by the society for the same purpose.

"King Charles I. was extremely fond of this exercise; and it is said that when he was engaged in a party of golf on the Links of Leith, a letter was delivered into his hands, which gave him the first account of the insurrection and rebellion in Ireland; on reading which, he suddenly called for his coach, and leaning on one of his attendants, and in great agitation, drove to the Palace of Holyrood House, from whence next day he set out for London."

"The Duke of York, afterwards James II., was not less attached to this elegant diversion. In the years 1681 and 1682, being then Commissioner from the King to Parliament, while the duke resided at Edinburgh, with his duchess, and his daughter the Princess Anne (afterwards queen), a splendid court was kept at the Palace of Holyrood House, to which the principal nobility and gentry resorted. The duke, though a bigot in his principles, was no cynic in his manners and pleasures. At that time he seemed to have studied to make himself popular among all ranks of men. Balls, plays, masquerades, &, were introduced for the entertainment of both sexes; and tea, for the first time heard of in Scotland, was given as a treat by the princesses to the Scottish ladies who visited at the Abbey. The duke, however, did not confine himself merely to diversions within doors. He was frequently seen in a party at golf on the Links of Leith, with some of the nobility and gentry. 'I remember,' says Mr. Tytler of Woodhouselee, 'in my youth to have often conversed with an old man, named Andrew Dickson, a golf club-maker, who said that, when a boy, he used to carry the duke's golf-clubs, and to run before him and announce where the balls fell.' Dickson was then performing the duty of what is now commonly called a *fore-caddie*."

At this time Burntsfield Links, now a much frequented field, does not seem to have been used for golfing. It formed part of the Burrowmuir, and perhaps had not been cleared. The usual places of recreation were Leith and Musselburgh Links—the former more especially of the Edinburgh golfers. In a poem entitled "The Goff" (by Thomas Mathison, at one period a writer in Edinburgh, but subsequently minister of Brechin), first published in 1743, and again by Mr. Peter Hill in 1793, the locality is thus alluded to:—

> North from Edina, eight furlongs and more
> Lies that famed field on Fortha's sounding shore;
> Here Caledonian chiefs for health resort—
> Confirm their sinews by the manly sport.

The author then goes on, in a lively strain, to describe some of the "chiefs"—the "cocks o' the green" at that period:

> Macdonald and unmatched Dalrymple ply
> Their ponderous weapons, and the green defy:
> Rattray for skill, and Corse for strength renowned,
> Stewart and Lesly beat the sandy ground;
> And Brown and Alston, chiefs well known in fame,
> And numbers more the muse forbears to name.
> Gigantic Biggar here full oft is seen,
> Like huge Behemoth on an Indian green;
> His bulk enormous scarce can 'scape the eyes;
> Amazed spectators wonder how he plies.
> Yea, here great Forbes,* patron of the just—
> The dread of villains, and the good man's trust;
> When spent with toils in serving human kind,
> His body recreates and unbends his mind.

The oldest golfing associations, or clubs, are the "Edinburgh Burgess" and "Burntsfield Links" Golfing Societies, instituted in 1735. The "Edinburgh Company of Golfers," under the patronage

---

* Duncan Forbes, Esq., Lord President of the Court of Session. It is reported of this great man that he was so fond of golf as to play on the sands of Leith when the Links were covered with snow.

of the city, originated in 1744. An act was passed by the Town Council, on the 7th of March, "appointing their treasurer to cause make a silver club, of £15 value, to be played for on the Links of Leith, the first Monday of April annually." Except in the years of 1746 and 1747, the club was regularly played for; and as a further encouragement, the society themselves gave two annual prizes— the one, a silver cup, value ten guineas, on which were engraved the winner's name and coat-of-arms, with a suitable inscription. The other prize was a gold medal, given to the best player at golf, and worn on the breast of the conqueror for a year, and as many years after as he might be able to maintain his superiority.

In 1768, about twenty-two members of the society having subscribed £30 each, they built what is called the "Goff-House," at the south-west corner of Leith Links, wherein the company might hold their meetings, social as well as connected with business. The company not being a corporate body, this property, feed from the city of Edinburgh, was "vested in Mr. St. Clair of Roslin, Mr. Keith of Ravelston, and Mr. W. Hogg, junior, banker, for behoof of the whole subscribers."

In 1800, the "Honourable Company of Golfers" was incorporated by a charter from the magistrates; and for more than twenty years afterwards, the meetings of the club—which could boast of the most illustrious Scotsmen of the day amongst its members— continued to be regularly held at Leith. Latterly, some alterations having been made on the Links, and the play-ground ceasing to be attractive, the stated meetings of the club were given up about seven years ago; and it was ultimately deemed advisable, or rather became necessary, from the state of the funds, to dispose of the Goff-House and furniture. This was accordingly done; and it is much to be regretted that various pictures of old members, and other articles, connected, it may be said, with the history of the club, were not preserved. These were sold for trifling sums, and, in many instances, to parties unconnected with the society, from whom they cannot now be repurchased. About three years ago, however, through the activity of some of the old members, the stated meetings were revived on Musselburgh Links; and a great accession of young members having taken place, the Edinburgh Golfing Company is once more in a flourishing condition.

The Links, or Commons, being free to all, there are innumerable players unconnected with any of the golfing societies, and many who resort to Burntsfield Links occasionally for amusement and exercise, are accommodated with the loan of clubs by the maker, for a trifling remuneration.

The handle of the bat or club is straight, generally about four feet and a half in length, and usually made of ash, or hickory, which is allowed to be better. The curvature, made of thorn, is affixed to the bottom, faced with horn, and backed with lead:—

> Forth rush'd *Castalio,* and his daring foe,
> Both arm'd with clubs, and eager for the blow.
> Of finest ash *Castalio's* shaft was made;
> Pond'rous with lead, and fac'd with horn the head;
> The work of *Dickson,* who in *Letha* dwells,
> And in the art of making clubs excels.

The ball is a little one, but exceedingly hard, being made of leather, and stuffed with feathers. There are generally two players, who have each of them his club and ball.* The game consists in driving the ball into certain holes made in the ground, and he who achieves this in the fewest strokes, obtains the victory. The golf lengths, or the spaces between the first and last holes, are sometimes extended—where the ground will permit, such as at St. Andrew's—to the distance of two or three miles; the number of intervening holes appears to be optional, but the balls must be struck into the holes, and not beyond them: when four persons play, two of them are sometimes partners, and have but one ball, which they strike alternately.

It is no unusual thing for a player to have along with him eight or ten clubs, of different forms, adapted for striking the ball in whatever position it may be placed.† These are usually carried by a boy denominated a *cadie;* and the players are generally

---

* It is almost indispensable for a player to have at least two clubs, a long one for driving, and a short one for putting near the hole; and on Links such as St. Andrew's, where there are many sand-holes, or bunkers, as they are termed, a club with an iron head (differing in form from the heads of the wooden clubs) is required. Of these iron clubs there are various kinds, adapted to the different situations of the green.

† By the rules of the game (with certain exceptions) the ball must be struck where it lies.

preceded by a runner, or *fore-cadie*, to observe the ball, so that no time may be lost in discovering it. Bets of a novel nature, which set the ordinary routine of the game entirely aside, are occasionally undertaken by the more athletic. An amusing and difficult feat, sometimes attempted from Burntsfield Links, is that of driving the ball to the top of Arthur's Seat! In this fatiguing undertaking, being a species of steeple chase, over hedges and ditches, the parties are usually followed by bottle-holders and other attendants, denoting the excessive exertion required.

When confined to its proper limits, the game of golf is one of moderate exercise, and excellently calculated for healthful recreation. In the west of Scotland it is comparatively unknown. One cause for this may be the want of commons, or links, sufficiently large for the pastime to be pursued to advantage. In Glasgow, a golf club was formed some time ago; but we understand the members were under the necessity of breaking up, in consequence of having been prohibited the use of the green, part of which is preserved with great care for the purposes of bleaching. In Stirling two or three golfers may occasionally be seen playing in the King's Park, but the game has evidently ceased to be popular there. An attempt was recently, very judiciously, made to stop the players by the tacksman, but ineffectually. About Edinburgh, Musselburgh, Perth, St. Andrew's, and other districts, where no restraints exist, golf maintains a decided superiority, and seems at the present time to be followed with new spirit. Indeed, the game was never more popular. In addition to the old clubs in the districts already mentioned, another has been recently established at New Berwick, the meetings of which are numerously attended. St. Andrew's, however, has been denominated the *Doncaster* of golfing. A great many of the nobility and gentry of the neighbouring counties are members of the club, which bears the name of the tutelar saint, and the autumn meeting may be said to continue for a week, during which the crack players from all quarters of the country have an opportunity of pitting their strength and skill against each other. On these occasions, the Links, crowded with players and spectators, present a gay and animated scene. Two medals are played for—the one belonging to the club, and the other a recent gift of King William IV., which was competed for at the last meeting (1837) for the first time, and attracted a very great assemblage of the best golfers. At the ordinaries in the evening, the parties "fight their battles o'er again," and new matches are entered into. The day on which the king's medal was played for, terminated with a ball, given by the club, which was numerously and fashionably attended. In London, a society of golfers still exists, principally composed, we believe, of Scotsmen, called the "Blackheath Golf Club," which was established prior to the year 1745.

ALEXANDER M'KELLAR, the "Cock o' the Green,"—whom the print represents as about to strike the ball—was probably one of the most enthusiastic golf-players that ever handled a club. When the weather would at all permit, he generally spent the whole day on Burntsfield Links, and he was frequently to be found engaged at the "short-holes" by lamp-light. Even in winter, if snow was sufficiently frozen, he might be seen enjoying his favourite exercise alone, or with any one he could persuade to join him in the pastime.* M'Kellar thus became well known in the neighbourhood of the green, and his almost insane devotion to golf was a matter of much amusement to his acquaintances. So thoroughly did he enter into the spirit of the game, that every other consideration seemed obliterated for the time. When victory chanced to crown his exertions, he used to give way to his joy for a second or two by dancing round the golf hole. M'Kellar, however, was not a member of any of the clubs; and, notwithstanding his incessant practice, he was by no means considered a dexterous player. This is accounted for by the circumstance of his having been far advanced in years before he had an opportunity of gaining a knowledge of the game. The greater part of his life had been passed as a butler, but in what family is unknown, nor indeed does it matter much. He had contrived to save a little money; and his wife, on their coming to Edinburgh, opened a small tavern in the New Town. M'Kellar had thus ample leisure for the indulgence of his fancy, without greatly abridging his income, and golf may be said to have virtually become his *occupation;* yet no perseverance could entirely compensate for the want of practice in his younger years.

* When snow happens to be on the ground, a *red* ball is used.

9

His all-absorbing predilection for golf was a source of much vexation to his partner in life, on whom devolved the whole duty of attending to the affairs of the tavern. It was not because she regretted his want of attention to business, for probably he would have been allowed to appropriate a very small portion of authority in matters which she could attend to much better herself, but she felt scandalised at the notoriety he had acquired, and was not altogether satisfied with the occasional outlay to which he was subjected, though he never speculated to any great amount.

No sooner was breakfast over than M'Kellar daily set off to the green, and ten to one he did not find his way home until dusk; and not even then, if the sport chanced to be good. As a practical jest on the folly of his procedure, it occurred to his "better half" that she would one day put him to the blush, by carrying his dinner, along with his nightcap, to the Links. At the moment of her arrival, M'Kellar happened to be hotly engaged; and, apparently, without feeling the weight of the satire, he good-naturedly observed, that she might *wait*, if she chose, till the game was decided, for at present he had no time for dinner!

So provoked at length was the good dame, that she abhorred the very name of golf, as well as all who practised it; and to her customers, if they were her husband's associates on the green, even a regard for her own interest could scarcely induce her to extend to them the common civilities of the tavern.

What betwixt respect for his wife, and his fondness of golf, M'Kellar must have been placed in a rather delicate situation; but great as the struggle might be, all opposition was eventually overcome, and he determined to enjoy his game, and be happy in spite of frowns, lectures, or entreaties. One thing alone annoyed him, and that was the little countenance he was enabled to give his friends when they happened to visit him. At length an opportunity occurred, apparently highly favourable for an honourable *amende* to his long-neglected acquaintances. Having resolved on a trip to the kingdom of Fife, where she calculated on remaining for at least *one* night, his "worthy rib" took her departure, leaving him for once, after many cautions, with the management of affairs in her absence. Now was the time, thought M'Kellar. A select party of friends were invited to his house in the evening: the hour had arrived, and the company were assembled in the best parlour —golf the theme, and deep the libations—when (alas! what short-sighted mortals are we!) who should appear to mar the mirth of the revellers, but the golf-hating Mrs. M'Kellar herself! Both winds and waves had conspired to interrupt the festivity; the ferry had been found impassable, and the hostess was compelled to return. What ensued may be imagined. The contemplated journey was postponed *sine die;* and M'Kellar internally resolved to make sure, before giving a second invitation, that his spouse had actually *crossed the ferry!*

Happening to be at Leith one day, where his fame as a golfer was not unknown, M'Kellar got into conversation, in the club-maker's shop, with a number of glass-blowers, who were *blowing* very much about their science in the game of golf. After bantering him for some time to engage in a trial of skill, a young man from Burntsfield Links opportunely made his appearance. "By gracious, gentlemen!" exclaimed M'Keller, whose spirit was roused, "here's a boy and I will play you for a guinea!" No sooner said than a match of three games was begun, in all of which the glass-blowers were defeated. The "Cock o' the Green" was triumphant; and, not waiting till the bet had been forthcoming, he ran to the shop of the club-maker, announcing the joyful intelligence —"By gracious, gentlemen, the old man and the boy have beat them off the green!"

By way of occupying his time profitably on the *seventh*—the only day in the week he could think of employing otherwise than in his favourite amusement—M'Kellar was in the habit of acting as door-keeper to an Episcopal chapel. On entering one day, old Mr. Douglas Gourlay, club and ball maker at Burntsfield, jocularly placed a golf ball in the plate, in lieu of his usual donation of coppers. As anticipated, the prize was instantaneously secured by M'Kellar, who was not more astonished than gratified by the novelty of the deposit.

It was at the suggestion of the late Mr. M'Ewan and Mr. Gourlay that Kay produced the etching of the "Cock o' the Green." Going out purposely to the Links, the artist found him engaged at his usual pastime, and succeeded in taking an accurate and characteristic likeness. When informed what Kay had been doing, M'Kellar seemed highly pleased. "What a pity," said he; "by gracious, had I known, I would have shown him some of my capers!"

In 1803, although pretty far advanced in life, M'Kellar continued to maintain his title of the "Cock o' the Green" for a considerable time. He died about twenty-five years ago.

FROM Chambers's Edinburgh Journal
June 22, 1839

THE SEPARATION OF MAN AND BOY

1952. Golfers will tell you that the Pine Valley course near Camden, New Jersey, is as difficult as any in the land. In the following story evidence is produced that once there was a man who was skilled in golf to a point where Pine Valley trembled.

Chances are, if you're a golfer, you've heard of Pine Valley. It's a course where par is a cruel man, and where man is separated from boy.

Pine Valley reclines like a vacuous serpent in Clementon, New Jersey, a meat and vegetable stand ten miles southwest of Camden. Through the years, Clementon has enjoyed a quiet existence, untouched by the turbulence of fame. Consolation for Clementon has come in the form of seeing its name in the paper whenever Pine Valley raises its frontage against human kind.

A favorite trick of the golfer familiar with Pine Valley is to bet the first-time starter he can't break a hundred. This is a standard wager and includes newcomers who normally shoot in the seventies. Few are the golfers who, having played Pine Valley for the first time, can claim that the round wasn't on them.

Suffice it to say that the course has narrows instead of fairways. That it has ravenous bunkers born with an insatiable appetite for a golf ball. And that a fellow who can't hit a green with a high frequency should prepare himself for circumstances over which only Pine Valley has control.

At this point, the reader should be notified that there's a plot to this story. At least we've got a villain and a hero. The ne'er-do-well is Pine Valley. The hero, who will require only slight introduction, is Woody Platt, amateur golfer, Philadelphian, fine shotmaker.

Friends of Platt, realizing the latter's great golf potential, didn't make any wagers with him on the first tee. The thought of watching him in hand-to-hand conflict with Pine Valley would be sufficient reward.

On the first hole, a par 4, Platt rammed a drive which cut the narrow-gauge fairway in two. His second found the green, and when he sank his putt for a birdie his companions politely applauded. They knew Pine Valley wouldn't tolerate this sort of onslaught all afternoon.

Pine Valley's second hole is also a par 4. Platt, showing less concern over hazards than his followers, blasted another perfect drive. Then he took a No. 6 iron and sank his second shot for an eagle two.

"How now?" wondered the onlookers. "What manner of golfer is this?"

They soon found out. On the third hole, a par 3, Platt took careful aim, stroked his shot with infinite finesse, and scored a hole in one. It was his second consecutive eagle.

Even today, people who were watching Platt will tell you that Pine Valley seemed to tremble a bit, like a human being about to lose a reputation. Platt, himself, was allergic to tremblings.

His drive from the fourth, another par 4, was straight and true. All that was needed to get home was an accurate iron and Platt plunked his ball on the carpet thirty feet from the pin.

A gallery, which by this time had grown to appropriate proportions, encircled the green as Platt approached his ball. Measuring the distance with a cursory glance, Platt asked a caddy to remove the pin and promptly sank his putt for a birdie three.

"Incredible," murmured a witness. "Imagine starting out at Pine Valley with a birdie—eagle—eagle—birdie!"

"Let's go to the fifth tee and see what happens next," said a second citizen.

Platt, meanwhile, had excused himself from the foursome in which he was playing. He mentioned something about having a drink, and since the Pine Valley clubhouse is situated between the fourth and fifth tee, no one expressed surprise.

So Platt retired, and the gallery waited. Platt had another, and the gallery waited. Truth of the matter is, Platt had one more and never did come out.

BY BOB COOKE

FROM *Wake Up the Echoes*

Don't carry more clubs than is absolutely necessary. Unless you feel full confidence in a weapon you had much better leave it in your locker. Six clubs are enough for anyone. If you have more you might be caught between two minds one day and not know which to take, and in that case the one you ultimately choose is always the wrong one. The less clubs you have, the less chance of making a mistake; besides, they are not so heavy to carry.

BY JOSHUA TAYLOR

FROM *The Art of Golf*

ONE STROKE PENALTY

Mary Queen of Scots was one lass who got more trouble from golf than she could handle—so she lost her head completely. She ended her career on the royal chopping block. A game of golf was one of the links in a chain of events which cut short Mary's political ambitions, and thus eliminated from further competition the world's first famous woman golfer.

It was on February 10, 1567, that Queen Mary's consort, one Lord Darnley, was murdered, and his house blown up with gun powder to hide the evidence. Foul play was suspected. The number one candidate for man-most-likely-to-have-committed-the-crime was the earl of Bothwell, a member of the local handicap committee.

The queen's subjects wept for her in the tragic loss of this, her second spouse, but Mary bore her grief with remarkable fortitude. In fact, only a few days after the murder she was seen "in the fields beside Seton" playing golf, hooking and slicing with rare abandon, and mourning only when a putt rimmed the cup. This fateful game brought down a storm of criticism on her royal brow. Political enemies, who recognized a good opening when they saw one, called it a shameless exhibition, hinting she not only had gone beyond all bounds, but had failed to mark the penalty shots on her score card. When, only three months later, she married chief suspect Bothwell, that did it.

Mary was forced to give up her card in the golf club, abdicate her throne, and flee to England. This proved as disastrous as blading a wedge shot in the sand trap, for Queen Elizabeth I promptly clapped her in irons, where she remained twenty years, before the penalty was exacted. It is said that Mary Queen of Scots, just before the blade swung, looked up—a true golfer to the last.

BY REG MANNING

FROM *From Tee to Cup*

15

The first lesson to be learned by the aspiring golfer is the value of practice. This is the beginning and end of excellence— the fundamental secret of improvement, other things being equal. Speaking for myself, I am convinced that the present position I hold in the golfing world is in a very great measure due to the faculty I am gifted with, of being able to proceed out to some quiet corner of the links, with just a couple of clubs and a dozen balls, and religiously set myself the task of trying to find out the peculiarities and idiosyncrasies of these particular weapons. To many this procedure may seem a somewhat dull and uninteresting task, but personally I have always found it to be a most fascinating pastime, and although nowadays my enthusiasm for practice may not be quite so marked as it was ten or twenty years ago, still I must candidly acknowledge enjoying even to this day an hour all alone by myself on the links more than the pleasure of participating in the most interesting and pleasant match one can imagine. Moreover, I consider that a young player is apt to gain more knowledge in such an hour of solitude than he is at all likely to acquire in playing thirty-six holes against even the finest players in the land.

BY HAROLD H. HILTON

FROM *Modern Golf*

When American players first came over to play on courses in Great Britain, some of them caused a degree of interest, not to say consternation, by appearing on the links minus their coats and vests; and it must be said in their favor, minus what they term in the States, their suspenders. This free and easy method of clothing for the links did not in any way meet with the approval of the older school of golfers in England, who had been brought up in a certain spirit of decorum that had been handed down to them by their forefathers from time immemorial. According to this tradition the correct garb in which to play the game of golf should be composed of a complete suit of more or less thick tweed, with footgear of a sufficiently ponderous character to correspond with the aforesaid heavy clothing.

This was the traditional garb, and tradition in connection with the game of golf is a hard taskmaster, at least it was in those days, and it was many years before the golfing public became acclimatized to a more rational form of garb in which to play the game. But by degrees the mind of the general golfing public has become sufficiently broad and independent to do away with many of the old set formulas or restrictions with regard to the golfing clothing, and although it is not yet customary in England to play coatless as American players are in the habit of doing, still it is not altogether unusual to see members of the younger generation of British players imitating their American cousins, particularly on such occasions as the summer of the year 1911, when the thermometer kept in the vicinity of ninety day after day. One cannot get away from the fact that in the hot summer days the methods of American players in playing the game with a minimum of covering is infinitely more rational and according to the views of common sense than the old time principles of playing in thick tweeds and heavy brogues to match.

But, notwithstanding the broader, and more enlightened

views of the present day, one cannot ignore the fact that there still lurks in the minds of the golfing public a certain degree of prejudice against what I once heard a disgusted old time golfer term "The half-naked stage." This is particularly noticeable at a championship meeting, when one would be considerably surprised to see a British player performing in the event in what may be termed regulation lawn tennis costume. Why this should be so is a little difficult to understand, as the Britisher plays most other games with as little clothing to hamper him as is consistent with respectability, but the old time prejudice is difficult to eradicate, and it undoubtedly supplies a serious drawback to American players who come over to play in the British Championship events.

One could not but feel sorry for young "Chick" Evans in 1911, when in order not to hurt British susceptibilities, he played right through the week in the sweltering heat in a comparatively thick tweed coat, and there cannot be much doubt that this act of courtesy toward British custom served to handicap the Chicago youth. Only once did he part with his coat, and that was in sheer desperation when he found himself in an almost hopeless position at the nineteenth hole—being bunkered badly beyond the green. Just for that last despairing effort he shed the garment which had been hampering him from the very start, and I do not think anyone would have blamed him had he discarded it somewhat earlier in the fight.

BY HAROLD H. HILTON

FROM Modern Golf

THE OPEN CHAMPIONSHIP OF 1913

The Sunday before the open tournament, I played at the Wellesley Country Club with friends. I bring this up merely to show you that one's form in golf is a mercurial affair. With the open championship two days away, I made two scores of 88 on a short and rather easy nine-hole course, the 88's being just twenty-two strokes higher than a record score I had established on one of my earlier rounds over the layout. The friend who invited me to play with himself and friends was broken-hearted, and thought he had ruined my game. I told him not to worry; that I had probably got all the bad golf out of my system—and, believe me, there must have been plenty of it in there. There was such a huge entry the field was divided into three qualifying sections and I was in the same group with Harry Vardon. With a 74 in my morning round, I finished a stroke ahead of Vardon. That was an accomplishment. In the afternoon I was playing quite as well until I reached the long fourteenth, and bumping into much trouble, I made a seven. At that I scored a 78 which ranked me next to Vardon, the leader in our section.

There is little to be said about the championship itself. After the first three rounds, I was tied with both Vardon and Ray at 225. Ray was finishing his final round as I walked to the first tee. I watched him hole out and learned he had made a 79. It was raining, but, even so, a 79 did not seem very low. It made his seventy-two-hole total 304. Playing the fifth hole, I was told that Vardon had tied Ray. The rumors in championship play, particularly if you happen to be in the running, come thick and fast. I was next told Barnes had the championship in the hollow of his hand. Then word came to me that Barnes had blown up.

I was having my own troubles out in that rain and nothing would go right. Out in 43, all hope seemed gone. Then someone said, "Tellier will win in a walk." The tenth hole was a par three. Owing to the sodden condition of the putting green, a high pitch was dangerous, because the ball would become embedded in the soft turf. I elected to use a jigger, intending to hit a low shot to the green. I forgot to look at the ball and hit it about fifteen feet. I put my next on the green eight feet from the hole and then took three putts for an inglorious five. Then I learned that Tellier had got into trouble and had finished behind both Vardon and Ray, who were still leading.

After that wretched five, walking to the eleventh tee between a lane of spectators, I heard one man say, "It's too bad, he has blown up." I knew he meant me, and it made me angry. It put me in the proper frame of mind to carry on. There was still a chance, I thought. People lined the fairway as I drove. A par four was helpful on the eleventh. A hard five on the twelfth helped not at all, because here was a hole where one might be expected to save a stroke, although it was a difficult four. Standing on the thirteenth tee, I realized I must play those last six holes in two under par to tie. There were two holes on the course where I thought I might save a stroke: the thirteenth, the one I had to play next, which was a drive and a short pitch, and the sixteenth, a short hole. I selected these two holes for reasons. I had been quite successful on the thirteenth and had scored threes there regularly. I had not made a two all the week, and I had a hunch I should get one at the sixteenth. It was just a hunch.

My drive to the thirteenth was satisfactory. With a simple pitch to the green, I mishit the ball and barely escaped a trap. My ball lay off the green thirty feet from the hole I had selected as one upon which to beat par. Instead of having a reasonably short putt, I was stuck with a chip shot. In any event, I chipped my ball right into the hole for my three and was still in the hunt. A routine five came on the long fourteenth. I missed my second to the fifteenth badly, so badly, I missed every trap. I pitched on and got my par four.

Then came the sixteenth, the hole I had been expecting to make in two. I not only did not get my two there, but actually had to hole a nine-footer for the three. One of the last two holes had to be made in three, the other in four. They were both testing holes. As I splashed along in the mud and rain, I had no further hunches. I just wanted an opportunity to putt for one of those threes. I got it on the seventeenth. A drive and second shot, played with a jigger placed my ball on the green fifteen feet from the cup. It was now or never. As I looked the line of putt over, I thought of one thing, giving the ball a chance—that is, getting it to the hole. I struck that putt as firmly as any putt I ever hit, saw it take the roll, bang smack against the back of the hole, and fall in for the three.

Now to get the four. A drive split the fairway to the last hole and was out far enough so that a long iron could reach the green.

Eddie Lowery, my ten-year-old caddie, handed me an iron and said, "Keep your eye on the ball and hit it." I did. I lifted my head just in time to see the ball sail toward the pin, saw it land and, as I thought, kick forward, and I can then remember saying to Eddie, "I have a putt to win this championship." I was certain I had seen my ball clear the embankment and hop forward. As a matter of fact, the ball struck the top of the bank, and stopped instantly just off the cut surface of the putting green. A chip shot left me a four-foot putt which I popped in. I had ended that seventy-two-hole stretch in a tie with Vardon and Ray for the championship I had been most reluctant to enter.

Friends hustled me into the locker-room building and the excitement was tremendous. One individual came to me and asked this question, "Were you bothered while putting on the seventeenth green?" "Not a bit," was my reply. "Why?" He went on to say that the highway directly in back of the green was littered with automobiles, so much so that it was impossible for machines to move in either direction. Just then a motor came along, and the driver, seeing his path blocked completely, kept up a constant tooting of his horn, as I was preparing to putt. I never heard a single sound, so thoroughly was my mind centered on the business of holing the putt.

After taking a bath, I walked home and turned in early for a real night's rest. I slept from nine-thirty until eight the next morning, and after a light breakfast, hustled over to the Country Club for my play-off with Vardon and Ray. I did not feel nervous or unduly excited. I slipped on my golf shoes, got hold of Eddie Lowery, and went out to the Polo Field to hit a few practice shots. There was nobody around. The shots I hit felt fine. Soon some people came along and watched me. After perhaps a half-hour's practice, I was told that Vardon and Ray were on the first tee waiting for the match to begin.

Johnny McDermott took my arm and said, "You are hitting the ball well; now go out and pay no attention whatsoever to Vardon or Ray. Play your own game." It was excellent advice and I promised Johnny I would do my best.

On the way to the tee my good friend Frank Hoyt ("Stealthy Steve") asked me if I would not permit him to carry my clubs. I had played much golf with Steve and he was a master in the finer points of the game. I told him he must see Eddie Lowery. He made one or two offers of money, but they did not tempt Eddie in the least. It was interesting to see the reaction of Eddie as he definitely and positively refused to be bought off. Finally, Hoyt appealed to me. I looked at the ten-year-old Eddie, his eyes filled, and I think he was fearful that I would turn him down. In any event, he seemed so sincere I did not have the heart to take the clubs away from him, and my final gesture was to tell Steve, Eddie was going to caddie for me.

It was raining, and the three of us were ushered into the tent near the tee to draw lots for the honor. I drew the longest straw and had to drive first. As I walked over to the sand box, and realized what I was up against and saw the crowd, I was terribly excited. If I could only get my tee shot away! Eddie stepped up as he handed me a driver and said, "Be sure and keep your eye on the ball." The opening salute was a drive well down the middle of the fairway and for good length. Vardon and Ray followed suit. Ray was the only one who was long enough to reach the green on his second, but he sliced a brassie to the right.

We all got on in three and took fives on the hole. I was left with a four-foot putt for my five, and I worried not a little over it. I tapped it in, and then almost instantly any feeling of awe and excitement left me completely. I seemed to go into a coma. Eddie kept telling me to keep my eye on the ball. He cautioned me to take my time. He encouraged me in any number of different ways. My first mistake was on the fifth hole where the slimy grip turned in my hand and my second shot went out of bounds. But Vardon and Ray both erred on the same hole, and I was safe for the time being. Ray had taken a five on the third to our fours, and that was the only difference in the scores up to that point.

Vardon made the sixth in three and went into the lead. Ray was now trailing Vardon by two strokes and me by one. The seventh hole at Brookline is a hard par three. Vardon was to the right of the green with his iron and needed four. I failed to lay a long approach putt dead, and took four. Ray was the only one to get a three and he pulled up on even terms with me.

The eighth hole was sensational. This hole measures three

hundred and eighty yards and the view of the green is more or less restricted by a hill. You can see the flag, but no part of the green. We all had fine drives. A tremendous crowd had gathered around the green to see the balls come up. I played my second with a mashie straight for the pin. In a few seconds a mighty roar went up. As I handed the club to Eddie, he said, "Your ball is stone dead." I wanted to think it was, but I wished also to prepare myself in case it was not. Therefore I said to Eddie, "It is not stone dead, but I believe I shall have a putt for my three." You see I did not wish to be disappointed.

As we walked toward the green and came to the top of the hill, I saw a ball twelve inches from the hole. It was mine. Ray was forty feet away with a sidehill putt and he tapped his ball as delicately as possible. It took the necessary turns and rolled right into the hole. Vardon had a four, and I got my three, which put us all even at the end of eight holes.

The next highlight was the short tenth. This green was so soggy that both Vardon and Ray, after pitching on, had to chip over the holes made by their balls as they bit into the soft turf and hopped back. I was fairly close in one. My opponents failed to make their threes, and I stepped into the lead by a stroke.

I added another stroke on the twelfth, where I got my four to their fives. Vardon dropped a nice putt for a three on the thirteenth, one under par, which brought him within a stroke of me. The long fourteenth was important. Ray might reach the green in two, but it was beyond the range of Vardon and myself. Ray drove last, and I saw him hurl himself at his ball to get just a little added length. When he played his second from the fairway, he put every bit of power into the shot, but his timing was poor and he hit the ball far to the right into a grove of chestnut trees. He recovered beautifully, and the hole was made in five by all.

I was paying as little attention as possible to the strokes of the others, because I did not wish to be unduly influenced by anything they did. I was simply carrying out McDermott's instructions and playing my own game. I could not help but notice, however, that Ray was struggling somewhat. I noticed, too, that Vardon, who seemed to be a master in mashie work, pulled his pitch to the green, which was not his natural way of playing such a stroke. Vardon normally played his pitches with a slight fade from left to right.

Ray got into all sorts of trouble on the fifteenth and he seemed out of the running. I never gave it a thought as he holed out in six. I still clung to my one stroke lead over Vardon through the sixteenth. Ray was now five strokes behind. Vardon had the honor on the seventeenth tee. This hole is a semi-dog-leg, and by driving to the right you eliminate all risk. On the other hand, if the player chooses to risk a trap on the left and gets away with it, he has a short pitch to the green. Vardon drove to the left. I saw his ball start, and that is all. I drove to the right. Ray tried to cut the trees on the left and hit a prodigious wallop that cleared everything, but his ball was in the long grass.

As we walked toward our balls, I saw that Vardon had caught the trap and his ball was so close to the bank he had no chance at all of reaching the green. He could just play out to the fairway. I knocked a jigger shot to the green, my ball stopping fifteen feet above the hole. Ray and Vardon took fives. As I studied my putt, I decided to take no liberties with the skiddy surface and simply tried to lay the ball dead for a sure four. I putted carefully and watched my ball roll quietly toward the hole. It went in for a three. With one hole left, I was now in the lead by three strokes over Vardon and seven over Ray.

The eighteenth hole was a hard two-shotter. The rains had turned the race-track in front of the green into a bog, and my one thought was to get over the mud. All hit fine tee shots. I placed my second on the green. It did not enter my head that I was about to become the open champion until I stroked my first putt to within eight or nine inches of the hole. Then, as I stepped up to make that short putt, I became very nervous. A veil of something that seemed to have covered me dropped from around my head and shoulders. I was in full control of my faculties for the first time since the match started, but terribly excited. I dropped the putt. Nothing but the most intense concentration brought me victory.

I was fearful at the beginning that I should blow up, and I fought against this for all I was worth. The thought of winning never entered my head, and for that reason I was immune to emotions of any sort. My objective was to play eighteen holes as well as I could and let the score stand for good or bad. I accomplished a feat that seemed so far beyond anything I ever hoped to do that, while I got a real thrill out of it, I felt I had been mighty lucky. Had I harbored the desire to win that championship or an open title of any kind, I might have been tickled beyond words. In sport one has to have the ambition to do things and that ambition in my case was to win the national amateur championship. Therefore, I honestly think I never got the "kick" out of winning the open title that I might have done if I had thought I could win it.

BY FRANCIS OUIMET

FROM *A Game of Golf*

Mr. Low has invited me to write my reminiscences of the late Mr. Frederick Tait. I comply out of affection for his memory; though, unhappily, my acquaintance with him was but slight. That, knowing him so little, and meeting him so rarely as I did, I yet felt the warmest regard for him, is a proof of his singularly winning nature. This proof is, indeed, the most that I have to offer to a record of his brief life, a life of real beneficence, for he brought sunshine wherever he came and a reflection of his own constitutional happiness.

Our additions to the well-being of the world rise not so much from what we do as from what we are, and the most ardent friend of his species may do less for it than the man or woman who merely shines upon it with a radiant presence. To do *that* was the unconscious virtue of Freddie. Genius, we know, has been defined as "an infinite capacity for taking pains." It is rather an infinite capacity for producing the right effect without taking any pains. All manner of painstaking is vain, says St. Paul, "if I have not

25

charity," by which he means universal goodwill. That was Freddie's quality: you had only to look at his kind, strong, friendly face, and honest eyes, to see that he was full of goodwill. A child would "lay his hand, unasked, in thine," Lord Tennyson says of his friend: and man, woman, and child had this spontaneous confidence in the friend of so many of us, whose face we shall not see, whose voice we shall not hear again, "till dreams depart and men awake."

He was a young man, a soldier, an athlete, in the fulness of joyous vigour, and I was—at the opposite pole. But, odd as it may seem, I had exactly the same sentiment for Freddie as, when at school, I used to have for a big, kind, football-playing elder kinsboy, if the word may be coined. He was so strong, so good, so jolly, so devoid of conceit, despite his immense popularity, and fame on the Links. It was on the Links at St. Andrews that I generally saw him, and a happy hour it was for many in that wintry little town when we heard that Freddie had come to lighten the murky days of December or January. You saw his broad, sunny smile brightening on you from far away, above his broad shoulders and undandified dress. I stop to "gaze across the glooming flats" of the sodden Links, and seem to see again him who is now but the brightest of the shadows that haunt this place of many memories. Bruce and Wallace, Culdees and grim Covenanters, the frail, wandering ghost of the exiled Henry VI., Knox in his vigour and Knox in his decline, the stern Regent Moray and the harmless Lyon King-at-Arms whom he burned; they are all among our haunting shades, with the Queen in her glad youth, and Chastelard, here condemned to die for her, and her French valet in like case, and the great Cardinal in his glory, and the anxious eyes of Mariotte Ogilvy, and Montrose in his boyhood—a thousand characters of immortal memory, with the same shroud around them all. But he who died in Africa, glad and kind as he was brave till his latest breath—he, too, will not be forgotten; he it is, next to one other, younger, and as brave and kind and good as he, whom I must remember best and long for most.

It was rarely except on the Links that I saw Freddie. It was my custom, and that of several others, to walk round and watch his play at golf, but I never even saw him compete for the Medal,

or in any greater contest than a match over both Links with
Andrew Kirkaldy. We used to make little bets with him, in ordinary matches, that he would not do the round under seventy-
eight, or some such figure, and we were apt to lose our half-
crowns.

At first, his extraordinary driving was the chief attraction, but
he later aimed more at accuracy, and drove much within his
powers. I remember his coming into the Club and asking whether
it was worth while to measure a drive he had made. He had, in
fact, "overpowered" the Heathery Hole, the thirteenth as you
come in, on the right-hand course. The drive has been disputed,
and I only narrate what I remember. Perhaps my recollection is
inaccurate. He was playing behind his brother Willie, and, when
the brother and partner had played their second, Freddie's ball
flew over their heads, and lighted on the long, narrow table-land
which there crosses the Links. Freddie, on approaching the hole,
could not find his ball, and, I think, gave up the hole, and then
found his ball about "hole-high." The day was of a light frost,
brilliantly sunny, and with the faintest flicker of air, no breeze. I
remember seeing Mr. Tait measuring the distance to the place
where the ball was found, and I think the whole extent was about
350 yards, the "carry" being about 250 yards. Probably there is a
more authentic record than my memory supplies.

Freddie became, as is well known, a master in every department of golf. He was not very careful, and usually smoked, laying
down his briar-root pipe on the grass when he was making a
stroke. His resource was wonderful. I remember his making a
beautiful approach with one foot in and one out of a steep bunker,
while his ball trembled on a blade of grass in the sand on the
brink. Perhaps the last time I ever saw him, his ball lay on thin
ice in the Scholar's Bunker. He walked in over the boots, for the
ice was a mere film, and flicked his ball on to the green, over the
slight declivity which stops so many an approach.

The best round I ever saw him do was 72: he was playing, I
think, with Tom Morris and Mr. Hull. The record previously was
73, and though he might have been down in 71, he left himself an
awkward shortish putt, on a difficult sticky green, for 72. When

he had holed out he said, "That putt took a year off my life": so great was the nervous tension.

These are trivial anecdotes. One day his game illustrated the feebleness of human evidence. He was playing in the Monthly Handicap, and winning easily. But at the hole beside the burn, coming in, he putted to run up a hill, and roll back to the hole. Forgetting that this was a solemn occasion, he replaced his ball, played his putt over again, and holed. Several people were looking on, and someone said that the putt was not orthodox. Then arose a dispute as to what he had done. A spectator, a townsman unknown to me, maintained with so much conviction that the putt was all right, that neither Tom Morris nor myself could venture to say exactly what had happened. Our critical memories were submerged in that of the earnest townsman. However, Freddie remembered, and explained—and lost the handicap. In weighing historical evidence as to more important events, one is occasionally reminded of this little incident.

One had no special forebodings when Freddie said good-bye, and went to take his part in the unhappy war. When the bitter news came of Magersfontein, it was currently reported in St. Andrews that Freddie had fallen. That element of the gloom was presently dissipated, and no calamity could have been less expected than the newspaper reports of his death. There was no official news for several days, and St. Andrews had begun to hope again, when the newspaper correspondents mentioned particulars which hardly admitted of doubt. We had supposed that his Magersfontein wound would have made it impossible for him to take part in a rapid march. Then the worst was confirmed beyond doubt, and these days of anxiety were over.

Hundreds of the finest young men, of both parties, have fallen, and the end no man foresees. All of these, in every rank, had friends to whom they were as dear as Freddie was to us. But none had more friends than he: who was so widely known, and, wherever he was known, was loved. His memory does not rest on his athletic prowess. Dozens of lads are acclaimed by the world of play, but he would have been as much endeared to those who knew him, if he had never handled a club. His golf merely made him known to a larger circle. I never heard a word said against him, except a solitary complaint that, in the lightness of his heart, he played pibrochs round the drowsy town at the midnight hour. What would I not give to hear his pipes again? For himself, a soldier's death, sudden and painless, was not the worst of fortunes. His memory lives among the glories of the Black Watch.

BEATI MORTUI QUI MORIUNTUR IN DOMINO.

Alleyne House,
St. Andrews,
December 3, 1900.

BY ANDREW LANG

FROM *F. G. Tait, A Record*
BY JOHN L. LOW

I had to leave on my tour of South America with Kirkwood a week before the first Masters tournament was staged in 1934. Missing the Masters was a severe disappointment to me. The following year I made sure that nothing would interfere with my being on hand for that event. I was extremely eager, in the first place, to see the Augusta National, the dream course that Bob Jones had talked of building for years and had constructed after his retirement with Dr. Alistair Mackenzie, the eminent Scottish golf architect. Today, the Augusta National is a magnificent monument to Bob Jones—the course itself, the classic clubhouse, the lovely avenue of trees leading to the clubhouse, the azaleas and the dogwood and the other beautiful flowering shrubs that frame the various holes. The Augusta National is for me the most picturesque course in the world.

But in 1935 on my first visit, I must admit, I was let down by Bob's layout. It has always been my contention that while great courses can be outlined on the drawing board, they can never attain their full potential until they are played on and the discovered weaknesses corrected. Bob always made it a point to ask his friends for criticism, and I never hesitated to express my honest opinion about holes I thought could be improved. With the assistance of Perry Maxwell and Robert Trent Jones, Bob has continually lengthened and remodeled the holes that were found to be wanting in true shot value. The 10th and the 16th, which were two of the weakest sisters, are now superb tests of skill. As the course stands today, I think it has only one poor hole, the 11th. I don't approve of the bunker in the middle of the fairway, 240 yards out. I can't see it from the tee, maybe because I'm too short. I hold with Jim Braid's statement that as long as you can see it, any bunker on a course is a fair hazard.

The Augusta National has many excellent features which ambitious clubs would do well to copy. You don't hear any of the tournament players complaining at Augusta, "That practice green threw me off." A golfer can pick up his putting stroke on the splendid practice green and carry it out onto the eighteen holes. On the course there are no silly traps 150 or 175 yards from the tee, which penalize only the average golfer who has enough on his hands without brooding about unjustified hazards. And any club that wants to see how a tournament should be conducted should dispatch a few emissaries to study the Masters. The galleries are intelligently marshaled. The spectators as well as the golfers are treated as gentlemen. Jones will not tolerate the faintest suspicion of burlesque-show atmosphere, which has been brought to golf tournaments by overcommercial promoters who love publicity better than the game itself. The flavor at the Masters reflects the personality of Robert Tyre Jones, Jr., and Bob has always epitomized the best in golf.

I was anxious to make a creditable showing in my first Masters, for a representative group of champions, the old and the new, had been invited, and the old master himself was competing. The experts didn't think that Bob could win. He had been away from tournament golf for over four years, and that's too long a time for even the greatest of golfers. Jones went for the highest price, though, in the Calcutta betting pool, with Craig Wood and myself also installed as favorites on the basis of the form we had shown tuning up.

My practice rounds, 65, 67, 72, and 67, represented straight hitting and accurate putting on the sharply contoured greens. I was using a cash-in putter, and the stroke I was getting with that model seemed to be precisely what was needed on the rye and Bermuda greens. I was also very pleased with the caddy assigned me, a lanky Negro well over six feet tall who had been nicknamed "Stovepipe," because of the battered tall silk hat he always wore when caddying. He was a very religious fellow and devoted a lot of his time to church activities. "Stovepipe," I used to ask him, "how are things going?" "Not so good, Mister Gene, not so good," he would drawl mournfully "Collections were mighty poor today. We done got to win."

It was very cold for April in Georgia, the week of the Masters, but the scoring was torrid. Henry Picard opened with 67–68 before striking a rough third round of 76. Picard's 211 at the 54-hole mark placed him two strokes behind the leader, Craig Wood. Craig, the golfer who looks like a tennis player, had fashioned three handsome rounds of 69, 72, and 68. That was too hot for me. I had held my practice form with a 68, 71, and 73, in that order, but I trailed Wood by three shots and Picard by one.

The night before the final day's play, I was cutting across the lobby of the Bon Air Hotel, heading for the elevators and an early-to-bed, when I ran into Bob Davis, my old globe-trotting friend. "Think you can catch 'em tomorrow?" Bob asked. Well, the way Craig was going, I replied, it was going to be a stiff assignment, but with a little luck I might still do it. "I've got just what you need," Bob said with dramatic inflection. He slid an elaborate ring from his finger and placed it in my palm. "Gene, this was given to me by a dear friend of mine in Mexico City. It's a lucky ring. Juárez was wearing it when he was murdered." I said I didn't see what was so lucky about that. "Don't worry, just wear it," Bob retorted. I told him I couldn't wear it because it would interfere with my grip, but that I'd carry it in my pocket.

On the last round I was paired with Walter Hagen. Walter was out of the running and in a mood for reminiscing about the good old days—how he had sent a wheelchair out on the course

31

for me when I was straggling home in the 1933 United States Open; how I had scoured St. Andrews later that season to find a similar chair or a taxi or a perambulator to help an exhausted Hagen limp into port in the British; how he had kept the Prince of Wales and President Harding waiting, and so on. We were followed by a sparse gallery, for the bulk of the spectators were watching either Jones or Wood and Picard, who were playing together three holes or so ahead of us. It was about five-thirty in the afternoon when Walter and I came to the 15th hole. Both of us lined out good drives, mine being exceptionally long as I had a tail-end hook on it and the ground was hard. As we were walking to our balls, an ear-splitting roar erupted from the gallery jammed around the 18th green watching Wood and Picard finish. It wasn't long before the news trickled down the valley: Wood had holed a birdie 3 on the 72nd for a total of 282. Picard was 286. As we neared the crest of the hill, I squinted at the clubhouse in the distance, where the photographers were snapping pictures of the happy winner and the newspapermen were hurrying to bat out their stories on Craig's victory.

Hagen played his second short of the pond that guards the approach to the green on the 485-yard 15th. I stopped for a moment and asked Stovepipe what I needed to win. "What do you mean, boss, to beat Craig Wood?" Stovepipe asked. I nodded. Hagen began to titter. "Oooh," Stovepipe groaned, as he checked our round, "you need four 3's, Mister Gene, 3, 3, 3, 3."

I did some calculating. I could possibly get a birdie 4 on the 15th . . . maybe a birdie 2 on the 16th . . . and then maybe a birdie 3 on either the 17th or the 18th which would give me a tie.

My high-flying optimism received a sudden jolt when I saw my lie. It was none too good. I went into a huddle with Stovepipe as to whether I should play a three-wood or a four-wood. The three, we decided, would never get the ball up from that close lie, being slightly deeper in the face than the four. The four, a new model called the Turfrider, had a hollow-back sole which enabled the club to go down after the ball. I knew that the only way I could reach the green with the four would be to toe the club in to decrease the loft and so give me extra yardage.

After it was settled that I would go with the four, I must have

32

been scanning the skies for some sign of approval or encouragement, for I was suddenly reminded of the lucky ring Bob Davis had given me. I extracted it from my pocket and rubbed it over Stovepipe's head to give its reputed powers every chance to go to work. I suppose the real contribution the ring made was that fooling with it tapered off the tension that had been building up in me. I took my stance with my four-wood and rode into the shot with every ounce of strength and timing I could muster. The split second I hit the ball I knew it would carry the pond. It tore for the flag on a very low trajectory, no more than thirty feet in the air. Running forward to watch its flight, I saw the ball land in the green, still dead on line. I saw it hop straight for the cup, and then, while I was straining to see how close it had finished, the small gallery behind the green let out a terrific shout and began to jump wildly in the air. I knew then that the ball had gone into the hole.

When I reached the green, the boy reporting the scores to the master score-board via telephone was trying to make it clear that Sarazen had got a 2 on the 15th. The operator at the master score-board kept telling him that he was mixed up and obviously meant to report a 2 on the 16th, the par 3, and the boy kept repeating that he didn't mean the 16th, he meant the 15th, the 485-yard 15th—Sarazen had holed a 235-yard wood shot for a 2, a double-eagle.

Within five minutes, five thousand frenetic fans had rushed down the hill to watch me finish. My own excitement had died down when I realized that after that miraculous shot I could tie Wood and perhaps beat him the next day. I had got my 3-under-par on one hole, and now all that I had to do to earn a tie was to match par on the last three holes.

On the 16th, a 135-yard 3, I had a grand chance for a birdie when my eight-iron stopped 10 feet from the cup, but I missed the straight putt. I secured my par 4 on the 17th without incident, since the wind, which was puffing up strong now, was behind me. The 18th was work. The wind was against me on that hole, 420 yards long and all uphill after the drive. What was normally a drive and a five or six was transformed into a drive and a long-iron or possibly a wood. Since the wind was blowing in slightly from the left, the surest way to hit the green with my second was to play a four-wood, making the left-hand edge of the green my target and trusting that the wind would cradle my ball into the pin. The shot came off well. My ball landed four feet past the pin and ran another thirty feet up the slope.

A great many expert putters, Ben Hogan for one, have three-putted the wickedly contoured home green at Augusta. It is a terror, and particularly when you have to gauge the delicate speed for a lengthy downhill putt. Hagen putted out while I studied the rolls and examined the grain. I stroked my approach putt gently and it trickled slowly down the rolls and died a slow death three feet short of the cup. Too much analysis would be a bad thing in that spot, I decided. I stepped up and hit the three-footer instantly. It dropped, and I had tied Wood.

Craig and I played off the next day over 36 frost-bitten holes, medal not match play. April in Georgia, and there we were blowing on our hands to keep them warm. For nine holes it was nip and tuck. Craig went out in front on the 1st when I went one over par. I made it up with a birdie on the 2nd. Craig, with a par, took the lead again on the short 6th. My birdie on the 7th squared our totals once more, and we both turned in 36. On the 10th I stuck my nose in front for the first time, and after that was never headed. By lunch I had built up a four-stroke advantage and I added another stroke in the afternoon. Craig is a notorious on-and-off putter, and he was "on" only during the last nine holes. His nines were 36, 39, 40, and 34—149. Mine were 36, 35, 36, 37—144. There is certainly nothing breathtaking about those figures, and yet I look back on those play-off rounds as constituting some of my finest golf. Certainly I was never straighter—in the rough only four times in 36 holes and never once bunkered. From the 11th hole through the 34th I put together a string of 24 consecutive pars. My play that entire week at Augusta, for that matter, was my best tournament effort since 1932, no question about that. During my four practice rounds, the four rounds of the championship proper, and the two rounds of the play-off, I went the full 180 holes without taking more than a 5 on my card.

But, of course, it was the double-eagle, that rarest of all golf birds, which was the talk of the fans at Augusta, and, I will readily admit, of Gene Sarazen, too. When Bobby Jones asked me if the Augusta National might have the ball and four-wood for permanent display in the clubhouse, he didn't have to coax me very hard. As a matter of fact, I was hoping that someone would suggest that a plaque, suitably inscribed, be placed on the 15th fairway to mark for posterity the spot from which I had played the shot. When I saw Stovepipe the day after the play-off, I asked him if he had picked up any talk around the club about possible plans to preserve my divot mark. "Mister Gene," Stovepipe answered with tantalizing slowness, "they went down there this morning, some of the greenkeepers, I mean, and they done sprinkled a little rye seed in the divot and covered it up."

I ran into Bob Davis in New York a week or so after the double-eagle. "About that ring, Gene," Bob said, clearing his throat, "I'm afraid I have a little confession to make. Juárez never saw that ring. It was just a trinket I picked up from a vendor one day while I was waiting to get my shoes shined."

BY GENE SARAZEN

FROM *Thirty Years of Championship Golf*

But we, the Four Million, discover sooner or later that something is lacking. We start out blithely, hit one ball on the nose, and decide we were cut out for crack golfers—only to find we were sewed up wrong. By devious paths we progress to a certain point, and there we stick, turning this way and that, striving sometimes to use our brains, if any, and at other times to proceed by dead reckoning or by the simple reflex action of the lowly angleworm, which travels straight ahead until he runs against something that stops him and then turns in whatever direction he may.

Yet always we hope to do better; always we keep a weather eye cocked for the Philosopher's Stone—possibly the eye we ought to keep on the ball. The eternal optimism of the game is upon us, and we never stop trying.

BY O. B. KEELER

FROM *Autobiography of an Average Golfer*

But the shot they still talk about in Atlanta is the one Ted Ray made on the old twelfth hole at East Lake; his second shot after a drive that seemed to everybody to have forced him away from a chance at a 4, on a hole four hundred and twenty yards in length. This hole extended north along the boundary line at the left with a cross-mound two hundred and eighty yards from the tee and a lone tree in the fairway just beyond the mound, and to the right of the line to the green. Ray's drive was the longest of the four but was pushed out enough to line up exactly with the tree, the ball being just short of the mound. The tree was about forty feet tall, with plenty of foliage. It was about twenty yards from the ball.

As the gallery scrambled along over the slippery dry grass in the afternoon sun, the golfers in it were debating what Ray would do. Would he slice an iron around the tree, or would he try a pulled shot? The green was fully one hundred and sixty yards away; the foliage of the tree was too thick to try a shot through it; and the tree was surely too close for him to hope to go over it and get anywhere near the green. The others played their second shots, full irons, and big Ted strode on up to his ball, puffing away at the inevitable pipe.

Scarcely glancing at the tree and the green beyond, he drew his pet mashie-niblick. And I am sure he hit that ball harder than any other while he was in Atlanta. He came down on it as if he would drive it through to China. From the "iron turf" flew a divot the size of his foot—an ample size—and from the gallery came a gasp and then a strangled sort of crow and then a roar as the ball, getting almost straight up in the air, went right over the tree-top, rose to an incredible height and completed an amazing parabola by landing on the green.

Men jumped up and down and pounded one another on the back and inquired of one another what they knew about *that*! I think that never since have I known a gallery so completely roused by a golf shot, apart from anything depending on that particular effort. And Ted Ray, his pipe in his mouth, the club tucked under his arm, was striding on toward the green long before the ball had come down, as if nothing at all had happened. He did not even look at it.

BY O. B. KEELER
FROM *The Autobiography of an Average Golfer*

The subject of applying the mind to a single stroke leads one to the question of concentration in general, concentration on the whole round. It varies with the individual according to his general outlook on life. A good many people cannot give of their best unless they play in silence: they like to lock themselves up in the strongholds of their minds and not to emerge until the round is done. Interruption breaks down their mental rhythm, and they find it difficult to recapture their tranquillity once it has gone.

One of the few great players who had the strength of mind to focus his thoughts at will upon the task in hand was Walter Hagen. In the height of an open championship he remained readily accessible to friends and acquaintances, to anyone who cared to talk to him as he went round. Measured in terms of distance, it took him about thirty yards of walking to re-harness his thoughts to the business in hand. At this distance from his ball he would cease to pay attention to the conversation, and the light of determination would come into his eye as he began to gather himself together for the next shot.

Harry Vardon's supremacy, as the other members of the Triumvirate would tell you, was due largely to the fact that it was almost impossible to put him off. Long delays and the marshalling of crowds, stupid remarks by spectators that would have aggravated a lesser man, all the trivial things that are calculated to upset the sensitive player, were as nothing to him. Where others were champing at the bit, anxious to get on with the job, Vardon sat contentedly on the tee box, puffing at his pipe and gazing peacefully at the landscape.

BY HENRY LONGHURST

FROM *Golf*

Yet not a little has been said, in a semi-sarcastic way, by devotees of other games than golf, about the comparative ease with which—as the sayers aver—a stationary ball can be, or should be, struck, compared with one in motion. These detractors forget the nicety of the stroke that is required. A tennis-player has a whole court into which to play; a cricketer a whole field; the golfer has to put his ball into a hole the size of a jam-pot, a quarter of a mile away.

BY ARNOLD HAULTAIN

FROM *The Mystery of Golf*

This course was of nine holes (it is now the site of several apartment houses), and the last hole called for a carry over a little pond, to a green immediately in front of the club-house. The somewhat elderly and irascible gentleman in question, playing in a foursome, had reached this ninth tee on the shore of the pond, and even from the club veranda it was evident that his temper was not of the best. Things had not been going right for him. His three companions carried the pond. Then he teed up, and drove—splash!—into the water. A remark was wafted through the still air. He teed again—another splash. Then followed an exhibition which I fear my wife would describe as childish. First this elderly gentleman spoke, in a loud, vexed voice. Then he hurled his driver into the pond. Then he snatched his bag of clubs from the caddie's shoulder, seized a stone from the pond side, stuffed it into the bag, grasped the strap as a hammer-thrower the handle of his weight, swung the bag three times around his head, and let it fly far out over the water. It hit with a great splash, and sank from sight. His three companions, respecting his mood, discreetly continued their game, while he came up to the club-house, sought a far corner of the veranda, and with a face closely resembling a Greek mask of Tragedy, sank down huddled into a chair.

On the veranda, too, his grief was respected. No one spoke to him. In fact, I think no one dared. We were careful that even our mirth did not reach his ears. He was alone with thoughts. The afternoon waned. His three companions again reached the ninth tee, drove the pond, and came into the club-house to dress. The caddies were about to depart. Then a strange thing happened; at its first intimation we tiptoed to a window to observe. He roused himself, leaned over the rail, and called a caddie.

"Boy," we heard him say, in a deep, tragic voice, "can you swim?"

"Yes, sir," the caddie replied.

"All right. About thirty feet out in front of the ninth tee there's a bag at the bottom of the pond. Go get it for me, and I'll give you five dollars."

The caddie ran, peeling his garments as he went. Modestly, retaining his tattered underclothes, he splashed in from the tee, while the somewhat elderly golf player gesticulated directions on the bank. Presently the boy's toes detected something, and he did a pretty surface dive, emerging with the bag strap in his right hand. He also rescued the floating driver, and we saw the promised bill passed to him, and watched him drag on his clothes over his wet undergarments. Slowly, even tenderly, the somewhat elderly gentleman emptied the water and the stone from his bag, and wiped the clubs on his handkerchief. With the wet, dripping burden over his shoulder he came across the footbridge and into the locker room, while we hastened to remove our faces from the door and windows, and attempted to appear casual.

He entered in silence, and strode to his locker. The silence grew painful. Somebody simply had to speak, or laugh. Finally somebody did speak, which was probably the safer alternative.

"Decided to try again, eh?"

The somewhat elderly gentleman wheeled upon the assemblage, his dripping bag still hanging from his shoulder.

"Yes, damn it!" he thundered.

BY WALTER PRITCHARD EATON
FROM *Penguins, Persons & Peppermints*

There are more "Don't's" in golf than there are in any other avocation in life. I put a few Don't's down here:—

1. Don't hurry—either before the game—or during the game —or after the game: otherwise you will contract the habit.

2. Don't hurry your stroke: time is of the essence of the impact.

3. Don't mind who your opponent may be; and

4. Don't watch your opponent: you are playing your game; let him play his.

5. Don't worry about your caddie. He may be an irritating little wretch; but for eighteen holes he is your caddie; accordingly

6. Don't lose your temper—about anything, anything whatsoever. If you lose your temper, you lose everything—self-control, self-respect, judgement, equanimity, decency of language,—and, of course, the hole, and probably the game.

7. Don't watch the pair behind—even if they drive into you. You can complain afterwards.

8. Don't experiment—unless you are in desperate difficulty— or are dormy.

9. Don't talk. If your opponent talks,

10. Don't listen to your opponent. Edge away from him. If your caddie talks,

11. Don't listen to your caddie; shut him up.

12. Don't fuss. Fussiness is inimical to seriousness.

13. Don't fidget. Fidgetiness is inimical to steadiness.

14. Don't argue. The rules are the rules. A moot point can be reserved.

15. Don't debate—even with yourself: there is the hole: there are your clubs.

16. Don't hesitate. Hesitation evinces weakness, and your opponent will notice it.

17. Don't be too polite; and

18. Don't be too sympathetic: golf is a combat.

19. Don't be cast down: it spoils one's game. On the other hand,

20. Don't be elated: that, too, spoils one's game.—Whether you are "up" or whether you are "down,"

21. Don't vary your game.

22. Don't put on airs. Lastly, and above all,

23. Don't take your eye off your ball—never. And, when the game is over,

24. Don't complain or explain.

BY ARNOLD HAULTAIN

FROM *The Mystery of Golf*

Alice in Bunkerland

"If forty pro's wrote forty books,
Besides what books there are,
Do you suppose," the Walrus said,
"I'd play this course in par?"
"I doubt it," said the carpenter,
And lit a fresh seegar.

BY BERT LESTON TAYLOR

FROM *A Line-o'-Gowf or Two*

Al Andereggen, veteran Chicago professional and golf range operator . . . now heads for Florida when the birds start winging south, or shortly thereafter, but still can't understand how a genuine golfer in any clime can put his clubs away on Labor Day, or ever, for that matter.

"Many a time I've played and watched the kids whizzing around on their ice skates. Golf's not a seasonal game. Once you learn to play it you play it as often as you can the rest of your life. I've played on Christmas Day and New Year's Day in Chicago, and when the weather was too bad I've driven to French Lick to play weekends. Anytime there's no snow on the ground and the temperature's 30 or above you can play. I had a putt one day for a sawbuck at Calumet. . . . It was the only putt I ever missed in my life on account of a blizzard. I had a groove cleared from my ball to the hole and thought I couldn't miss. But by the time it got up to the hole it looked like a snowball.

"We used to play for a few bucks," he went on. "And before we started I'd take three new balls into the clubhouse and get 'em like a hot potato by soaking 'em in hot water. Then I'd wrap two of 'em up in a handkerchief and put 'em in my back pocket. I'd play the other one a few holes, then switch. The guys would say: 'Boy, Al, are you hitting 'em! What'll you do when the weather gets warm?' They didn't know I was using those hot potatoes."

Al admits he likes a wager when he plays, but says he'd much rather play a fellow professional than an amateur.

"Those amateurs lie too much," he says with a grin. "They plead insanity on the first tee. The thing to do is just get a bunch of pros cutting each other up, the way they do in Florida in the winter time. Just count arms and legs and if the count's the same, spring even. A pro will always play another pro, even if he thinks he's gonna lose. He doesn't want the other guy to think he's a hacker. Many a day I've played the real top pros, figuring to myself: 'If I can just win one way I'll only drop a fin.'

"All those guys want to send each other back to the snow country. But if a guy's too sharp you put him on the fox list. I once shot a 68 and lost fifty bucks to a pro from New Jersey. I told him: 'Buddy, you better shellac it and put it on the wall. That's all you're gonna get from me.' He began screaming, telling me I still got $150 of his money I won earlier. I told him: 'Yeah, but I gotta file that.'"

Andereggen says he had a string of 19 rounds in succession in Florida in the winter of 1950–51 during which he shot 69 or better.

"I emptied out many a guy," he adds cheerfully. "They bet pretty good down there. You start out polite with a two dollar Nassau, and step off the last green stuck for $40."

He believes that one of the big differences between the top player and the hacker is this:

"The top player knows you don't hit it as hard as you can. When I hit a good one I always feel I could have hit it 20 yards further. Snead only lets it go when he has to. When Samuel Jackson wants to release he can hit it 300. But he knows he can let it go only twice a round or so. Otherwise he'd lose his timing."

Someone asked why Al ran a range instead of being a club pro.

"I like to run a driving range," he answered. "There's nobody to holler at you but yourself, and that relieves the pressure. I like to be my own boss. If you don't feel like working you can stay in the sack.

"And if I wasn't in this business I'd be in the golf ball business. I think I've recovered a million and a half golf balls. I been in many a photo-finish with big alligators and water moccasins looking for balls down south, and if anyone wants up to a million balls I know where to get 'em. Once in a while I still dip the body for a lark. I get a kick out of it. Especially if I think the bottom's paved with 'em. Some places, in two hours, a couple of guys can come up with three or four thousand balls. That's just like stepping on dimes and quarters."

Al glanced out at the tee line and indicated a nearby customer.

"He tells me he's shortened his backswing," Al said. "He nearly unties his shoelaces with it now, I wonder where he used to go before?"

Al paused, then shook his head.

"Man," he said reflectively, "I could show you swings out here that would stop your heart!"

BY PAUL NORTH
FROM *Chicagoland Golf* "One Man Sports Reel"

44

To be worth getting into, any particular brand of trouble must offer something more than the mere prospect of getting out of it alive. There must be a "reward" sensation. The man bounding from a dental chair, the mountain climber atop his crag, each experiences a moment of gratification which wipes out memory of trouble that has gone before. While no man can expect a happier climax of woe than the dental patient, tooth pulling has certain other drawbacks which retard its popularity. For one thing, you eventually run out of teeth. And the climber's big moment is a lonely triumph at best.

Golf provides a point of exhilaration which erases all pain, can be experienced often, and never dulls with repetition. A golf hole is sometimes called a "cup" or "can" because of the metal liner inserted in each. This metal golf cup is endowed with a rare tonal quality never noted by the music world, because it can only be detected by the super-sensitive ear of an ardent golfer.

A ball dropping into a golf cup produces a unique sound, which, to the untrained ear, might seem nothing more than a hollow "thump." Actually it is a combining, in one vibrant chord, of all the world's most inspiring symphonies. It's a hymn—an aria—taps in the night—a mother's lullaby—a Sousa march—a girl's soft laughter—pulsing jungle drums—sighing flutes—tolling bells—Scottish bagpipes—trumpets—cymbals—and an angel's song, all rolled into one. It's the "lost chord" rediscovered. No sweeter sound is known to ear of mortal.

BY REG MANNING

FROM *From Tee to Cup*

WOODCRAFT FOR GOLFERS

Do not become panicky when you have to pursue a golf ball into a wooded wilderness area. Remember, most of the time, the woods are full of golfers. Threshing in the underbrush seldom marks the presence of anything more menacing than a lost twenty-handicapper. Of course, a twenty-handicapper is dangerous enough, but you'll be reasonably safe if you approach him with due caution.

The most deadly thing in the woods is a wild ricocheting golf ball. Be alert. At the first warning signal (the anguished cry of "Oh, NO-O-O" in the distance), drop to the ground and remain covered until you hear the "all clear" (sound of a ball thudding to ground). When scouting through timberland, it's a good idea to crook one arm over your head to ward off stray ricochets.

Golfers should hunt in pairs while penetrating dense forested regions. If you are alone, however, and get lost, follow this simple procedure: stand quiet for a moment; then, in a loud, clear voice, call out these words, "Did anybody lose a new (brand name) ball?" Within a matter of seconds, golfers will come rushing from all directions to find you.

BY REG MANNING

FROM *From Tee to Cup*

Some men feel preternaturally aggrieved when asked to hole out a short putt; it should be scarcely necessary to say that they have absolutely no grounds whatever for annoyance at such a request. The extreme shortness of putts that *are* missed every now and again is justification enough and to spare; those of twelve inches, say, the length of the grip of a club, have been muddled over and over again; and once the present writer saw one missed, so ludicrously short, that he had the curiosity to measure it—just inside six inches; no mistake about it, and the misser thereof is in the front rank of amateurs, a winner of many medals; and the occasion was a medal round in which the writer was playing with the gentleman in question. It has always appeared matter of regret, emphasized by the reminiscence just recorded, that the custom of giving putts ever came into vogue at all. "Shall we say halved?" says the player eighteen inches away to you who are two-feet six from the hole; for well he wots that you will hole out, and for himself—well, perhaps that is his shaky distance. In "serious golf" the reply should be the courteous one: "Putt it out, mine enemy;" in fact, the occasion should not arise, for, in important matches, everything ought to be holed out just as in medal play, or the hole given up; if this were the universal practice, it would save much misunderstanding. Under the present system annoying things may happen, and often do; for instance, your adversary says to you, "you can't miss that, I suppose," or makes some similar remark; he has no business to say so: either he should frankly say "that's enough," or stand like an image till you have taken your precautions, and, let us say, holed out. But what *may* follow is this: the fact of the remark having been made is to create in your mind a feeling of uncertainty as to whether you are expected to putt out or not; this destroys your concentration of purpose; you play in a half-hearted way, and do miss; the hole, of

47

course, is lost, or you failed to win it; you stride off to the teeing ground fuming and incontinently miss your next drive. What, then, to do in the circumstances? Why, this—the advice has been given before . . . but is sound, and will bear repetition—have a decided policy and stick to it; when an opponent "supposes you can't miss that," say, "No, I can't," but on no account whatever try to play it, for possibly the result might falsify your bold assent— pick the ball up—kick it away to the teeing ground, and follow there yourself; you have right on your side, for by any such remark a man gives away his position. Or again, impropriety has been known to assume this form; the opponent says nothing, but turns and walks away; tyro, in a weak moment, plays, and misses: "What, did you miss it?" says the other: gnashing of teeth, and the result as before. Here again, the last thing you should ever do is to try to hole that putt; when a man says nothing, but turns and walks away, that action is tantamount to an admission that the subsequent proceedings interest him no more. It seems a pity that such a loophole should exist; but so long as the system of giving putts remains, we must be prepared for such contingencies as those mentioned.

BY H. S. C. EVERARD
FROM *Golf in Theory and Practice*

THE AMERICAN WOMAN AND GOLF

Golf is no longer a fad. At the beginning of its history in this country it was the fashion, and every woman who was or wished to be fashionable thought it necessary to flock to the golf clubs and wear a red coat, many of them being entirely ignorant of the difference between a caddy and a niblick. In those days all women had faith that a little effort would make them champions. Of all this number, the names of few of the early devotees remain in the entry list of the national tournaments. Few women have real persistence, and when they discovered that to play well meant unremitting toil, and that it was not a question of divine right or inherited genius, they became disheartened at the real problem of hard work and persistent practice.

The contestants for honors in these days are women and girls who really love the game and who mean business. They do not play because it is fashionable, but because they wish to excel and because they have a true fondness for sport. This being the case, the standard of golf has improved incredibly, almost to the extent of our being able to compete with the women players in England.

During last year American women's golf took a particularly long stride. For several years there were but two first-class players in America, viz., Miss Beatrix Hoyt, who held the championship for three years, and Mrs. Butler Duncan, who played equally well, but who for some reason never entered the championship tournaments, although able to beat the champion each year in private matches. The year when Miss Underhill won the championship it was anyone's game, and there were two or three who seemed equally deserving of the honor, while the same could be said of the following season. At the last championship tournament, however, the standard of golf had so improved that there were at least ten women who had apparently equal chances of success; the greatest improvement being in the extraordinarily long driving of the players.

Not many years ago 115 yards was a more than usually good drive or brassey shot, but now no one who cannot clear a 135 or 140 bunker can hope to compete for championship honors. This being the case, one would think that the game would be on the wane, but the list of entries was never so long as at Morristown and the contestants were representative of clubs all over the country. Golf is on the wane as a fashionable pastime, but is more of a recognized sport than ever before in the country at large.

The custom of having professional caddies at national or even club tournaments is one to be deplored. While technically within the rules, a professional caddy is not in the spirit of the game as played in this country. The best men players have long ago discarded them, but some of the women still cling to their support. If a woman does not know enough golf to play without eleventh-hour instruction she should not consider herself a fit competitor for national honors. If there was any possibility of framing a rule against professional caddies, it would be a wise action on the part of the United States Golf Association, but it is so difficult to tell where a caddy stops and an instructor begins that no rule could be made which could not be evaded, and one must hope that the women themselves will develop sportsmanship sufficient to dispense with such extraneous aid.

Golf is more of a game for general use than any other that has been at one time a fad. It has become an institution. The reason for this is that it requires so much less absolute strength and because it increases endurance rather than lessens it. This is because it is never, or should never be, violent. It is much more a question of skill than of force, and needs nicety and intelligence more than any other game. A mere practice of golf is excellent for exercise, but will never mean skill, because it is a game which almost everyone has to learn through the mind rather than by instinct. This being the case, one must acquire the essential rule from the beginning, or one merely goes from bad to worse. Practice does not make perfect, unless the practices are perfect, and this must come of much care and absolute attention to the regulations.

The reason why the Eastern women play better than the Western women is because the latter have not taken it so seriously as a science, and have merely regarded it as a pastime, with no ulterior motive. In the oldest club in the West, for example, the professionals have been so unable to impart their knowledge of the game that they have not even turned out a second-class player. Not one of the women has been taught to play in correct form, and they have played for years without any apparent improvement, although they have practiced daily. While this is deplorable, it is really more the fault of the professionals than of the women themselves, and proves first of all that effort wrongly applied is entirely useless.

Adults never learn anything by imitation, and it is only through intelligence and by intelligence that the game can be taught. The reason why so many people start with enthusiasm and stop in discouragement is on this account. They see no improvement, and believe they are incapable of learning, when in reality it is only a case of misdirected energy and uninstructed instinct.

The best instructor that has been teaching in this country is one who did not have any given rule upon which he insisted with every woman. He advocated a full swing with some and a half swing with others, recognizing each one's possibilities and limitations. He was an educated man who used his intelligence and told as well as showed one how. He taught successfully many players, and they all knew why they played every stroke. It never was a question of being off one's game; it was an almost exact science and did not depend upon that broken reed, instinct, but rather upon abstract knowledge.

In England almost all the women are long drivers, and the reason for it is that they were taught originally just when, how and where to put in their strength and get the velocity at the right spot, which is the whole secret of the business. It will always be a fascinating game for women, because it permits them to take out-of-door exercise without fatigue. No other game brings so much pleasure, so much exercise and so little fatigue when continued for hours, and for this reason it is particularly suited to our sex.

The great difficulty in the road to real excellence is the necessity for constant and unremitting practice, and there is no doubt that extreme nervousness is the result, particularly in the case of tournaments. For some reason, many days of continuous playing is particularly trying to the nerves. Even in the men's tournaments this is evident. The runner-up in a recent national championship lost ten pounds during the week's play, and many women lose all freshness of face as well as all semblance of calm during a summer spent in golfing events. For this reason medal play is more advisable than match play, as it is then purely a case of skill rather than endurance; also it would seem advisable that the national champion should not have to play down during the matches, but simply meet the winner as is done in the tennis tournaments.

There is no game where accident of weather or ill health can so entirely upset all calculation; even so small a matter as an unsympathetic or injudiciously advising caddy has often caused unnecessary and undeserved defeat. This year the new Haskell ball has given a new cause for inaccuracy. It is more resilient, no doubt, and carries a longer distance, but it is much more difficult to putt. Of the players in last year's tournament many had recently begun to play with it, though not with any degree of accuracy, which is a most important factor in every sport, particularly golf.

Now that golf has ceased to become a fad and has become a sport, it takes its place with the other recognized sports of the country, such as tennis, yachting, etc. Because it is possible to play it in youth and old age, it should have a greater number of devotees than any other sport in which women indulge, and if taken in moderation is a real assistance in the preservation of youth and health.

BY MRS. CHATFIELD TAYLOR
FROM *Collier's Magazine*

What self-deceivers golfers are! When they do a round far beyond anything they have ever done before they claim this as their true form. "I was in something like my best form today," airily said a 13-handicap who by a succession of inconceivable flukes had holed the course in a dozen strokes less than he had ever taken before. "Something like," be it noted, intending his audience to realize that his golf was capable of still higher flights. Poor self-deceiver! He reverted to his normal 90's the next day and has never since been known to leave that decade save to soar above it into the 100's.

Alas! it is our average round that is our true form, and the performance that gives us our handicap. And if by virtue of a series of good "breaks" we get round in 6 strokes less than our previous best, let us not make too much of this feat. Far better to join the humble company of a certain golfer who, after playing rather worse than usual, said he had come to the conclusion that when he played well he was off his game.

BY CECIL LEITCH

FROM *Golf*

Jimmy McDonald was Hagen's caddie throughout the 1925 season and made himself so indispensable that he was taken abroad for the British open. He was sole custodian of Hagen's famous golf bag, which housed, besides its quota of a dozen or more clubs and balls, an umbrella, a clock, a ball-cleaner and brushes, a case for tees, a thermomenter, a wind-gauge, a caddie whistle, a rule-book, an extra sweater, and a change of shoes. It may give you an idea of the demands upon a "big-time" caddie to state that Jimmy not only carried this bag, but mastered the use of each bit of its assorted contents.

BY GLENNA COLLETT

FROM *Ladies in the Rough*

When a preacher wants to scare his congregation into being good, he invariably goes back to ancient Rome for parallels to modern corruption. Love of fine clothes, jewels, wine; the desire to spend more money than one's neighbours, to have more divorces in the family than the people across the street—all those weaknesses of twentieth-century New York were present, we are told from the pulpit, in the Imperial City. But the Romans didn't play golf, thank heavens; and, with their unerring aptitude for all the vices in the catalogue, the Romans certainly would have invented golf and played it for all it was worth if it had been inherently evil. Therefore, by a logic that is ingenious even though faulty, I say that golf must be by nature a good clean sport, one that can't urge us into crime unless it's scandalously abused.

BY GLENNA COLLETT

FROM *Ladies in the Rough*

I did not play any golf whilst a prisoner, although Major C. R. Hutchinson had laid out a six—I think it was—hole course at Clousthal. Apparently the majority of people there played every day, and it must have been extremely dangerous. I am told it was an everyday occurrence to be hit by two balls at the same moment, and one man was hit by three at the same time on one occasion. Apparently all the holes crossed each other, the longest being about 100 yards long. Most of the players were but indifferent performers. In the afternoons a German under-officer used to parade about the course, and everybody tried to hit him, as he was very unpopular, but nobody ever remembered him being hit, which rather points to the players being a little erratic.

BY CYRIL J. H. TOLLEY

FROM *The Modern Golfer*

THE MECCA OF GOLF

Every golfer surely desires to see St. Andrews. It was the dream of my boyhood and like many another dream, it came true. I have seen the ancient city of golf twice, once when I was very happy, and once when I was very sad and both times I loved it.

There were many reasons for that, and one of them is as simple as a matter of color. I have always loved grey; women I have loved have worn it, and St. Andrews, as I have seen it, is always one shade of grey or another, and sometimes several. It is the mist from the sea that gives the color and name to the old grey city and the vigorous life to its inhabitants.

On both my visits I was alone, but it is the first one that I am always glad to describe. It was in 1911, and I had been traveling part of the time with Mr. Silas H. Strawn and Mr. William V. Kelly, two noted Chicagoans and golfers. It happened that they had already been at St. Andrews and preferred to finish their playing around Edinburgh. I felt, however, that an ardent golfer, although very young and a stranger, would be welcome at St. Andrews. For the old city beckons.

St. Andrews is just north of Edinburgh, about an hour by train. At this time I went by train and I was thrilled by the sound of the cars rattling over the Firth of Forth Bridge. I bore a letter from Mr. Strawn to the Secretary of the Royal and Ancient Club, which I presented immediately on my arrival, and I asked him to recommend some inexpensive place for me to stay. In consequence, I was lodged in a house overlooking the putting course and the sea, and the mistress of that household had lived there all her life. Her husband was dead, and maybe because I was feeling very far away from my own mother, she, at least, appeared to take a very kindly interest in me, and she will always be a part of my remembrances of St. Andrews. When I went back in that sad year of 1921, I asked for her and was told that she had taken the last long journey. It seemed a year of futile questions.

On that first visit the Secretary of the Royal and Ancient fixed me up with games, and I played thirty-six holes a day three days in succession. The first round was a disappointment, for I had expected too much, but from then on my interest grew enormously. When one is completely enveloped in the golfing atmosphere, has wandered in the city and has talked with the citizens, then the actual St. Andrews feeling is his.

Strange to say I seemed to learn most about St. Andrews from the sixty-year old motherly woman in whose house I found lodging. Sometimes we walked in St. Andrews in the long twilight after dinner, and sometimes we went down, a hundred feet or so, to the sea, and there we talked while the water rolled softly to the sandy shore.

I learned from her that golf is played in St. Andrews from January to December on regular greens without winter covering, in the most equable temperature in the United Kingdom, and with plenty of sunshine—but I have to confess that I saw little sunshine. Sometimes we walked up into the town, by the quaint shops, and twice to the University, the oldest in Scotland, with its timeworn buildings and its lovely shrubbery and grass; and up the miles of glorious sand along the beach, and into the inspiring scenery of the heights where the cemetery is. There we read the epitaphs in that strange graveyard of golfers, the records of golf shots and scores carved in cold marble that will live longer than any we have made. I wish that I could reproduce some of them here.

The Royal and Ancient Golf Club at St. Andrews is about the

fourth oldest club in the world, having been instituted in 1754. When you play on the old course where golf was played a hundred years before, you feel that every yard is enshrined in the memories of golfers. There can be seen the sweeping galleries and the outstanding figures of the game. Your thoughts dwell upon Freddie Tait, the most peculiarly beloved golfer of Britain. The British have a genius for friendship, and Freddie Tait was a fine golfer with an extraordinary charm.

There are four courses of eighteen holes now at St. Andrews, and a ladies' private putting course, and three public putting courses of eighteen holes each. Visitors have equal rights with the Royal and Ancient Club members and residents, during all months except August and September. The tariff was decreed by the St. Andrews' Act of 1913, in operation the whole year round; the new course is one shilling and the jubilee course is three pence.

Overlooking these courses are hotels and shops. Just opposite to where you play the second shot to the eighteenth green is the shop of R. Forgan and Sons. That fact brings to my mind Mr. J. B. Forgan and the big bank in Chicago, of which he was the honored head. It seems strange to think of a life beginning in a little quiet town far up in Scotland and ending in the big, bustling city beside the waters of Lake Michigan.

In visiting St. Andrews, one must not fail to spend a great deal of time in the clubhouse of the Royal and Ancient wherein the old equipments of the game can be read, dating back to the early history of golf. A half hour here may serve to make us a little more patient with all the innovations that shall surely come.

I think, too, that every pilgrim to the shrine of St. Andrews, masculine though the old saint be, will think of the city named for him, as a lovely grey lady sitting in her quiet beauty beside that Northern sea.

BY CHICK EVANS
FROM *Ida Broke, The Humor and Philosophy of Golf*

GOLFSMITH'S DESERTED VILLAGE

The location of the club in question doesn't matter. Suffice it to say that I stumbled on it by accident while making a motor tour. It was the condition of the course that first aroused my curiosity. An ideal natural layout, with little need for artificial hazards, but covered with weeds four feet high! When I saw the palatial clubhouse the mystery increased. The building was the length of three city blocks and the cheapest material in the whole structure was marble! But the whole place seemed deserted, except for a caretaker. I called the man out and questioned him.

"This is the Hianmitee Country Club," he explained. "It's the most exclusive golf club in the world. Piping Rock is a municipal course compared to this."

"Who plays here?" I asked.

"Nobody: It's too exclusive!"

"Whom does it exclude?"

"Everybody!"

"You mean—?"

"Listen. The twelve men who first organized the Hianmitee Club were leading figures in the social life of America. They planned to make it an upstage and Ritzy-nth-power-super-exclusive outfit. The qualifications for membership would make your hair curl into a permanent wave. The applicant must be worth a hundred millions. He must be from a First Family. He must furnish proof that his ancestors were first-cabin passengers on the Mayflower. His name must apear on the first page of the Social Register in large red type. His pedigree must show an unbroken record of gentlemanly conduct, free from moral stain, from the applicant clear back to the monkeys. And proof must be given that the said ancestors were monkeys of the very highest type. And so forth. The idea was to limit the membership to one hundred."

"Where did they find the hundred?"

"They didn't. Nobody could pass the test. At the end of a year's time the membership still consisted of the original twelve. A little later the roster had dwindled to ten. Reginald De Pupster, Third, and Montmorency K. Jackson-Jackson-Jackson had been eliminated. It came out that Reggie's great uncle had once run for Congress, and Monty's cousin had sung (though the critics said not) in vaudeville.

"Other scandals came to light as time went on and one by one the membership dwindled. Well, to make a long story less boresome, the club finally reached the point where it had a large and flourishing membership named Cornelius J. Rockerstall. Being the only member he was naturally the President of the Club. It was a pitiful sight to see the old boy playing alone, trying to defeat himself in the final round of the club championship, and yelling 'Fore' for no reason in particular."

"And what became of him? He doesn't play here now, and—"

"No. In looking through some old documents he discovered that his distant cousin, Pauline De Razzle-Tazzle, had once eloped with a garbage man. Being a conscientious man he felt it his duty to kick himself out of the Club. So Cornelius J., Member, submitted the case to the membership committee consisting of Cornelius J. and by the unanimous vote of Cornelius J., decided to ask for the resignation of Cornelius J. Accordingly Cornelius J., President, wrote a letter to himself demanding his own resignation, with the postscript 'I hope this will cause no hard feelings between us' and the next day Cornelius J. resigned."

BY BARRIE PAYNE

FROM *Ida Broke, The Humor and Philosophy of Golf*

ONE IN A TRILLION

Once upon a time there was a golfer who had a perfect wife.

When he told how his drive on the Sixth hit the pin, described in detail his birdie on the Tenth that should have been an eagle, and drew a diagram of the heelprint that ruined his shot on the Twelfth, she listened with rapt attention and begged him to tell the story all over again.

She applauded his many shots on the Nineteenth and said she just adored the odor of gin.

When, after being held up by a funeral procession threesome, he arrived home late for dinner, she kissed him and said, "I'm glad you took plenty of time for your game. Why didn't you stay and play nine more holes?"

In reply to his dutiful request to play with him on Sunday The Perfect Wife said, "I'm sorry, dear, but I've got a foursome arranged with three other ladies. I hope you don't mind."

One day he broke his pet mashie on a hidden rock and came home heart-broken. Instead of the usual, "Well, what of it? Can't you buy another?" his peerless mate wept sympathetically and offered to wear mourning for the dear departed.

The Wonder Woman was constantly urging him to play more golf, even at the risk of neglecting his business. "Golf means health," she said, "and health is more important than money."

If she happened to be present when he hit a long drive she always cried, "Attaboy! Two-eighty right down the middle!" instead of the customary "Where did it go? Into the rough? I didn't see it."

This Miracle of Femininity never tried to putt with a driver. She never attempted an explosion-shot with a brassie. She never lingered in the fairway on a crowded course to pick four-leaf clovers. She never chose a moment in the middle of his swing to remind him that his tie was twisted. She never laughed when he topped one into the creek.

When she dubbed a shot she invariably blamed herself. She always said, "I guess I didn't do what you told me" instead of "I did exactly as you said and look what happened! As a golf instructor you're the worst foul ball in the National League."

When her ball was lost she immediately said, "Let 'em go through" instead of "Let 'em wait. They shouldn't be so impatient."

When he came home tired after playing thirty-six holes she usually said, "I'll phone the Smiths we can't play bridge tonight. You ought to get some sleep."

Another of her favorite remarks: "I wrote mother not to come this month. I knew you were busy with golf and wouldn't have time to entertain her."

When her husband happened to mention the name of Bobby Jones she didn't ask, "Who's Bobby Jones?"

On a certain occasion she sent him this telegram: "Our house burned down today, but don't worry. We managed to save your golf clubs."

As I remarked in the beginning, once upon a time there was a golfer who had a perfect wife.

All fairy tales begin with "Once upon a time—."

BY BARRIE PAYNE

FROM *Ida Broke, The Humor and Philosophy of Golf*

SMOLLETT ON GOLF

In the fields called the Links, the citizens of Edinburgh divert themselves at a game called Golf, in which they use a curious kind of bat tipped with horn, and small elastic balls of leather, stuffed with feathers. . . . These they strike with such force and dexterity from one hole to another, that they will fly to an incredible distance. Of this diversion the Scots are so fond that, when the weather will permit, you may see a multitude of all ranks, from the senator of justice to the lowest tradesman, mingled together, in their shirts, and following the balls with the utmost eagerness. Among others, I was shown one particular set of golfers, the youngest of whom was turned fourscore. They were all gentlemen of independent fortunes, who had amused themselves with this pastime for the best part of a century, without ever having felt the least alarm from sickness or disgust; and they never went to bed without having each the best part of a gallon of claret in his belly. Such uninterrupted exercise, co-operating with the keen air from the sea, must, without all doubt, keep the appetite always on edge, and steel the constitution against all the common attacks of distemper.

BY TOBIAS SMOLLETT

FROM *Humphry Clinker*

I am a golfer. I have played for twenty years but I have recently made a discovery. I *hate it!*

Golf is a game only to the dub: he alone gets any fun, any satisfaction and any considerable benefit out of it. To the man who takes his game seriously, it is a torment. Annoyance, impatience, disappointment, rage—the confirmed addict suffers all of these. If he likes golf enough to try and play it well its pleasure vanishes: if he sets out to shoot a low score he dooms himself to anxiety, anguish and chagrin. For him all pleasure in the sport evaporates and the residue upon his tongue is wormwood.

The duffer, on the other hand, tastes nothing but pure satisfaction. He speeds to the links with joy in his heart, he dresses with the inflammatory eagerness of a bridegroom and he capers to the caddy house. He plays an explosion shot from the first tee, removing a great chunk therefrom with his driver. It is a shot which Kirkwood couldn't duplicate and it gains him nearly thirty yards. But is he disturbed? By no means. He goes blithely ahead lacerating the ball as he kicks it along, drinking in the sunshine, enjoying the exercise and caring little whether he does a hole in four or in multiples thereof. If by some accident he occasionally hits the ball squarely on the button he drops ten years from his age: if not, it doesn't matter. There's another hole coming.

That, without doubt, is the spirit in which golf should be played by the average man—carelessly, gladly, terribly. The advantage, mental, physical, and spiritual, which the cluck player enjoys over the low-handicap man is that he gets a great kick out of one or two good shots during a round, whereas the other, if he muffs a couple, decides to drink iodine and jump off a bridge.

But let the dub beware. He is toying with razor blades, he is juggling hand grenades. If he ever makes a decent score, ten to one he will be lost. He will begin to take lessons. He will study the science of the thing. He will sneak off and practice. He will buy a set of matched clubs. There isn't much hope for him after that. Gone are the days when he could top a ball and say something funny. As he explores the mysteries, parts the veil and gradually improves his game, a complete change in his mental and physical metabolism occurs. He grows pessimistic and apprehensive. He develops temperament and gets so jumpy that he can't putt if an ant stirs. He may, and probably will, remain a duffer—few graduate from that class—but his peace of mind is gone forever. The worst has happened. Thereafter he will be no stranger to torment of soul and bitterness of spirit.

Not long ago, in the locker room of a club, I noticed a globular little man, pink-faced and beaming. He was surrounded by half a dozen members who were clinking glasses and patting him on the bare back. I learned that they were congratulating him on having broken a hundred for the first time and he radiated happiness like a base-burner. He glowed, he expanded until he had fewer wrinkles than a grape: he was a boy again.

Presently the club champion slouched in dragging his heels. His pallid face was seamed, his shoulders drooped and in his eyes was that expression of hope abandoned which one saw in the eyes of people bent over the ticker tape in that ghastly month of October, 1929. With a deep sigh, half moan, he sank onto a bench and sat gazing at the floor, his cupped hands supporting his face.

"Hello, Jim!" somebody called. "Will you join us in a snifter?"

The champion's shoulders heaved, he shook his head without looking up.

"How'd it go today?" the other asked.

"Oh, my god!" Jim ran a trembling hand through his wet hair: in a voice that seemed to issue from the tomb, he answered: "I hooked one out of bounds and three-putted two greens! . . . A lousy seventy-seven! I guess I'll quit the game. There's no hope for me."

Hope! It is all the serious-minded golfer has to cling to. And how he clings! To him the game is a dull chore, a battle in which he invariably meets defeat. Day after day it beats him and he only licks his wounds and comes back for more. But it breaks his spirit finally.

Women have the right idea. Never hurry, enjoy a cosy chat on every green, take four or five practice swings to each shot and never let anybody go through—the brutes! And don't be fussy about rules, either—they're only technicalities; improve your lie; if there's any doubt about a putt, concede it to yourself.

BY REX BEACH

FROM *A New Way to Better Golf*

The golf pioneers were brave men, not unlike our sturdy Pilgrim Fathers, who kept pegging away at the foundations of this nation in the face of terrible hardships. Without detracting one iota from the fortitude of these early settlers, I doubt whether their courage exceeded that of the heroes who introduced Uncle Sam to golf and tried to convince him it was a he-man affair. Uncle Sam couldn't see the he-manism of it; and he dismissed it as a sissy game and those who played it as dudes. So positive were the denizens of the Gas House District on this score that none was so bold as to venture into those quarters with a golf bag swung over his shoulders. Going over the top in France never held such terrors as this.

BY JEROME TRAVERS AND JAMES CROWELL
FROM *The Fifth Estate*

Travis' English triumph is a golf epic. The late Waldo Burton, who was at Sandwich at the time and fancied the long odds quoted against Travis' chances, a foresight which repaid him handsomely, gave me a first-hand account of it. Let me give a brief outline of the incident as Burton related it to me.

The outstanding feature of Travis' play had been the accuracy of his shots. The precision of his putting was uncanny. To many an American opponent the click of his putter had been as a funeral dirge of the links. He was never beaten on any hole until he and his adversary had attended to the formalities of putting. If it

65

happened that his opponent lay six feet from the pin in 2 and Travis twenty feet away in 3, it was no safe bet that this could be counted as a lost hole for the Old Man. In fact, the reverse has happened many times. Travis has sunk his twenty-footer and the other player, unnerved by this exhibition has floundered around with three putts before holing the ball.

But in the 1904 British championship the bottom seemed to drop out of America's hope for success when Travis suffered an unaccountable slump in his putting a few days before the start of the tournament. It was a complete reversal of his usual putting form, and the distressing part of it was that the trouble showed no evidence of disappearing as the day for the championship to start drew close. In fact, as Burton told me, Travis awoke on the morning of that day itself with his putting troubles in their most aggravated form and with none but an outside hope that a sudden windfall would put him back on his game.

The windfall came. It came in the form of a putter which he borrowed from an American friend as he went into action. It was a type of putter the English people were wholly unaccustomed to, a product of golf in America and known as the Schenectady putter because it was invented by a man named Wright, who worked for the General Electric Company at the Schenectady plant. I do not know whether Travis had ever used one of these clubs before, but the effect which the change produced on his play was amazing. Waldo Burton told me he sank the first putt he made with it and from that moment he was invincible on the greens.

Through the various rounds of the British championship Travis literally putted his way to the final round, in which he faced Edward Blackwell, a capable veteran of the game and a demon driver, who some twelve years before had driven a gutta-percha ball three hundred and sixty-six yards at St. Andrews. His streak of phenomenal putting never faltered. The English critics admitted they had never seen anything to equal it. Hole after hole which seemed to be lost to him on Blackwell's advantage from the tee and through the fairway was won by the deadly putts which Travis kept dropping into the cup. One hole may be used as an illustration. Travis had used a cleek from the tee, but the shot was so bad he had to use the same club for his second, which found him on the edge of the green about thirty-five feet away from the cup. Blackwell was on in 1. Travis dropped his thirty-five-footer for a 3, and Blackwell took three putts for a 4.

The match was marked by an incident which is unquestionably without parallel in all golf history and stands small chance of ever being duplicated. After Travis had sunk two or three long putts, Waldo Burton seemed to sense that the American champion had embarked on a remarkable exhibition of putting. It was something more than a hunch. It was a conviction.

A hole or two later Travis' ball lay some distance from the cup, the chances being about two to one that he would not sink it. As the Old Man surveyed the ground preparatory to tapping the ball, Burton turned to one of his English friends and offered to bet him even money that Travis would hole the putt. The Britisher snapped him up, and Travis obliged his American admirer by dropping the ball into the hole.

When Travis' ball lay twenty, twenty-five, thirty, and thirty-five feet away from the pin on subsequent greens, Burton kept offering to bet all comers that the putt would be made, increasing the stakes as he went. The Englishmen, believing that this weird streak of accuracy could not keep up, accommodated him by covering every wager. And Travis continued rewarding Burton for his unwavering faith by shooting the ball into the cup from all distances and all angles.

Burton had won so much money toward the final stages of the match that his English friends were not only broke but refused to make further bets against Travis, no matter if his ball lay thirty-five feet from the pin. I have never heard of a similar situation and never expect to hear of one. The odds against a player sinking a thirty-five-footer should be at least ten to one. I cannot see how the time will ever come again when a gallery will have a chance to get an even bet on the proposition, and certainly no gallery of the future will ever refuse to make the most of such an opportunity, if it comes.

BY JEROME D. TRAVERS AND JAMES R. CROWELL
FROM *The Fifth Estate*

ORDEAL BY GOLF

A pleasant breeze played among the trees on the terrace outside the Manhooset Golf and Country Club. It ruffled the leaves and cooled the forehead of the Oldest Member, who, as was his custom of a Saturday afternoon, sat in the shade on a rocking-chair, observing the younger generation as it hooked and sliced in the valley below. The eye of the Oldest Member was thoughtful and reflective. When it looked into yours you saw in it that perfect peace, that peace beyond understanding, which comes at its maximum only to the man who has given up golf.

The Oldest Member has not played golf since the rubber-cored ball superseded the old dignified gutty. But as a spectator and philosopher he still finds pleasure in the pastime. He is watching it now with keen interest. His gaze, passing from the lemonade which he is sucking through a straw, rests upon the Saturday foursome which is struggling raggedly up the hill to the ninth green. Like all Saturday foursomes, it is in difficulties. One of the patients is zigzagging about the fairway like a liner pursued by submarines. Two others seem to be digging for buried treasure, unless—it is too far off to be certain—they are killing snakes. The remaining cripple, who has just foozled a mashie-shot, is blaming his caddie. His voice, as he upbraids the innocent child for breathing during his up-swing, comes clearly up the hill.

The Oldest Member sighs. His lemonade gives a sympathetic gurgle. He puts it down on the table.

How few men, says the Oldest Member, possess the proper golfing temperament! How few indeed, judging by the sights I see here on Saturday afternoons, possess any qualification at all for golf except a pair of baggy knickerbockers and enough money to enable them to pay for the drinks at the end of the round. The ideal golfer never loses his temper. When I played, I never lost my temper. Sometimes, it is true, I may, after missing a shot, have broken my club across my knees; but I did it in a calm and judicial spirit, because the club was obviously no good and I was going to get another one anyway. To lose one's temper at golf is foolish. It gets you nothing, not even relief. Imitate the spirit of Marcus Aurelius. "Whatever may befall thee," says that great man in his "Meditations," "it was preordained for thee from everlasting. Nothing happens to anybody which he is not fitted by nature to bear." I like to think that this noble thought came to him after he had sliced a couple of new balls into the woods, and that he jotted it down on the back of his score-card. For there can be no doubt that the man was a golfer, and a bad golfer at that. Nobody who had not had a short putt stop on the edge of the hole could possibly have written the words: "That which makes the man no worse than he was makes life no worse. It has no power to harm, without or within." Yes, Marcus Aurelius undoubtedly played golf, and all the evidence seems to indicate that he rarely went round in under a hundred and twenty. The niblick was his club.

Speaking of Marcus Aurelius and the golfing temperament recalls to my mind the case of young Mitchell Holmes. Mitchell, when I knew him first, was a promising young man with a future before him in the Paterson Dyeing and Refining Company, of which my old friend, Alexander Paterson, was the president. He had many engaging qualities—among them an unquestioned ability to imitate a bulldog quarrelling with a Pekingese in a way which had to be heard to be believed. It was a gift which made him much in demand at social gatherings in the neighbourhood, marking him off from other young men who could only almost play the mandolin or recite bits of "Gunga Din"; and no doubt it was this talent of his which first sowed the seeds of love in the heart of Millicent Boyd. Women are essentially hero-worshippers, and when a warm-hearted girl like Millicent has heard a personable young man imitating a bulldog and a Pekingese to the applause of a crowded drawing-room, and has been able to detect the exact point at which the Pekingese leaves off and the bulldog begins, she can never feel quite the same to other men. In short, Mitchell and Millicent were engaged, and were only waiting to be married till the former could bite the Dyeing and Refining Company's ear for a bit of extra salary.

Mitchell Holmes had only one fault. He lost his temper when playing golf. He seldom played a round without becoming piqued, peeved, or—in many cases—chagrined. The caddies on our links, it was said, could always worst other small boys in verbal argument by calling them some of the things they had heard Mitchell call his ball on discovering it in a cuppy lie. He had a great gift of language, and he used it unsparingly. I will admit that there was some excuse for the man. He had the makings of a brilliant golfer, but a combination of bad luck and inconsistent play invariably robbed him of the fruits of his skill. He was the sort of player who does the first two holes in one under par and then takes an eleven at the third. The least thing upsets him on the links. He missed short putts because of the uproar of the butterflies in the adjoining meadows.

It seemed hardly likely that this one kink in an otherwise admirable character would ever seriously affect his working or professional life, but it did. One evening, as I was sitting in my garden, Alexander Paterson was announced. A glance at his face told me that he had come to ask my advice. Rightly or wrongly, he regarded me as one capable of giving advice. It was I who had changed the whole current of his life by counselling him to leave the wood in his bag and take a driving-iron off the tee; and in one or two other matters, like the choice of a putter (so much more important than the choice of a wife), I had been of assistance to him.

Alexander sat down and fanned himself with his hat, for the evening was warm. Perplexity was written upon his fine face.

"I don't know what to do," he said.

"Keep the head still—slow back—don't press," I said, gravely. There is no better rule for a happy and successful life.

"It's nothing to do with golf this time," he said. "It's about the treasurership of my company. Old Smithers retires next week, and I've got to find a man to fill his place."

"That should be easy. You have simply to select the most deserving from among your other employees."

"But which *is* the most deserving? That's the point. There are two men who are capable of holding the job quite adequately. But then I realise how little I know of their real characters. It is the treasurership, you understand, which has to be filled. Now, a man who was quite good at another job might easily get wrong ideas into his head when he became a treasurer. He would have the handling of large sums of money. In other words, a man who in ordinary circumstances had never been conscious of any desire to visit the more distant portions of South America might feel the urge, so to speak, shortly after he became a treasurer. That is my difficulty. Of course, one always takes a sporting chance with any treasurer; but how am I to find out which of these two men would give me the more reasonable opportunity of keeping some of my money?"

I did not hesitate a moment. I held strong views on the subject of character-testing.

"The only way," I said to Alexander, "of really finding out a man's true character is to play golf with him. In no other walk of life does the cloven hoof so quickly display itself. I employed a lawyer for years, until one day I saw him kick his ball out of a heel-mark. I removed my business from his charge next morning. He has not yet run off with any trust-funds, but there is a nasty gleam in his eye, and I am convinced that it is only a question of time. Golf, my dear fellow, is the infallible test. The man who can go into a patch of rough alone, with the knowledge that only God is watching him, and play his ball where it lies, is the man who will serve you faithfully and well. The man who can smile bravely when his putt is diverted by one of those beastly wormcasts is pure gold right through. But the man who is hasty, unbalanced, and violent on the links will display the same qualities in the wider field of everyday life. You don't want an unbalanced treasurer, do you?"

"Not if his books are likely to catch the complaint."

"They are sure to. Statisticians estimate that the average of crime among good golfers is lower than in any class of the community except bishops. Since Willie Park won the first championship at Prestwick in the year 1860 there has, I believe, been no instance of an Open Champion spending a day in prison. Whereas the bad golfers—and by bad I do not mean incompetent, but

71

black-souled—the men who fail to count a stroke when they miss the globe; the men who never replace a divot; the men who talk while their opponent is driving; and the men who let their angry passions rise—these are in and out of Sing-Sing all the time. They hardly find it worth while to get their hair cut in their brief intervals of liberty."

Alexander was visibly impressed.

"That sounds sensible, by George!" he said.

"It is sensible."

"I'll do it! Honestly, I can't see any other way of deciding between Holmes and Dixon."

I started.

"Holmes? Not Mitchell Holmes?"

"Yes. Of course you must know him? He lives here, I believe."

"And by Dixon do you mean Rupert Dixon?"

"That's the man. Another neighbour of yours."

I confess that my heart sank. It was as if my ball had fallen into the pit which my niblick had digged. I wished heartily that I had thought of waiting to ascertain the names of the two rivals before offering my scheme. I was extremely fond of Mitchell Holmes and of the girl to whom he was engaged to be married. Indeed, it was I who had sketched out a few rough notes for the lad to use when proposing; and results had shown that he had put my stuff across well. And I had listened many a time with a sympathetic ear to his hopes in the matter of securing a rise of salary which would enable him to get married. Somehow, when Alexander was talking, it had not occurred to me that young Holmes might be in the running for so important an office as the treasurership. I had ruined the boy's chances. Ordeal by golf was the one test which he could not possibly undergo with success. Only a miracle could keep him from losing his temper, and I had expressly warned Alexander against such a man.

When I thought of his rival my heart sank still more. Rupert Dixon was rather an unpleasant young man, but the worst of his enemies could not accuse him of not possessing the golfing temperament. From the drive off the tee to the holing of the final putt he was uniformly suave.

When Alexander had gone, I sat in thought for some time. I was faced with a problem. Strictly speaking, no doubt, I had no right to take sides; and, though secrecy had not been enjoined upon me in so many words, I was very well aware that Alexander was under the impression that I would keep the thing under my hat and not reveal to either party the test that awaited him. Each candidate was, of course, to remain ignorant that he was taking part in anything but a friendly game.

But when I thought of the young couple whose future depended on this ordeal, I hesitated no longer. I put on my hat and went round to Miss Boyd's house, where I knew that Mitchell was to be found at this hour.

The young couple were out on the porch, looking at the moon. They greeted me heartily, but their heartiness had a rather tinny sound, and I could see that on the whole they regarded me as one of those things which should not happen. But when I told my story their attitude changed. They began to look on me in the pleasanter light of a guardian, philosopher, and friend.

"Wherever did Mr. Paterson get such a silly idea?" said Miss Boyd, indignantly. I had—from the best motives—concealed the source of the scheme. "It's ridiculous!"

"Oh, I don't know," said Mitchell. "The old boy's crazy about golf. It's just the sort of scheme he would cook up. Well, it dishes *me!*"

"Oh, come!" I said.

"It's no good saying 'Oh, come!' You know perfectly well that I'm a frank, outspoken golfer. When my ball goes off nor'-nor'-east when I want it to go due west I can't help expressing an opinion about it. It is a curious phenomenon which calls for comment, and I give it. Similarly, when I top my drive, I have to go on record as saying that I did not do it intentionally. And it's just these trifles, as far as I can make out, that are going to decide the thing."

"Couldn't you learn to control yourself on the links, Mitchell darling?" asked Millicent. "After all, golf is only a game!"

Mitchell's eyes met mine, and I have no doubt that mine showed just the same look of horror which I saw in his. Women say these things without thinking. It does not mean that there is

73

any kink in their character. They simply don't realise what they are saying.

"Hush!" said Mitchell, huskily, patting her hand and overcoming his emotion with a strong effort. "Hush, dearest!"

Two or three days later I met Millicent coming from the post-office. There was a new light of happiness in her eyes, and her face was glowing.

"Such a splendid thing has happened," she said. "After Mitchell left that night I happened to be glancing through a magazine, and I came across a wonderful advertisement. It began by saying that all the great men in history owed their success to being able to control themselves, and that Napoleon wouldn't have amounted to anything if he had not curbed his fiery nature, and then it said that we can all be like Napoleon if we fill in the accompanying blank order-form for Professor Orlando Rollitt's wonderful book, 'Are You Your Own Master?' absolutely free for five days and then two dollars sixty-five, but you must write at once because the demand is enormous and pretty soon it may be too late. I wrote at once, and luckily I was in time, because Professor Rollitt did have a copy left, and it's just arrived. I've been looking through it, and it seems splendid."

She held out a small volume. I glanced at it. There was a frontispiece showing a signed photograph of Professor Orlando Rollitt controlling himself in spite of having long white whiskers, and then some reading matter, printed between wide margins. One look at the book told me the professor's methods. To be brief, he had simply swiped Marcus Aurelius's best stuff, the copyright having expired some two thousand years ago, and was retailing it as his own. I did not mention this to Millicent. It was no affair of mine. Presumably, however obscure the necessity, Professor Rollitt had to live.

"I'm going to start Mitchell on it today. Don't you think this is good? 'Thou seest how few be the things which if a man has at his command his life flows gently on and is divine.' I think it will be wonderful if Mitchell's life flows gently on and is divine for two dollars sixty-five, don't you?"

At the club-house that evening I encountered Rupert Dixon. He was emerging from a shower-bath, and looked as pleased with himself as usual.

"Just been going round with old Paterson," he said. "He was asking after you. He's gone back to the city in his car."

I was thrilled. So the test had begun!

"How did you come out?" I asked.

Rupert Dixon smirked. A smirking man, wrapped in a bath towel, with a wisp of wet hair over one eye, is a repellent sight.

"Oh, pretty well. I won by six and five. In spite of having poisonous luck."

I felt a gleam of hope at these last words.

"Oh, you had bad luck?"

"The worst. I over-shot the green at the third with the best brassey-shot I've ever made in my life—and that's saying a lot—and lost my ball in the rough beyond it."

"And I suppose you let yourself go, eh?"

"Let myself go?"

"I take it that you made some sort of demonstration?"

"Oh, no. Losing your temper doesn't get you anywhere at golf. It only spoils your next shot."

I went away heavy-hearted. Dixon had plainly come through the ordeal as well as any man could have done. I expected to hear every day that the vacant treasurership had been filled, and that Mitchell had not even been called upon to play his test round. I suppose, however, that Alexander Paterson felt that it would be unfair to the other competitor not to give him his chance, for the next I heard of the matter was when Mitchell Holmes called me up on the Friday and asked me if I would accompany him round the links the next day in the match he was playing with Alexander, and give him my moral support.

"I shall need it," he said. "I don't mind telling you I'm pretty nervous. I wish I had had longer to get the stranglehold on that 'Are You Your Own Master?' stuff. I can see, of course, that it is the real tabasco from start to finish, and absolutely as mother makes it, but the trouble is I've only had a few days to soak it into my system. It's like trying to patch up a motor car with string. You never know when the thing will break down. Heaven knows

75

what will happen if I sink a ball at the water-hole. And something seems to tell me I am going to do it."

There was silence for a moment.

"Do you believe in dreams?" asked Mitchell.

"Believe in what?"

"Dreams."

"What about them?"

"I said, 'Do you believe in dreams?' Because last night I dreamed that I was playing in the final of the Open Championship, and I got into the rough, and there was a cow there, and the cow looked at me in a sad sort of way and said, 'Why don't you use the two-V grip instead of the interlocking?' At the time it seemed an odd sort of thing to happen, but I've been thinking it over and I wonder if there isn't something in it. These things must be sent to us for a purpose."

"You can't change your grip on the day of an important match."

"I suppose not. The fact is, I'm a bit jumpy, or I wouldn't have mentioned it. Oh, well! See you tomorrow at two."

The day was bright and sunny, but a tricky cross-wind was blowing when I reached the clubhouse. Alexander Paterson was there, practising swings on the first tee; and almost immediately Mitchell Holmes arrived, accompanied by Millicent.

"Perhaps," said Alexander, "we had better be getting under way. Shall I take the honour?"

"Certainly," said Mitchell.

Alexander teed up his ball.

Alexander Paterson has always been a careful rather than a dashing player. It is his custom, a sort of ritual, to take two measured practice-swings before addressing the ball, even on the putting-green. When he does address the ball he shuffles his feet for a moment or two, then pauses, and scans the horizon in a suspicious sort of way, as if he had been expecting it to play some sort of a trick on him when he was not looking. A careful inspection seems to convince him of the horizon's *bona fides*, and he turns his attention to the ball again. He shuffles his feet once more, then raises his club. He waggles the club smartly over the ball three times, then lays it behind the globule. At this point he suddenly peers at the horizon again, in the apparent hope of catching it off its guard. This done, he raises his club very slowly, brings it back till it almost touches the ball, raises it again, brings it down again, raises it once more, and brings it down for the third time. He then stands motionless, wrapped in thought, like some Indian fakir contemplating the infinite. Then he raises his club again and replaces it behind the ball. Finally he quivers all over, swings very slowly back, and drives the ball for about a hundred and fifty yards in a dead straight line.

It is a method of procedure which proves sometimes a little exasperating to the highly strung, and I watched Mitchell's face anxiously to see how he was taking his first introduction to it. The unhappy lad had blenched visibly. He turned to me with the air of one in pain.

"Does he always do that?" he whispered.

"Always," I replied.

"Then I'm done for! No human being could play golf against a one-ring circus like that without blowing up!"

I said nothing. It was, I feared, only too true. Well-poised as I am, I had long since been compelled to give up playing with Alexander Paterson, much as I esteemed him. It was a choice between that and resigning from the Baptist Church.

At this moment Millicent spoke. There was an open book in her hand. I recognised it as the life-work of Professor Rollitt.

"Think on this doctrine," she said, in her soft, modulated voice, "that to be patient is a branch of justice, and that men sin without intending it."

Mitchell nodded briefly, and walked to the tee with a firm step.

"Before you drive, darling," said Millicent, "remember this. Let no act be done at haphazard, nor otherwise than according to the finished rules that govern its kind."

The next moment Mitchell's ball was shooting through the air, to come to rest two hundred yards down the course. It was a magnificent drive. He had followed the counsel of Marcus Aurelius to the letter.

An admirable iron-shot put him in reasonable proximity to the pin, and he holed out in one under bogey with one of the nicest putts I have ever beheld. And when at the next hole, the danger-

77

ous water-hole, his ball soared over the pond and lay safe, giving him par for the hole, I began for the first time to breathe freely. Every golfer has his day, and this was plainly Mitchell's. He was playing faultless golf. If he could continue in this vein, his unfortunate failing would have no chance to show itself.

The third hole is long and tricky. You drive over a ravine—or possibly into it. In the latter event you breathe a prayer and call for your niblick. But, once over the ravine, there is nothing to disturb the equanimity. Par is five, and a good drive, followed by a brassie-shot, will put you within easy mashie-distance of the green.

Mitchell cleared the ravine by a hundred and twenty yards. He strolled back to me, and watched Alexander go through his ritual with an indulgent smile. I knew just how he was feeling. Never does the world seem so sweet and fair and the foibles of our fellow human beings so little irritating as when we have just swatted the pill right on the spot.

"I can't see why he does it," said Mitchell, eyeing Alexander with a toleration that almost amounted to affection. "If I did all those Swedish exercises before I drove, I should forget what I had come out for and go home." Alexander concluded the movements, and landed a bare three yards on the other side of the ravine. "He's what you would call a steady performer, isn't he? Never varies!"

Mitchell won the hole comfortably. There was a jauntiness about his stance on the fourth tee which made me a little uneasy. Over-confidence at golf is almost as bad as timidity.

My apprehensions were justified. Mitchell topped his ball. It rolled twenty yards into the rough, and nestled under a dock-leaf. His mouth opened, then closed with a snap. He came over to where Millicent and I were standing.

"I didn't say it!" he said. "What on earth happened then?"

"Search men's governing principles," said Millicent, "and consider the wise, what they shun and what they cleave to."

"Exactly," I said. "You swayed your body."

"And now I've got to go and look for that infernal ball."

"Never mind, darling," said Millicent. "Nothing has such power to broaden the mind as the ability to investigate systematically and truly all that comes under thine observation in life."

"Besides," I said, "you're three up."

"I shan't be after this hole."

He was right. Alexander won it in five, one above bogey, and regained the honour.

Mitchell was a trifle shaken. His play no longer had its first careless vigour. He lost the next hole, halved the sixth, lost the short seventh, and then, rallying, halved the eighth.

The ninth hole, like so many on our links, can be a perfectly simple four, although the rolling nature of the green makes bogey always a somewhat doubtful feat; but, on the other hand, if you foozle your drive, you can easily achieve double figures. The tee is on the farther side of the pond, beyond the bridge, where the water narrows almost to the dimensions of a brook. You drive across this water and over a tangle of trees and undergrowth on the other bank. The distance to the fairway cannot be more than sixty yards, for the hazard is purely a mental one, and yet how many fair hopes have been wrecked there!

Alexander cleared the obstacles comfortably with his customary short, straight drive, and Mitchell advanced to the tee.

I think the loss of the honour had been preying on his mind. He seemed nervous. His up-swing was shaky, and he swayed back perceptibly. He made a lunge at the ball, sliced it, and it struck a tree on the other side of the water and fell in the long grass. We crossed the bridge to look for it; and it was here that the effect of Professor Rollitt began definitely to wane.

"Why on earth don't they mow this darned stuff?" demanded Mitchell, querulously, as he beat about the grass with his niblick.

"You have to have rough on a course," I ventured.

"Whatever happens at all," said Millicent, "happens as it should. Thou wilt find this true if thou shouldst watch narrowly."

"That's all very well," said Mitchell, watching narrowly in a clump of weeds but seeming unconvinced. "I believe the Greens Committee run this darned club purely in the interests of the caddies. I believe they encourage lost balls, and go halves with the little beasts when they find them and sell them!"

Millicent and I exchanged glances. There were tears in her eyes.

"Oh, Mitchell! Remember Napoleon!"

"Napoleon! What's Napoleon got to do with it? Napoleon

79

never was expected to drive through a primeval forest. Besides, what did Napoleon ever do? Where did Napoleon get off, swanking round as if he amounted to something? Poor fish! All he ever did was to get hammered at Waterloo!"

Alexander rejoined us. He had walked on to where his ball lay.

"Can't find it, eh? Nasty bit of rough, this!"

"No, I can't find it. But to-morrow some miserable, chinless, half-witted reptile of a caddie with pop eyes and eight hundred and thirty-seven pimples will find it, and will sell it to someone for a dime! No, it was a brand-new ball. He'll probably get a quarter for it. That'll be ten cents for himself and fifteen for the Greens Committee. No wonder they're buying cars quicker than the makers can supply them. No wonder you see their wives going about in mink coats and pearl necklaces. Oh, dash it! I'll drop another!"

"In that case," Alexander pointed out, "you will, of course, under the rules governing match-play, lose the hole."

"All right, then. I'll give up the hole."

"Then that, I think, makes me one up on the first nine," said Alexander. "Excellent! A very pleasant, even game."

"Pleasant! On second thoughts I don't believe the Greens Committee let the wretched caddies get any of the loot. They hang round behind trees till the deal's concluded, and then sneak out and choke it out of them!"

I saw Alexander raise his eyebrows. He walked up the hill to the next tee with me.

"Rather a quick-tempered young fellow, Holmes!" he said, thoughtfully. "I should never have suspected it. It just shows how little one can know of a man, only meeting him in business hours."

I tried to defend the poor lad.

"He has an excellent heart, Alexander. But the fact is—we are such old friends that I know you will forgive my mentioning it—your style of play gets, I fancy, a little on his nerves."

"My style of play? What's wrong with my style of play?"

"Nothing is actually wrong with it, but to a young and ardent spirit there is apt to be something a trifle upsetting in being compelled to watch a man play quite so slowly as you do. Come now, Alexander, as one friend to another, is it necessary to take two practice-swings before you putt?"

"Dear, dear!" said Alexander. "You really mean to say that upsets him? Well, I'm afraid I am too old to change my methods now."

I had nothing more to say.

As we reached the tenth tee, I saw that we were in for a few minutes' wait. Suddenly I felt a hand on my arm. Millicent was standing beside me, dejection written on her face. Alexander and young Mitchell were some distance away from us.

"Mitchell doesn't want me to come round the rest of the way with him," she said, despondently. "He says I make him nervous."

I shook my head.

"That's bad! I was looking on you as a steadying influence."

"I thought I was, too. But Mitchell says no. He says my being there keeps him from concentrating."

"Then perhaps it would be better for you to remain in the club-house till we return. There is, I fear, dirty work ahead."

A choking sob escaped the unhappy girl.

"I'm afraid so. There is an apple tree near the thirteenth hole, and Mitchell's caddie is sure to start eating apples. I am thinking of what Mitchell will do when he hears the crunching when he is addressing his ball."

"That is true."

"Our only hope," she said, holding out Professor Rollitt's book, "is this. Will you please read him extracts when you see him getting nervous? We went through the book last night and marked all the passages in blue pencil which might prove helpful. You will see notes against them in the margin, showing when each is supposed to be used."

It was a small favour to ask. I took the book and gripped her hand silently. Then I joined Alexander and Mitchell on the tenth tee. Mitchell was still continuing his speculations regarding the Greens Committee.

"The hole after this one," he said, "used to be a short hole. There was no chance of losing a ball. Then, one day, the wife of one of the Greens Committee happened to mention that the baby needed new shoes, so now they've tacked on another hundred and fifty yards to it. You have to drive over the brow of a hill, and if you slice an eighth of an inch you get into a sort of No Man's Land, full of rocks and bushes and crevices and old pots and pans. The Greens Committee practically live there in the summer. You see them prowling round in groups, encouraging each other with merry cries as they fill their sacks. Well, I'm going to fool them to-day. I'm going to drive an old ball which is just hanging together by a thread. It'll come to pieces when they pick it up!"

Golf, however, is a curious game—a game of fluctuations. One might have supposed that Mitchell, in such a frame of mind, would have continued to come to grief. But at the beginning of the second nine he once more found his form. A perfect drive put him in position to reach the tenth green with an iron-shot, and, though the ball was several yards from the hole, he laid it dead with his approach-putt and holed his second for a four. Alexander could only achieve a five, so that they were all square again.

The eleventh, the subject of Mitchell's recent criticism, is certainly a tricky hole, and it is true that a slice does land the player in grave difficulties. To-day, however, both men kept their drives straight, and found no difficulty in securing fours.

"A little more of this," said Mitchell, beaming, "and the Greens Committee will have to give up piracy and go back to work."

The twelfth is a long, dog-leg hole, par five. Alexander plugged steadily round the bend, holing out in six, and Mitchell, whose second shot had landed him in some long grass, was obliged to use his niblick. He contrived, however, to halve the hole with a nicely-judged mashie-shot to the edge of the green.

Alexander won the thirteenth. It is a three hundred and sixty yard hole, free from bunkers. It took Alexander three strokes to reach the green, but his third laid the ball dead; while Mitchell, who was on in two, required three putts.

"That reminds me," said Alexander, chattily, "of a story I heard. Friend calls out to a beginner, 'How are you getting on, old man?' and the beginner says, 'Splendidly. I just made three perfect putts on the last green!'"

Mitchell did not appear amused. I watched his face anxiously. He had made no remark, but the missed putt which would have saved the hole had been very short, and I feared the worst. There was a brooding look in his eye as we walked to the fourteenth tee.

There are few more picturesque spots in the whole of the countryside than the neighbourhood of the fourteenth tee. It is a sight to charm the nature-lover's heart.

But, if golf has a defect, it is that it prevents man being a whole-hearted lover of nature. Where the layman sees waving grass and romantic tangles of undergrowth, your golfer beholds nothing but a nasty patch of rough from which he must divert his ball. The cry of the birds, wheeling against the sky, is to the golfer merely something that may put him off his putt. As a spectator, I am fond of the ravine at the bottom of the slope. It pleases the eye. But, as a golfer, I have frequently found it the very devil.

The last hole had given Alexander the honour again. He drove even more deliberately than before. For quite half a minute he stood over his ball, pawing at it with his driving-iron like a cat investigating a tortoise. Finally he despatched it to one of the few safe spots on the hillside. The drive from this tee has to be carefully calculated for, if it be too straight, it will catch the slope and roll down into the ravine.

Mitchell addressed his ball. He swung up and then, from immediately behing him came a sudden sharp crunching sound. I looked quickly in the direction whence it came. Mitchell's caddie, with a glassy look in his eyes, was gnawing a large apple. And even as I breathed a silent prayer, down came the driver, and the ball, with a terrible slice on it, hit the side of the hill and bounded into the ravine.

There was a pause—a pause in which the world stood still. Mitchell dropped his club and turned. His face was working horribly.

"Mitchell!" I cried. "My boy! Reflect! Be calm!"

"Calm! What's the use of being calm when people are chewing apples in thousands all round you? What *is* this, anyway—a golf match or a pleasant day's outing for the children of the poor. Apples! Go on, my boy, take another bite. Take several. Enjoy yourself! Never mind if it seems to cause me a fleeting annoyance.

Go on with your lunch! You probably had a light breakfast, eh, and are feeling a little peckish, yes? If you will wait here, I will run to the club-house and get you a sandwich and a bottle of ginger-ale. Make yourself quite at home, you lovable little fellow! Sit down and have a good time!"

I turned the pages of Professor Rollitt's book feverishly. I could not find a passage that had been marked in blue pencil to meet this emergency. I selected one at random.

"Mitchell," I said, "one moment. How much time he gains who does not look to see what his neighbour says or does, but only at what he does himself, to make it just and holy."

"Well, look what I've done myself! I'm somewhere down at the bottom of that dashed ravine, and it'll take me a dozen strokes to get out. Do you call that just and holy? Here, give me that book for a moment!"

He snatched the little volume out of my hands. For an instant he looked at it with a curious expression of loathing, then he placed it gently on the ground and jumped on it a few times. Then he hit it with his driver. Finally, as if feeling that the time for half measures had passed, he took a little run and kicked it strongly into the long grass.

He turned to Alexander, who had been an impassive spectator of the scene.

"I'm through!" he said. "I concede the match. Good-bye. You'll find me in the bay!"

"Going swimming?"

"No. Drowning myself."

A gentle smile broke out over my old friend's usually grave face. He patted Mitchell's shoulder affectionately.

"Don't do that, my boy," he said. "I was hoping you would stick around the office awhile as treasurer of the company."

Mitchell tottered. He grasped my arm for support. Everything was very still. Nothing broke the stillness but the humming of the bees, the murmur of the distant wavelets, and the sound of Mitchell's caddie going on with his apple.

"What!" cried Mitchell.

"The position," said Alexander, "will be falling vacant very shortly, as no doubt you know. It is yours, if you care to accept it."

84

"You mean—you mean—you're going to give me the job?"

"You have interpreted me exactly."

Mitchell gulped. So did his caddie. One came from a spiritual, the other from a physical cause.

"If you don't mind excusing me," said Mitchell huskily, "I think I'll be popping back to the club-house. Someone I want to see."

He disappeared through the trees, running strongly. I turned to Alexander.

"What does this mean?" I asked. "I am delighted, but what becomes of the test?"

My old friend smiled gently.

"The test," he replied, "has been eminently satisfactory. Circumstances, perhaps, have compelled me to modify the original idea of it, but nevertheless it has been a completely successful test. Since we started out, I have been doing a good deal of thinking, and I have come to the conclusion that what the Paterson Dyeing and Refining Company really needs is a treasurer whom I can beat at golf. And I have discovered the ideal man. Why," he went on, a look of holy enthusiasm on his fine old face, "do you realise I can always lick the stuffing out of that boy, good player as he is, simply by taking a little trouble? I can make him get the wind up every time, simply by taking one or two extra practice-swings! That is the sort of man I need for a responsible post in my office."

"But what about Rupert Dixon?" I asked.

He gave a gesture of distaste.

"I wouldn't trust that man. Why, when I played with him, everything went wrong, and he just smiled and didn't say a word. A man who can do that is not the man to trust with the control of large sums of money. It wouldn't be safe. Why, the fellow isn't honest! He can't be." He paused for a moment. "Besides," he added, thoughtfully, "he beat me by six and five. What's the good of a treasurer who beats the boss by six and five?"

BY P. G. WODEHOUSE

FROM *Wodehouse on Golf*

THE LAND OF PAR

There are days when my drives wing far,
   When my iron shots clear the rut;
But then when I get on the green in two
   I putt and I putt and I putt.

There are days when my chip shots roll
   Like a Vardon's to the pin,
But I've missed my drive and I've taken six
   At last when the putt drops in.

There are days when my putts run true
   And straight to the waiting hole;
But these are the days when my mashie shots
   Have shattered my aching soul.

Oh, gods of the golfer's realm,
   Over the bunkered heather,
When is the day to come when I
   Hook three fine shots together?

From over the mystic seas
   The answer clears the foam—
"On the day St. Peter turns the key
   And Heaven calls you home."

BY GRANTLAND RICE

FROM *Songs of the Stalwart*

Putting looks easy. As Mr. John Low, once one of England's greatest golfers, remarked, "All that is necessary is to hit the ball with freedom, grace, and accuracy in the middle of the club." How true, yet how difficult! Putting seems to be the easiest part of golf and yet is the most exasperating. Everybody can hit a ball on a lawn into a small hole with ease and certainty. To the on-looker nothing seems simpler, yet under the tension of tournament play the same onlooker cannot believe his eyes as he watches the ball pass by one side of the cup, far from the hole. And neither can the player! The mental hazard plays an overwhelming part in this little drama of the cup and ball and club.

BY GLENNA COLLETT

FROM *Ladies in the Rough*

The golfer's life and habits, when not upon active duty, are very much what might be expected. Of course he talks shop and that incessantly. Now, all shop is intolerable to those who neither know nor care about the subject; but we do not think that golfing shop is worse than any other.

We do not know whether it falls within the scope of this chapter to give the golfer any advice in regard to his diet; we presume not, because he would certainly pay no attention to the advice given. Thanks to the healthy nature of his occupation and the fine air he breathes, the golfer can and does eat and drink everything with impunity—for a season; and nothing but a gastric crisis, or losing two or three matches in succession will open his eyes to the fact that he is abusing his advantages. There is a weird story of a mysterious stranger who had been taken into a foursome, who was interrupted in the heroic attempt to putt *through* a large black retriever dog which was standing between himself and the hole. On being remonstrated with by his partner, the stranger asked him quietly whether that was a real dog; and on being assured that it was, seemed much relieved. *His* explanation, which was received politely but without comment, was that he was suffering from an indigestion produced by his having for two or three days been emboldened by the fine air to take a glass of port after his cheese—a thing which never agreed with him.

The golfer's home bears traces of his noble infirmity. For the sake of domestic peace our advice is, that he should not be permitted to take a club home with him. But he is very sly, and has a trick of walking about with a cleek and pretending to use it as a walking-stick; and whenever he finds a bit of turf he begins at once to exercise his destructive art. If he possesses a lawn he is sure to have a round of short holes upon it. If his girls have a tennis-ground, he slyly punches putting holes in the corners; and if he is driven from that, he practises wrist iron shots among the flower beds. Even within the house on a wet day he practises his swing in the lobby, and putts into tumblers laid upon their side upon the dining-room floor. That is to say, he does all these things if his wife permits him, or if he can escape her eye. If she is a wise woman, she will give in at once; the disease is incurable and ends only with life. The golfer's night thoughts are even as his day thoughts, so far as the god of dreams will permit; but golfing dreams are apt to be inconsecutive and grotesque. Our own special forms of nightmare are that we are driving or putting with an umbrella (the badge of a respectable professional man), or shooting rocketing balls. Others have been known to use a fishing-rod as a driver in their dreams. Now all this is magnificent sport, but it is not golf. Others, again, have protracted quarrels with their partners, or opponents, in which they get very angry, but never a bit nearer a satisfactory conclusion. To all at last comes oblivion till another golfing day dawns, and they begin the round of their daily work again.

If, at any time, we have seemed to treat the golfer with levity, our excuse must be that it is due to the same impulse which makes schoolboys, released from school, shout and gambol to work off the effects of the enforced restraint of the hours of tuition. The real business of golf is so earnest and exacting, that while it is in progress all joking and superfluous comment are sternly repressed; but, although we may not speak or laugh at the time, we see and hear a good deal which must find expression in some way.

BY LORD WELLWOOD

FROM *Golf*

It will be convenient to consider this delicate question under three heads: (1) the abstract right of women to play golf at all; (2) their right to play the "long round" with or without male companions; and (3) their right to accompany matches as spectators.

On the first question our conscience is clear. We have always advocated a liberal extension of the right of golfing to women. Not many years ago their position was most degraded. Bound to accompany their lords and masters to golfing resorts for the summer months, they had to submit to their fathers, husbands, and brothers playing golf all day and talking golfing shop the whole of the evening, while they themselves were hooted off the links with cries of "fore," if they ventured to appear there. We therefore gladly welcomed the establishment of a ladies' links . . . which have now been generously provided for them on most of the larger greens. Ladies' links should be laid out on the model, though on a small scale, of the "long round"; containing some short putting holes, some longer holes, admitting of a drive or two of seventy or eighty yards, and a few suitable hazards. We venture to suggest seventy or eighty yards as the average limit of a drive advisedly; not because we doubt a lady's power to make a longer drive, but because that cannot well be done without raising the club above the shoulder. Now, we do not presume to dictate, but we must observe that the posture and gestures requisite for a full swing are not particularly graceful when the player is clad in female dress.

Most ladies putt well, and all the better because they play boldly for the hole without refining too much about the lie of the ground; and there is no reason why they should not practise and excel in wrist shots with a lofting iron or cleek.

Their right to play, or rather the expediency of their playing the long round, is much more doubtful. If they choose to play at times when the male golfers are feeding or resting, no one can object. But at other times—must we say it?—they are in the way; just because gallantry forbids to treat them exactly as men. The tender mercies of the golfer are cruel. He cannot afford to be merciful; because if he forbears to drive into the party in front he is promptly driven into from behind. It is a hard lot to follow a party of ladies with a powerful driver behind you if you are troubled with a spark of chivalry or shyness.

As to the ladies playing the long round with men as their partners, it may be sufficient to say, in the words of a promising young player who found it hard to decide between flirtation and playing the game: "It's all mighty pleasant, but it's not business."

But it is to their presence as spectators that the most serious objection must be taken. If they could abstain from talking while you are playing, and if the shadow of their dresses would not flicker on the putting-green while you are holing out, other objections might, perhaps, be waived. But, apart from these positive offences against the unwritten laws of golf, they unintentionally exercise an unsettling and therefore pernicious influence, deny it who can. You wish to play your best before them, and yet you know they will not like you any the better if you beat their husband or brother. Again, it seems churlish not to speak to them; but if you do the other players will justly abuse you. It may be stated parenthetically that one of the party is sure to speak to them; because (to their praise or blame be it said) few foursomes do not contain one ladies' man.

Thirdly, if they volunteer to score, they may, and probably will, score wrong (not in your favour, you may be sure); yet you cannot contradict them. An outraged golfer once said to his opponent in a single who had brought his wife to score for him three days in succession, "My good fellow, suppose we both did it!" This was in the circumstances a very strong and cogent way of putting the case; because there was no manner of doubt what the speaker's wife would do if she came. But the remonstrance was not well received, and the match was not renewed.

BY LORD WELLWOOD

FROM *Golf*

The golfer does not, as a rule, appear at his best at Christmas. A painful alternative is before him. Either he must wholly neglect his duty, fly to a golf course, and leave his wife to hang the Christmas tree and his children to enjoy it alone, or else he must stay at home and go through with it all, in a state of Stygian and dyspeptic gloom, in which case, although his conduct will be the less base, the sum total of unhappiness produced by it will probably be the greater.

* * *

The golfing winds have characters just as distinct, though no one has had sufficient imagination to christen them. The wind against is an implacable, relentless enemy, but he is an honest one, and plays the game according to his lights. He has no shifty tricks, and, mercifully, he is rather stupid. He can be rendered comparatively innocuous if you do not play his game by hitting too hard, and he affords you now and then, one of the most perfectly satisfactory of human sensations, in the cleanly-struck ball that flies low and straight into the wind's eye. Moreover, he is not nearly so formidable as he used to be in gutty days, since he has never discovered how to make a rubber-cored ball soar and soar till it comes back almost over the striker's head. That is, I suppose, because he is stupid, and for the same reason, he over-reaches himself when it comes to the approaching. By blowing so hard he makes things in some ways easier, since the ball can be pitched right up to the hole and will stop there of its own accord, with no need for recondite back spins.

The wind behind is entirely well meaning. He is a cheerful wind of rollicking and jovial disposition. If we could see him he would, I am convinced, wear a blue coat with brass buttons and drab breeches and gaiters like a jolly old gentleman in one of Caldecott's pictures. He would like to see everyone happy and, since he does not understand much about golf, he thinks everyone must be happiest when he is hitting the ball furthest. So he just takes the ball and whirls it along as far as he can, and, which is really friendly of him, minimises as far as possible any little tendency to slice or hook. In the short game he overdoes his good intentions. He thinks it a poor niggling business, which should not be taken too seriously. He cannot imagine anyone being really annoyed because a perfectly struck mashie shot has sent the ball bounding over the green into a bunker beyond; he cannot in the least understand the agonies of putting when you are being blown forward on to your nose. Golf, he thinks, is a game to be played with roars of boisterous laughter.

I wish I could think that the two side winds, the wind on your back and the wind on your face, had characters half so pleasant. They have nothing of the sort, being, in fact, cunning and evilly disposed persons. There is nothing honest and straightforward about them, and there is a good deal both of the bully and the snob. Thus they oppress most cruelly the poor player who has not strength or skill enough to resist them, but when they meet a really fine player, who cannot merely fight them but use them for his own ends, they become his allies. Watch such a player as Mr. Hilton at his best using the wind first with a pull and then with a cut, and you will see what curs these side winds really are, and how they cringe when they recognize their master.

Even much humbler players can, in a measure, conquer them. The poor terrified slicer with a wind on his back is apt to make more and more allowance for his weakness, and aim further and further to the left. The wind at once perceives that he has a beaten enemy to deal with, and hurtles the ball still further to the right. But if the slicer will stand up to him like a man, make no allowance, and even stand for something of a hook, the wind loses half its bluster, and lets the ball fly, not very far indeed, but reasonably straight.

BY BERNARD DARWIN

FROM *A Friendly Round*

THE STRANGER

"Who's that stranger, mother dear?
Look, he knows us. . . . Ain't he queer?"

"Hush, my own, don't talk so wild;
He's your father, dearest child!"

"He's my father? No such thing!
Father died away last Spring!"

"Father didn't die, you dub!
Father joined a golfing club.

"But they've closed the club, so he
Has no place to go, you see—

"No place left for him to roam—
That is why he's coming home.

"Kiss him . . . he won't bite you, child;
All them golfing guys look wild."

BY J. P. McEVOY

FROM *Lyrics of the Links*

THE REASON

"You are old, Father William," the young man said.
    "And your swing has become very flat,
And yet you incessantly lay the ball dead.
    Pray what is the reason for that?"

"In my youth," Father William replied, "it is that
    I studied and practised and swore;
But now I just step up and give it a swat—
    What reason for anything more?"

ANONYMOUS

FROM *Lyrics of the Links*

IN MIDDLE AGE

We have grown rather tired in this country of having pointed out to us the virtuous qualities of the young American golfer, how he practises and thinks and trains and plays with professionals and so on. Let me, by way of a slight change, praise the middle-aged American golfer. He is wonderfully and splendidly keen, not merely about playing the game, but about trying to play it in the right way. On an American golf course, in my experience, one does not, as one does here, see stout elderly gentlemen playing in innumerable self-taught styles which have only this quality in common, that they are utterly prohibitive of any success in striking the ball. Nearly all the players, whatever their age, are trying to hit the ball in the right style, and the results reflect the greatest credit on themselves and on their teachers. For they take lessons; that is the real point, and if any middle-aged beginner will read that sentence, take it to heart and act upon it, he need not read another word. I shall have done my duty by him.

BY BERNARD DARWIN

FROM *Golf*

Yet what I am prepared to say is that the putting of the best golfers has definitely improved. The Americans began it and our players have tried very hard to imitate them. They have not yet quite caught them but they putt better than their predecessors. They take fewer putts in the course of a round and so down go the scores. I think too that on the whole they chip better from near the green and so give themselves the chance of holing more putts. The thing that I really feel sure about as an improver of scores is the wedge. I am now so long incapacitated that I have never owned a wedge: I do not really understand the art of it, but I see what it can do in a bunker and that is enough. There it has in skilful hands produced a new stroke, and it merely laughs at the sand. John Ball said that he liked to see his enemy in a bunker where he had to scratch his head to find any way out of it. Today he would see that enemy, equipped cap-à-pie with an armoury of wedges, play an easy smooth sliding shot, as it were right through the ball, and lay it as likely as not stone dead. The head-scratching comes no doubt in learning that stroke, which I would never deny is a lovely and skilful one, but once learnt it seems to perform these miracles with perfect regularity. It is this infernal machine, and I wish it had never been invented, that has in my belief made more difference than anything else, clubs, balls, green-keeping and all, and I was glad to read the other day that Tommy Armour, a great golfer who knows American golf inside out, says so too. What a heavenly feeling it must be not to mind in the least getting into a bunker! I wish I had ever enjoyed it.

BY BERNARD DARWIN

FROM *The World that Fred Made*

THE SOUL OF GOLF

Nearly every one who writes about a game essays to prove that it is similar to "the great game, the game of life." Golf has not escaped; and numberless scribes in endeavoring to account for the fascination of golf have used the old threadbare tale. As a matter of fact, golf is about as unlike the game of life as any game could well be. As played now it has come to be almost an exact science, and everybody knows exactly what one is trying to do. This would not be mistaken for a description of the game of life. In that game a man may be hopelessly "off the line," buried "in the rough," or badly "bunkered," and nobody be the wiser. It is not so in golf. There is no double life here. All is open, and every one knows what the player is striving for. The least deflection from his line, and the onlooker knows he did not mean it. It is seen instantly. In that other game it may remain unseen for years, for ever.

BY P. A. VAILE

FROM *The Soul of Golf*

SEASIDE GOLF

How straight it flew, how long it flew,
    It clear'd the rutty track
And soaring, disappeared from view
    Beyond the bunker's back—
A glorious, sailing, bounding drive
That made me glad I was alive.

And down the fairway, far along
    It glowed a lonely white;
I played an iron sure and strong
    And clipp'd it out of sight,
And spite of grassy banks between
I knew I'd find it on the green.

And so I did. It lay content
    Two paces from the pin;
A steady putt and then it went
    Oh, most securely in.
The very turf rejoiced to see
That quite unprecedented three.

Ah! seaweed smells from sandy caves
    And thyme and mist in whiffs,
In-coming tide, Atlantic waves
    Slapping the sunny cliffs,
Lark song and sea sounds in the air
And splendour, splendour everywhere.

BY JOHN BETJEMAN

FROM *Collected Poems*

ON GOLF

"An' what's this game iv goluf like, I dinnaw?" said Mr. Hennessy, lighting his pipe with much unnecessary noise. "Ye're a good deal iv a spoort, Jawnny: did ye iver thry it?"

"No," said Mr. McKenna. "I used to roll a hoop onct upon a time, but I'm out of condition now."

"It ain't like base-ball," said Mr. Hennessy, "an' it ain't like shinny, an' it ain't like lawn-teenis, an' it ain't like forty-fives, an' it ain't"—

"Like canvas-back duck or anny other game ye knows," said Mr. Dooley.

"Thin what is it like?" said Mr. Hennessy. "I see be th' pa-aper that Hobart What-d'ye-call-him is wan iv th' best at it. Th' other day he made a scoor iv wan hundherd an' sixty-eight, but whether 'twas miles or stitches I cudden't make out fr'm th' raypoorts."

" 'Tis little ye know," said Mr. Dooley. "Th' game iv goluf is as old as th' hills. Me father had goluf links all over his place. An', whin I was a kid, 'twas wan iv th' principal spoorts iv me life, afther I'd dug the turf f'r th' avenin', to go out and putt"—

"Poot, ye mean," said Mr. Hennessy. "They'se no such wurrud in th' English language as putt. Belinda called me down ha-ard on it no more thin las' night."

"There ye go!" said Mr. Dooley, angrily. "There ye go! D'ye think this here game iv goluf is a spellin' match? 'Tis like ye, Hinnissy, to be refereein' a twenty-round glove contest be th' rule iv three. I tell ye I used to go out in th' avenin' an' putt me mashie like hell-an'-all, till I was knowed fr'm wan end iv th' county to th' other as th' champeen putter. I putted two men fr'm Roscommon in wan day, an' they had to be took home on a dure.

"In America th' ga-ame is played more ginteel, an' is more like cigareet-smokin', though less onhealthy f'r th' lungs. 'Tis a good game to play in a hammick whin ye're all tired out fr'm social duties or shovellin' coke. Out-iv-dure golf is played be th' follow-in' rules. If ye bring ye'er wife f'r to see th' game, an' she has her name in th' paper, that counts ye wan. So th' first thing ye do is to find th' raypoorter, an' tell him ye're there. Thin ye ordher a bottle iv brown pop, an' have ye'er second fan ye with a towel. Afther this ye'd dhress, an' here ye've got to be dam particklar or ye'll be stuck f'r th' dhrinks. If ye'er necktie is not on sthraight, that counts ye'er opponent wan. If both ye an' ye'er opponent have ye'er neckties on crooked, th' first man that sees it gets th' stakes. Thin ye ordher a carredge"—

"Order what?" demanded Mr. McKenna.

"A carredge."

"What for?"

"F'r to take ye 'round th' links. Ye have a little boy followin' ye, carryin' ye'er clubs. Th' man that has th' smallest little boy it counts him two. If th' little boy has th' rickets, it counts th' man in th' carredge three. The little boys is called caddies; but Clarence Heaney that tol' me all this—he belongs to th' Foorth Wa-ard

Goluf an' McKinley Club—said what th' little boys calls th' players 'd not be fit f'r to repeat.

"Well, whin ye dhrive up to th' tea grounds"—

"Th' what?" demanded Mr. Hennessy.

"Th' tea grounds, that's like th' homeplate in base-ball or ordherin' a piece iv chalk in a game iv spoil five. Its th' be-ginnin' iv ivrything. Whin ye get to th' tea grounds, ye step out, an' have ye're hat irned be th' caddie. Thin ye'er man that ye're goin' aginst comes up, an' he asks ye, 'Do you know Potther Pammer?' Well, if ye don't know Potther Pammer, it's all up with ye: ye lose two points. But ye come right back at him with an' upper cut: 'Do ye live on th' Lake Shore dhrive?' If he doesn't, ye have him in th' nine hole. Ye needn't play with him anny more. But, if ye do play with him, he has to spot three balls. If he's a good man an' shifty on his feet, he'll counter be askin' ye where ye spend th' summer. Now ye can't tell him that ye spent th' summer with wan hook on th' free lunch an' another on th' ticker tape, an' so ye go back three. That needn't discourage ye at all, at all. Here's yer chance to mix up, an' ye ask him if he was iver in Scotland. If he wasn't, it counts ye five. Thin ye tell him that ye had an aunt wanst that heerd th' Jook iv Argyle talk in a phonograph; an', onless he comes back an' shoots it into ye that he was wanst run over be th' Prince iv Wales, ye have him groggy. I don't know whether th' Jook iv Argyle or th' Prince iv Wales counts f'r most. They're like th' right an' left bower iv thrumps. Th' best players is called scratch-men."

"What's that f'r?" Mr. Hennessy asked.

"It's a Scotch game," said Mr. Dooley, with a wave of his hand. "I wonder how it come out to-day. Here's th' pa-aper. Let me see. McKinley at Canton. Still there. He niver cared to wandher fr'm his own fireside. Collar-button men f'r th' goold standard. Statues iv Heidelback, Ickleheimer an' Company to be erected in Washington. Another Vanderbilt weddin'. That sounds like goluf, but it ain't. Newport society livin' in Mrs. Potter Pammer's cellar. Green-goods men declare f'r honest money. Anson in foorth place some more. Pianny tuners f'r McKinley. Li Hung Chang smells a rat. Abner McKinley supports th' goold standard. Wait a minyit. Here it is: 'Goluf in gay attire.' Let me see. H'm. 'Foozled his approach,'—nasty thing. 'Topped th' ball.' 'Three up an' two to play.' Ah, here's the scoor. 'Among those prisint were Messrs. an' Mesdames—'"

"Hol' on!" cried Mr. Hennessy, grabbing the paper out of his friend's hands. "That's thim that was there."

"Well," said Mr. Dooley, decisively, "that's th' goluf scoor."

FROM *Mr. Dooley in Peace and in War*

What boots it? Aye, though you be bunkered sore
When you had thought to do the hole in four,
Haply the next you may achieve in three;
How well a three looks on a duffer's score!

* * *

Many months are since the prime of year
When first I teed the ball with cynic sneer;
　An hundred fold I trust the time will be
Ere I shall cease to chase the little sphere.

For, though I falter on the path to fame,
And ne'er in medal-play behold my name,
　Nor cut a figure on the winning side,
A solace to my soul remains the game!

The game remains; and I shall swear thereby,
Whate'er the season, and whate'er the "lie,"
　Although it sorely crucify my pride,
And I remain a duffer till I die!

* * *

You, the Ungolfing, who have never seen
The lofted ball fall dead upon the green,
     Who have not known the skilly putter's bliss,
Alas, alas, what sterile fields you glean!

The Spring is robbed of half its triumph thrill,
For what to you the last snows on the hill!
     And what the young year's apotheosis,
When brooks roar full, and April has its will!

And what the Summer orientry, and all
The pennoned pageant and the pomp of Fall!
     And what the Winter sovereignship austere,
And what the earth beneath a samite pall!

But to the Golfer even the bleak snows
That swirl without, the while the ingle glows,
     Bring happy omens; in his bosom dear
Anticipation bourgeons like a rose;

Or in the embers clear-eyed Memory
Pictures some wondrous stroke from off the tee,
     Some marvelous brassie to a hidden hole,
And the inspiring magic of a three.

Such kindling visions hold his heart elate
While wild Euroclydon is at the gate;
     Content abides within his steadfast soul,
And though mayhap impatient, he can wait.

Yes, he can wait until the vernal chord
Is softly smitten, and the umbered sward
     Quickens beneath the sun's renewing fire,
And stripling Spring is Winter's overlord.

Then feel his feet the tempting turf once more,
While down the distance floats his ringing "fore!"
     And he is brother to the hale desire
That is of all reviving things the core.

Others may catch the scattered scrap and shard
Of exultation, but to them is barred
   The keen elation that the Golfer knows
When Spring's first ball is teed and driven hard.

High ride the clouds as white as wind-tossed foam—
The Ariel clouds—across the sky's deep dome;
   A day in May is goldening to its close;—
Just one more round before the sun goes home!

BY CLINTON SCOLLARD

FROM The Epic of Golf

THE PERFECT GOLFER

His drives are rather ragged and his iron shots are punk;
His putting's an amazing thing; he's rarely ever sunk
A putt much longer than a foot; his mashie stroke's a sin;
Somehow he cannot seem to get a touch of Hagen spin
To hold it safely on the green; his brassie shot's the type
The devil teaches when the lads are slightly under-ripe.
And more than that he know all traps; not one but has its charms
And welcomes him with encores and, it seems, with outstretched
                              arms;
But somehow it can't feaze him much; a song is in his heart
And on his lips a whistle and a jest of golfing art.
When he comes in he always has the graciousness to say
"This Club is perfect, I have had a most delightful day."
And though we jest and laugh at him, we'll tell the wide world
                              flat
God made the golf course brighter when he made a man like that.

BY JOHN E. BAXTER

FROM Locker Room Ballads

103

The strange case of Sir Archibald Strand is one that caused much excited attention among the members of the golf community in general some months ago, and it is still discussed in the club-houses. Sir Archibald Strand, Bart., is a fair example of the thorough, enthusiastic, middle-aged player, who treats golf as something rather more than a game, which is as it should be. He is one of tolerably equable temperament, a good sportsman, and a man of strong character and physique, who did a long term of military service in India. Nowadays he spends an appreciable portion of his time in golfing, and a fair part of the remainder in contemplating the enduring mysteries and problems of the links. The game worries him exceedingly, occasionally it leads him to unhappiness, but, on the whole, he feels he likes it. He is a member of several London clubs, including Sunningdale, Walton Heath, Mid-Surrey, Coombe Hill, and Woking, and of his seaside clubs those he most frequents are the Royal St. George's at Sandwich, and Rye. His handicap is 5, and generally he is what we consider and call a good reliable 5.

He and his opponent, to whom, as a matter of discretion and confidence, we must refer as Mr. A., had just ended their match at Mid-Surrey one pleasant day, and Sir Archibald was trying his last putt over again as golfers often do. It was a putt of two feet. He had missed it before; but now, of course, he rolled the ball in every time. A question arose about circumstances altering cases, as they so commonly do in golf, and of responsibility weighing heavily on the mind that hesitates; and Sir Archibald declared that nobody in good health could be such a fool as to miss a two-feet putt like that, if he really examined the line thoroughly and took the proper pains. Just then the open champion of the period was passing by the green, and they called him up and asked his views upon the missing of two-feet putts. Taylor denied that a man was a fool for missing them. He mentioned the psychology of the business, and very forcibly argued that a two-feet putt was a very difficult thing, that the more important it was the more difficult it became, and that the longer one thought about it the more impossible did it seem to hole it. "Ah!" said he, with the solemn countenance he assumes when discussing the terrors of this game, and the deep emphasis he makes when he admits the difficulties it creates for him, "Ah!" he murmured, "if I had never missed any putts of one foot, let alone the putts of two! I tell you, sir, the two-feet putt, when it has to be done—mind you when it has got to be done—is one of the most difficult things in the world to do, and never mind the fact that your babies can do it all the time! Take that from me, sir!" This was a touch of the real Taylor, the true philosopher, one who knows the game.

Mr. A., who is sometimes aggressive in manner, brought the matter in discussion to a pretty point at once. "Look here, Strand," said he, "I will tell you what I will do. I will place this ball here, so, exactly two feet from the hole, and I will give you a fortnight, but not less than a fortnight, to hole that putt. You are not to practise it here at this hole on this green in the meantime; but you may place the ball in position if you like, and look at it. And a fortnight to-day, at ten o'clock in the morning, you must make the putt, and I will bet you fourteen guineas, being a guinea a day for waiting, that you do not hole it. We will have the position of the hole properly marked, so that a fortnight hence it shall be in the same place."

The champion said he would tell Lees, the greenskeeper, and that should be done. Strand, with a laugh, accepted the wager, and the matter was settled.

The events that followed were curious. In the club-house there was then little disposition to attend to the accounts of the proceedings that were furnished by both parties. The men who had finished their rounds were too much occupied with their own troubles or joys.

At his club in town that evening, Sir Archibald, over dinner, related the circumstances of the wager to a few friends, with an appearance of considerable satisfaction with himself, and seemed a little surprised that the other members of the party did not at once approve of his proceeding as sound and business-like.

"Of course, you know, Strand, my good man," said Mr. Ezekiel Martin, a successful stockbroker, "these putts are missed sometimes, and I don't suppose it makes it any easier for you by waiting a fortnight. It's like carrying over in the House till one is a very tired bull."

"Nonsense!" exclaimed Sir Archibald, "I could go out now and hole that putt nineteen times out of twenty in the dark!"

"I believe you could," answered Martin, "but doing it in the dark, when you cannot see the hole and realise all the imaginary difficulties, is very different from doing it in broad daylight; and putting now, on the spur of the moment, as it were, is very different from putting when you have a whole fortnight to think about what you are going to do."

"I don't see it," replied Sir Archibald, yet he began to feel a little uneasy. On returning home that night, instead of going to bed at once he went into his study, laid a tumbler on its side on the carpet, and putted from a measured two feet for about half an hour. He holed most of them, and tumbled into bed feeling that Martin had been "pulling his leg," as people say. In the morning he engaged a gardener to smooth down a piece of his lawn, planting in a little putting-green turf, and he had a hole made in it, and a circle with two feet radius drawn round the hole, so that he could putt from every point. When this work was done, he spent an hour in practising there, and succeeded well. He only missed about one in ten. He tried seven different putters, with approximately equal results. In the afternoon he went down to Mid-Surrey, played a match, and lost it by missing a short putt at the home hole. After tea, he went out on to the eighteenth green, found the spot where the hole was the day before, examined it carefully, and saw that there were slight differences in the texture of the grass round about, and that there was a little depression to the left side. He had not noticed this before. However, he said to himself, it would be easy to make allowances for these things, but he began now to doubt whether thirteen days ahead he would use his wry-necked putting cleek or bolt the putt with an aluminum putter. Where there are troubles of that kind it is often better to make short work of the putt by the bolting way, and have an end of it. At home that evening he did more putting practice on the carpet, and did not hole them quite so well. Lady Strand, who understands her husband thoroughly, and is the sweetest, gentlest sympathiser, coaxed him to telling her the trouble, for she saw that one existed. With perfect wisdom she suggested that he should wipe the fourteen guineas from the current account as already lost, and face the task as one who had all to gain and nothing to lose. Of course, her husband said, it was not the money, but the frightful jackass he would look if he missed the putt.

He went to his club in town the next day instead of going to golf, and took with him a book containing a chapter on putting, by Willie Park. He stretched himself out on a Chesterfield in a corner of the library, and gazed at two spots on the carpet which he had measured as being two-feet from each other. Eventually, he decided that that was not good enough for him, since equal distances in furnished rooms, as is well known, look longer than they look outside. He lunched with a few friends, and brought up the subject again.

"Give him the money and have done with it, Strand. You are sure to lose!" said the brutish Martin.

"I wish I had not to wait for a fortnight," murmured Strand.

"Ah! He knew! The other man knew!" rejoined Martin. "He knows the game of golf! What I cannot understand is why he did not give you a year and make it 365 guineas. You would have sold out in six weeks at 200 pounds!"

Sir Archibald wrote a letter to Mr. A. that evening, intimating that he would probably have to leave town the week after next. He hinted that it might be convenient if they got their wager out of the way beforehand, and if he putted a week from then. Mr. A. replied that he was sorry it would not be convenient for him to attend then, and that the signed terms of the contract had better be abided by.

Sir Archibald bought two new putters on the following day, and in the afternoon he had Taylor out for an hour, and they went practising on the putting lawn just outside the garden gate. Sir Archibald was putting very well then; but he insisted that it would be a good thing to change the ball he was using, which was rather lively. After he had done with Taylor, he went to look at the place on the eighteenth green where he would have to putt, and it seemed that the coarse grass had fattened up considerably with the rain that had fallen, and that the sand below it was distinctly gritty. It began to seem that he would have to run the ball in at the right side of the hole. He asked Lees some questions about the grasses on that green, and was sorry he could not take a little Mid-Surrey turf home with him. He was feeling a little tired when he reached his home that night, and as it was Thurday he suggested to Lady Strand that they should go to Folkstone for the week-end, and not bother at all about golf, which they did accordingly. He found it delightful to linger on the leas and not be worried with the game.

This kind of thing continued and became worse and worse again during the days that followed. There was practice, thought, and purchase continually, and unfortunately the proportion of missed putts at two feet, both on the carpet, on the practice lawn, and on the greens at Mid-Surrey, Coombe Hill, and Woking, began to increase. At putts of three feet, four, and five, Sir Archibald was marvellous, and, of course, he never missed the very little ones; but the two-feet putts bothered him all the time. He attributed it to his liver; and he was certainly looking worn. matters were not improved by such inconsiderate remarks as were made by Martin, Evans, and others, whenever he had a two-feet putt to make, such as, "Now, Strand, that's just your distance!" It was only a joke; but in the circumstances it was not perhaps in good taste.

On the evening of the twelfth day Strand, after deliberation, wrote a letter to A. in which he said he feared he would not be able to go down to the course at the appointed time, and intimated that, according to the terms of the wager, he would hand over the fourteen guineas to him when next they met. Before posting this letter he went and did a little practice in the dusk on the lawn outside the house. He seemed to get them down with some confidence on this occasion, and Lady S., watching him, called out cheerily, "Silly boy! as if you could really miss! Now what shall I buy with the fourteen guineas?"

So Strand tore up the letter and went to bed for rest.

On the night before the appointed day he slept badly. He was putting in his mind until three o'clock in the morning. Then he rose, went in his pyjamas into the study, made a line on the top of his aluminum putter indicating the striking point, and went back to bed, but did not sleep. For some time he tried an imaginary humming of the "Jewel Song" from *Faust*, and repeated a few lines from Scott's "Lady of the Lake"—old dodges of his for assisting distraction and sleep—but they did not serve, nor did a fixed vision of millions of balls falling in an endless stream from the mouth of a pump and disappearing instantly through a golf hole in the ground.

At five-thirty he rose again and took his bath. He hesitated as to what golfing suit he should wear. Finally, for the sake of complete ease, and that there should be nothing to attract his eye from the ball, he put on some dark-blue flannels.

He looked at his breakfast, pecked at a sole, and at nine-fifteen, feeling distinctly unwell, he took a taxi for the course. He had one great consolation upholding him. At five minutes past ten it would all be over. He felt that he knew how glad a condemned criminal must be that at five minutes past eight on a certain morning—or a minute or two earlier with a little luck—a black flag would be hoisted on the prison pole.

At seven minutes to ten he drank a large brandy and soda and went out to the eighteenth green. Mr. A. and a few others were there to see the business properly carried out. Taylor placed the ball exactly two feet from the hole, which was cut in the proper place. He had his watch in his hand.

Sir Archibald bent down and examined the putt with great care. He essayed to pick up what seemed to be a "loose impediment" on his line, but saw that it was not loose. The putt seemed very difficult now, and he wished he had brought his plain putting cleek out with him, but it was too late.

At ten o'clock exactly, Taylor said, "Now, Sir Archibald, will you kindly putt?"

Sir Archibald Strand looked like a man who had been hunted down. He made one swift glance around him, but saw no escape, so he pulled himself together, smiled a little sadly, and said to himself, "Don't be a fool, Archie!" Then he faced the putter to the ball; the club was trembling slightly. He swung it back much too far, checked it in the return swing, and came on to the ball in a nervous, stupid way, doing little more than touch it. The ball took a line to the right of the hole, and did not run more than fourteen inches.

You may have thought that Sir Archibald used unfortunate words and was dismayed. He did not. A look of established happiness and placid contentment spread upon his countenance, as a streak of sunlight might flash across a plain. "Ha!" he sighed in relief. He took from his pocket a cheque for fourteen guineas already made out, and handed it to Mr. A., and then joyfully exclaimed: "Thank heaven, it is finished! Now, my friends, we will honour this unusual occasion in a suitable manner at your convenience, and this afternoon I leave for Sandwich for a week of golf. And no letters are being forwarded."

BY HENRY LEACH

FROM The Happy Golfer

In St. Andrews are the hopes of the golfer fixed. The very air seems to be impregnated with the spirit of the game. At the tee with the brave old towers behind, the rolling waters of the Bay to the right, and in front the mounds, and hillocks, and levels of the links, one feels that he has reached the end of his pilgrimage to the Shrine of Golf. A new glamor is thrown about the game: the Golfer's "spirit leaps within him to be gone before him then": the

Swilcan may receive his second or third shot in its liquid shallows: he may foozle on the green under the critical eye of a bystanding professional, but "his heart's his own, his will is free." And standing at the end hole with his round half accomplished, he can survey the towers of the ruined Cathedral, and the ragged masonry of the Castle, and the grey old city itself with the feelings of one who has found life worth living and Golf a game for men.

BY Andrew Lang

FROM *A Batch of Golfing Papers*

LINES ON BEING ASKED TO CONTRIBUTE TO THIS BOOK

Some words on Golf I am desired to utter:
   I, who care nothing for the noble game,
Who do not know a niblick from a putter
   (Perhaps they are the same);

I, who have suffered by the hour together
   From idle blockheads talking golfer's shop,
Until I had to introduce the weather
   Or the potato crop.

Not that all golfers are such bores to be with;
   Some, I believe, are reasonable men.
Some, whose acquaintance Fate has favored me with,
   I will not meet again.

And now the terror of their conversation
  Confines itself no more to living speech.
Take any paper for an illustration:—
  Golf is the theme of each.

The *Scotsman* and *Dispatch* a column lavish
  When Old Tom Morris opens a new green;
They grudged five lines when Doctor Neil M'Tavish
  Opened a church at Skene.

The papers find the game seductive,
  The very magazines and the reviews
Print verse and prose which is, I hope, instructive,
  For it does not amuse.

If devotees of football and of cricket
  Should clog the press with innings and with maul,
And rabid scribes be always on the wicket,
  Or always on the ball—

As devotees of golf, with frenzy drunker,
  Riot in type and suffer no control,
And rabid scribes are always in a bunker,
  Or always in a hole—

Would people stand the former like the latter?
  An answer to the question might be guessed,
But since this is a book on Golf, no matter—
  Silence perhaps is best.

BY R. F. MURRAY

FROM *A Batch of Golfing Papers*

The first team match created so much favorable comment and was such good sport that everyone looked forward to another day on the links with the same good fellows competing. Many home-and-home matches were played later. Tuxedo succeeded in beating the crack St. Andrews team by 1 up on one occasion, but the Yonkers stalwarts insist that only unusual circumstances brought about their catastrophe. The story is worth relating.

Walker Breeze Smith, president of the Tuxedo Club, was pitted against John C. Ten Eyck who was humiliated by losing 4 down. Ten Eyck told the story of his misfortune and he had a lot of sympathizers. "We had not played three holes," said Ten Eyck, "when my opponent, a most gracious monster, got in his deadly work. He told me that golf was a matter of courage and one other important thing—keeping your eye on the ball. He pulled out a flask of good Scotch whiskey and invited me to have a drink, insisting that this supplied the courage. I refused politely, but he drank his own liquor without apology. To my amazement when he teed up the ball he took out his glass eye (he was a one-eyed man) and placed it on top of the ball. 'That,' he said, 'means keeping your eye on the ball!' Then he proceeded to wallop it down the fairway. The loss of that eye did not deter him, as he had a whole box full of them in his pocket, and on every tee he went through the same performance. You can imagine what this would do to a fellow's game."

Smith played golf for the enjoyment of the game and what fun he could get out of it. He often pulled this stunt as a joke, but it didn't always make a hit, especially with golfers who took their games seriously.

BY H. B. MARTIN

FROM *Fifty Years of American Golf*

113

Yes, golf must be played conscientiously. Recklessness never pays in golf. It may once in a great while bring off a thundering drive or an accidentally brilliant approach; but in nine hundred and ninety-nine cases out of a thousand it gives your opponent the hole. Few things prove this necessity for conscientiousness more than the disastrous results which always follow a yielding to that fatal temptation to "press," to force your stroke, that is, to try to go farther than you can. One moment's consideration will tell you that you must hit accurately, not wildly; yet player after player, at hole after hole, omits that moment's consideration; hits with all his might; and—perhaps goes fifty yards. I have seen him go six inches. I have seen him not go at all, though no doubt the solid earth received a jar. My learned friend was right. The game must be played with a resolute determination not to yield to temptation.

This is why the books tell you always to take the honour at the first tee if you win it, and always to keep the lead if you can; inasmuch as a terrific drive by your opponent is so apt to cause you to forget that determination and to try to outdrive him—which always means to "press." And temptations like this crop up all through the game, all through the game. Thousands of matches have been lost by nothing more or less than pressing; thousands perhaps won by avoidance of that sin. —I know a hale, hearty, kindly septuagenarian who stands high up in the Club Handicap, far above many men years his junior. Why? Because he never presses. He cannot drive very far; but he never tries to. It never disconcerts him to be "away." He never objects to taking two strokes to your one. He never makes distance. But he always goes straight. And—he is one of the hardest men to beat I ever met.

*   *   *

114

Almost unconsciously in golf one finds oneself ranking men, estimating them, summing them up, by the way they play; and many a man, I venture to say, has found companionship come to him or go from him according to the estimate formed of him on his links. One man, to my actual knowledge, got himself dearly beloved by numberless men, men who only knew him as they met him on the links.—Where his house was I don't even know. The just and generous way he played; his kindliness to younger players; his manliness, straightforwardness, and courage; the way he got out of difficulties; his quietness and meekness; his unselfishness; his carefulness; his consideration . . . instinctively one felt that if one did meet him in business or in official or in social life one would have trusted him. —His portrait hangs in my locker. —Be these my thanks to thee, departed mentor, for lessons more valuable than many received from pulpit or dais or platform.

BY ARNOLD HAULTAIN

FROM *The Mystery of Golf*

The pupils of the St. John Ambulance classes are taught what to do in case of accident, and the first thing to be done is always, *"Send for the doctor."* The first thing to do if you are really going to play golf with your head is to *take lessons from a golf professional.* Take good advice early. Don't teach yourself golf, or law, or medicine. It is too expensive.

BY C. W. BAILEY, M.A.

FROM *The Brain and Golf*

How often one hears the remark, "So-and-so is a born putter"! In my long experience of thirty years in first-class golf I have never seen a golfer whom I should call a born putter; some have a more delicate touch than others, but how few players gifted with this right touch have made proper use of it! The few that have become real good putters have practised on highly scientific lines.

BY JACK WHITE

FROM *Putting*

LET GOLF PLAY YOU

I am confident that golf would play itself pretty well if we didn't interfere with it.

Almost every error we make is the result of our putting the brakes on somewhere.

When a golf swing goes wrong, it is usually the result of our locking some set of muscles. We tighten up, hug in, hold back, cramp, and indulge in various and sundry constrictive spasms which produce abortive results.

If you pinch in on a putt instead of letting the putter float out in a straight line toward the hole, the ball will go to the left of the hole as sure as the Lord made little apples. And so on, up through every stroke of the game.

Every expert at any game, or at any art involving physical

116

skill, has had to learn how to let go of muscles. They tell me it is very hard for pianists to learn how to let go of back muscles. I took hundreds of dancing lessons during one decade of my life and one of the hardest things I had to learn was to let go in the muscles in my shoulders. In golf, there are a dozen points at which you can lock your muscles and defeat your swing.

You can even look at the ball too hard, and lock a lot of muscles in the back of your neck which will spoil your swing.

You can lock arm muscles, back muscles, leg muscles, knee muscles and muscles all over your body—all to the detriment of your game.

Percy Boomer says that golf is a *passive* game—that its dominating sensation should be passivity. He says that the worse he feels, the better he plays. I've seen some mighty good golf out of guys with hangovers. They're too bushed to play too hard.

Percy Boomer says that all the good golf maxims of the ages enjoin passivity—"Take it easy," "Don't press," etc.

Tommy Armour, sitting at the lesson tee at Boca Raton, said, "I want to set them the example of *educated languor.*"

All my life I've been trying to learn cartooning, and one of the first things I learned about comic art was that if you want to draw funny you have to let go. I learned early in life that *the hardest thing on earth to control is abandon.*

To quote Chick Evans again: "One should hit the ball in a carefree way, but not carelessly."

The semantics of the game can sometimes add to its tension. For instance, "grip" is the wrong word for the action of holding a golf club. Harry Vardon speaks of the grip being sometimes improved by finger injuries, which enforce a lighter grip.

Golf lacks the "flow" of tennis and other sports. You have, in golf, the opportunity to stand there and work yourself up into a cataleptic state every time you swing at the ball.

Most of us can take a pretty swing at a dandelion. But a golf ball in front of us terrorizes us into a fine set of tensions.

Tension is the main cause, too, of hurry. We go back with a jerky backswing and zip down into a lightning-like downswing because we are tense. We try to play golf instead of letting golf play itself—instead of letting golf play *us.*

117

Without relaxation there can be no golf. Even if you knew perfectly every paragraph of a perfect book on how to play perfect golf, you couldn't do it without complete relaxation. Relaxation is the number one requisite of a good golf swing.

At no point in your swing should there be any evidence of jerk or sudden effort.

You are not in the stockyards killing a steer.

Smoothness adds to force, because it is momentum and rhythm, not mauling, which gives power to your swing.

Sammy Snead says that the force of a golf swing is "gathered." You can't wham it from the top.

"Good golf is easy to play," says Ernest Jones, "and easy golf is enjoyable golf." This man, Ernest Jones, should be in every golfer's life to some extent. As I've suggested before, get his book, and when and if you go to New York and can arrange it, take a few lessons from him, at Spalding's on Fifth Avenue.

He'll teach you that a golf club is not a club. (Wrong semantics again.)

"Unless you can feel what you are doing with the club head, you cannot possibly have any idea or sense of timing."

Jones says you must feel the "pull" outward of the club head, as you do in whirling a weight on a string.

After all, golf is more like playing with a yo-yo than ringing the bell with a sledgehammer at a county fair.

Even pivoting will take care of itself, if you let golf play you.

One serious point of possible tension is in the right knee on the downswing. Keep that knee stiff and you can't possibly let go out at the ball.

Sammy Snead says, "You must be more rubber than iron."

The Scots tell us to "play sloppy." (But, just the same, you have to be a little crisp about it.)

The habit some of us have of "firing and falling back" is nothing more or less than tension. As we hit the ball, we're opposing it with every muscle in our body. We finish on our right foot instead of our left. We constrict every limb. Common sense should tell us that if we respond to the pull of the club head it will take us naturally over onto the left foot.

Bobby Jones says that the three things that contribute most to tension are (1) a hard grip, (2) undue extension of the arms because we stand too far from the ball, (3) a too-wide separation of the feet. When we combine the three, we might as well be tied in chains.

Bobby says the chief center of relaxation is the knees.

Golf is easy. We just make it hard by getting all ossified when we swing.

Let golf play you.

BY Don Herold

FROM *Love That Golf*

THE LAY OF THE TROUBLED GOLFER

His eye was wild and his face was taut with anger and hate and
     rage,
And the things he muttered were much too strong for the ink of
     the printed page.
I found him there when the dusk came down, in his golf clothes
     still was he,
And his clubs were strewn around his feet as he told his grief to
     me:
"I'd an easy five for a seventy-nine—in sight of the golden goal!—
An easy five and I took an eight—an eight on the eighteenth hole!

"I've dreamed my dreams of the 'seventy men,' and I've worked
     year after year,
I have vowed I would stand with the chosen few ere the end of
     my golf career;
I've cherished the thought of a seventy score, and the days have
     come and gone.

And I've never been close to the golden goal my heart was set
upon.
But today I stood on the eighteenth tee and counted that score of
mine,
And my pulses raced with the thrill of joy—I'd a five for a seventy-
nine!

"I can kick the ball from the eighteenth tee and get this hole in
five,
But I took the wood and I tried to cross that ditch with a mighty
drive—"
Let us end the quotes, it is best for all to imagine his language
which,
But he topped that ball, as we often do, and the pill stopped in
the ditch.
His third was short and his fourth was bad and his fifth was off
the line,
And he took an eight on the eighteenth hole with a five for a
seventy-nine.

I gathered his clubs and I took his arm and alone in the locker
room
I left him sitting upon the bench, a picture of grief and gloom;
And the last man came and took his shower and hurried upon his
way,
But still he sat with his head bowed down like one with a mind
astray,
And he counted his score card o'er and o'er and muttered this
doleful whine:
"I took an eight on the eighteenth hole, with a five for a seventy-
nine!"

BY EDGAR A. GUEST

FROM *The Passing Throng*

A mutual contempt exists between those who play golf and those who do not. Those who have not played are sure they could become expert in a week, if they had so little sense as to waste time on so simple and objectless a game. Those who are familiar with the game know that no man living can ever hope to approach its possibilities, and they also know that it is the grandest sport designed since man has inhabited this globe.

BY JOHN HENRY SMITH

FROM *Frederick Upham Adams*

FOG GOLF

For this sport there are three essentials—a fog, a golf-course, and two enthusiastic lunatics. My uncle is neither a golf-course nor a fog, but—well, every Saturday morning he is accustomed to meet his old friend Bolter in a round of golf *à outrance*. Both are twenty handicap men, but the affair is conducted with the solemnity of a championship. The stake, half a crown, never varies, and forfeit is exacted if either combatant is absent.

One Saturday he remarked at breakfast, "I want you to help me with my clubs to-day, my boy." (My uncle does not care for professional caddies. He dislikes their manner of smiling, in which he traces a supercilious air. Mr. Bolter's must be either a greater nature or a more callous one.)

We were breakfasting by gaslight, owing to the thick yellow

121

fog that rolled outside the windows. I seldom argue with my uncle, because he does not like it, but I looked my amazement.

"Yes, yes, I know!" he said testily. "There *is* a little mist. Well, it may frighten Bolter into paying forfeit. He is five shillings up!"

The fog seemed to have thickened when we reached the club-house. It crept into your eyes and stung. My uncle found his clubs, and we groped our way towards the first tee. As we approached it, a muffled voice came to our ears out of the clinging vapour.

"I shall wait five minutes more, my lad," it said triumphantly, as though in answer to a protest, "After that, I shall claim forfeit!"

Two nebulous figures, a large and a little one, became discernible. They resolved into Mr. Bolter and a small, red-haired, shivering caddy. At sight of each other the faces of my uncle and Mr. Bolter fell. It appeared that both had hoped for forfeit. I know that *I* had, and I fancy that the caddy had been clinging to a similar wistful aspiration.

Our principals bowed coldly to each other. Off the golf-course they are old and dear friends; upon it they assume the bearing of duellists. Mr. Bolter took the honour. He is the untrammelled type of driver that rises slowly upon both toes, and then leaves the ground altogether at the moment of problematical impact with the ball. His wholehearted style tends to variety. Upon this occasion chance willed it that he should hit the missile.

"It felt straight and clean," he remarked to his caddy with pleasant optimism. "We should have no difficulty in finding it."

The child answered unemotionally that Mr. Bolter had achieved a high slice. He added that they might find the ball, and then again they mightn't. It struck me that there was probably Scotch blood in his puny body. Mr. Bolter appeared annoyed and disappointed.

My uncle relies for his drive (with perhaps misplaced confidence) upon a short, quick, powerful jerk. The tawny, remorseless fog engulfed his ball.

"A clinker, Harry!" he cried exultantly. "One of the very best, wasn't it?"

Silently I led my uncle away to the left. Both of us, despite his incurably sanguine nature, knew that in all human probability he had pulled. He *always* pulls—except when he clean misses, or when there is more danger in slicing. Before we had gone six paces Mr. Bolter and his small victim were invisible.

My instinct had not failed me. Unerringly, like some trained and patient hound, I led my uncle along the left-hand hedge, and there in the ditch we found his ball. He did not appear over-grateful to my instinct.

That first hole is always a long one. To-day it seemed somehow to have been lengthened. Sooner or later you should come to a pond across which you have to play. Everything looked altered and unreal in the fog. I will say for my uncle that we did not have much trouble in finding his ball after each stroke.

"Short, straight, steady play is needed to-day, Harry!" he kept saying. . . . But somehow we did not come to the pond.

The next thing that I remember is finding ourselves upon a green. I removed the pin, and my uncle holed out and picked up with some quiet triumph. Nothing in the least offensive, you understand. But— "Where's Bolter?" he asked, with just a trace of superiority.

"Where's the pond?" I rejoined, for a horrid doubt had come to me.

"We must have gone right round it," my principal answered hopefully. "Good Lord! . . . I do believe this is the *sixth* green!"

It was, and my uncle had handled his ball and lost the hole. We made a wide cast to the right, my uncle frankly grumpy, and I more than ever convinced that a compass and some one who understood the use of it were essential.

"We must be near the pond," he said at last. "Do I or do I not hear splashing and violent language? Yes, by the Lord, there's some one in the water!"

It was Mr. Bolter. It appeared that he had walked straight into the pond. Fortunately, from a humane point of view, to which Mr. Bolter neglected to give expression, his caddy had been warned in time by his first scream. Mr. Bolter cheered up on hearing that we had lost the hole; his caddy seemed to think that even tears were vain.

"You are very wet, Bolter," my uncle said solicitously. "If you would rather abandon the match and pay forfeit—"

"I am one up!" Mr. Bolter answered very curtly, and led the way vaguely towards the second tee. We found it quite by chance after a protracted search.

Both of them drove, apparently in the same direction, but we could not find my uncle's ball. Mr. Bolter, a being in whom golf brought out the basest instincts of humanity, made but a half-hearted effort to assist us in the search. He went back to his own ball and played it three times within a space of twenty yards. As we searched on, my uncle suddenly gave a short shriek of pain. A ball had sailed out of the fog and had struck him a stinging blow. A blurred shape came running towards us. It was Mr. Bolter.

"I am sorry for hitting you," he said triumphantly, "but I am afraid I must claim the hole! You were in front of me, and the rules are clear upon the point."

My uncle could only gobble with excusable rage. I, too, felt that the case was hard. Then his eye fell upon the missile that had struck him, and he gave a yell of triumph.

"By heaven, Bolter, you've played with my ball, more than once!" he howled. "It's my hole, after all."

Mr. Bolter's jaw fell. "I'm afraid you're right," he admitted dolefully. "That makes us all square, and—and I fancy my caddy has run home!"

"Mine is still here," responded my uncle, glancing at me with the complacence of a successful trainer of lions. "However, I will accept no advantage over you, Bolter—"

"Perhaps he can carry for us both?" suggested Mr. Bolter hopefully.

And it was then that I followed slavishly the example set by that intelligent, red-haired Scottish child.

BY J. R. STAGG

FROM *Mr. Punch on the Links*

DID SHAKESPEARE PLAY GOLF?

In a recent issue of *Punch* the above question was answered in the negative, but it is impossible for a discerning reader of *The Tempest* to come to any other conclusion than that the immortal William was at least familiar with the fine points of the game. Indeed, we are inclined to the view that, after his retirement to Stratford, his declining years were solaced with many a joyous round on the municipal links. James I undoubtedly introduced the game from Scotland, and what is more natural than that the courtly poet should take the opportunity of paying a delicate compliment to his sovereign by hinting that the chief character in his play was a golfer?

It is generally admitted that in Prospero we see Shakespeare himself, and there are many lines in the play suggesting that the magician had, possibly with the assistance of Ariel, laid out a private course on the island. Thus, in the masque, Iris is sent by Juno to bid Ceres—

> "Here on this grass plot, in this very place,
> To come and sport."

Ceres, in answer, says:

> "Why hath thy queen
> Summon'd me hither to this short-grass'd green?"

Then there is ample evidence that Caliban had an occasional round with his master, whose canny methods he appears to resent as unfair.

> "And here you sty me,"

he indignantly exclaims.

It would appear that Caliban was also frequently employed as caddy, and found that Prospero was no better than other golfers are said to be, for in the same scene he remarks:

125

> "You taught me language; and my profit on 't
> Is, I know how to curse."

Nevertheless we can readily sympathize with the unfortunate master's indignation when Caliban proposes to transfer his services to a more even-tempered player (Stephano):

> "I'll bear him no more sticks, but follow thee,
> Thou wondrous man."

The previous scene abounds in references to the Royal and Ancient game. Indeed, when Antonio, Francisco and Sebastian are teasing poor old Gonzalo, one could easily imagine oneself listening to the comments of some unsympathetic onlookers at the trial of an enthusiastic beginner:

> *Gon.:* How lush and lusty the grass looks! How green!
> *Fran.:* With his good arms in lusty stroke—
> *Ant.:* What a blow was there given!
> *Seb.:* An it had not fallen flatlong!

Our old friend has evidently decided not to hand in his card, which he hides away:

> *Ant.:* If but one of his pockets could speak, would it not say he lies?
> *Seb.:* Ay, or very falsely pocket up his report.

Again, Sebastian, as if encouraging a partner who has got into the rough, says:

> "One stroke shall free thee."

Stephano, however, who is evidently a player of little resource, replied (oddly enough, not till the next scene):

> "I will leave him; I have no long spoon."

Passing over Gonzalo's somewhat cryptic remark in Act III, sc.3:

> "Each putter-out of five for one,"

we are compelled to the conclusion that *all* of the lines quoted in support of our contention cannot be mere coincidences.

BY W. F. CANDY

FROM *Mr. Punch on the Links*

One day not long ago, a St. Louis hotel detective tipped off a cop friend of his that there was a fellow in a room on the eighth floor who packed a gun. They decided to do a little further research. They went into the room without knocking, and it didn't take long to find the gun. It was pointing at them. The man who held it was tall, dark, thin, well dressed and fiftyish.

"Take it easy," he said. Then, observing the cop's uniform, he set down the gun, a small Army model, on a table, and smiled pleasantly. "I thought it might be a stick-up," he said. "I have to be careful."

Down at the station house, where the man was taken to explain why he was armed and why he drew his hardware so quickly, they got a polite and possibly a truthful answer. He happened to have $3,930 on him. He was expecting to claim a race horse with it. When he carried cash, he liked to feel protected. He had a license for the gun. His name was Alvin C. Thomas. At this point, the police lost interest in the details of the story and merely sat looking at the speaker with the frank curiosity of zoo-goers looking at a duck-billed platypus—for Alvin C. Thomas, as they knew and as he readily confirmed, is also Titanic Thompson. All the cops in the house took a good, long stare. Then they released him, and he went on his way.

On a small scale, Titanic Thompson is an American legend. I say a small scale, because an overpowering majority of the public has never heard of him. That is the way Titanic likes it. He is a professional gambler. He has sometimes been called the gamblers' gambler. He does not resent his fame among fellow hustlers as a "man with a million propositions," as a master of percentage, but he likes to have it kept within the lodge. In the years of his early manhood, no one knew of him except gamblers, a few rich suckers, a few golf pros, and, by rumor, the police of New York City, the Middle West, and California, his favorite bases of operation. The cops had heard that he clipped people at everything, from golf to throwing quarters at a crack in the floor. But the people he clipped were mostly members of his own profession. Those outside it, honest suckers, did not complain. Suckers seldom do. Besides, they believed—and often they were right— that they had been beaten by pure skill.

One night in 1928, the most celebrated card game in American criminal history took place. As a result of it, Arnold Rothstein, a so-called underworld king, was murdered. And then it turned out that someone named Titanic Thompson had sat in on the game, and might know something about the killing.

That was the end, for a while, of Titanic's obscurity. Members of the Grassy Sprain Country Club, near New York City, blurted out a story that had been on their minds for a month. One day, some time between the Rothstein killing and Titanic's arrest as a material witness, Leo P. Flynn, a big-time fight manager and matchmaker who once handled Jack Dempsey, had brought a stranger out to the club. Leo was known there as a sport and a pretty fair golfer. This time, though, he didn't want to play golf himself. He wanted to match the stranger, whom he called Titanic, against the club professional, George McLean.

A side bet of $2,500 was arranged, with Flynn backing Thompson and several members pooling their funds in support of the local pride. That day, McLean won. He won with ease—the stranger, though he hit some good shots, did not seem to be in George's class. Besides, he was left-handed, and top-notch left-handed golfers are almost as rare as left-handed catchers. The McLean faction listened to Flynn's talk of a return match. McLean listened to the stranger's mild appeal for a ten-stroke handicap.

"I'm not in your league," said the unknown, running his hand through his floppy dark hair, "but I think I can do better than I did today. Give me a real edge in strokes, and we'll bet real dough."

The handicap, after some needling back and forth, was fixed

at eight strokes. The real dough, supplied mostly by Mr. Flynn and another golfing sport, a Mr. Duffy, was $13,000, and the members covered every dime of it in behalf of their pro. Mr. Duffy, it happened, was Big Bill Duffy, a jolly henchman of Owney Madden, the racketeer. The members did not know this, but it would probably have made no difference if they had. They did not see how an amateur could beat a good pro. It may not have occurred to them that for $13,000 Titanic was not, strictly speaking, an amateur.

The stranger shot much better, or luckier, golf this time than he had in the first match, but at the end of sixteen holes he had used up his eight-stroke advantage. The match was dead even, and McLean prepared to close in. On the short seventeenth, his tee shot stopped six feet from the pin. Titanic studied the distance and dropped one four feet closer. Perhaps that shot unnerved McLean. At any rate, he missed his putt. The stranger sank his. Titanic stood one up. He halved the last hole in par, and Mr. Flynn and Mr. Duffy picked up the $13,000—of which they gaily gave Mr. Thompson his share—and called for drinks for the house. The members went home to brood on the fact that a golf match can indeed be fixed—"fixed upward," as gamblers say—if the fixer is a talented athlete who knows how to hide the symptoms till the price is right.

On the day the news broke of Titanic's arrest in the Rothstein case, Grassy Sprain started the legend rolling. It has been gathering strength ever since. Generally speaking, New York newspaper readers forgot Thompson soon after the trial of George A. McManus for Rothstein's murder (Titanic was a state witness who gave the state no help at all). To most of the rest of the world, he was then, and still is, unknown. But in the small circle in which his name is famous, Titanic Thompson stories have been collected, pooled, and warmed over slow fires for nearly a quarter of a century, till now they amount to a kind of saga—the sharpshooter's Adventures of Robin Hood.

Rothstein's death reminded Broadway story-swappers of what might on other levels be called the Adventure of the White Horses. The horse-playing set to which Titanic and Rothstein belonged had formed the habit of spotting white horses from the train that took them to the Belmont or Jamaica track. One morning, some twenty of these smoking-car handicappers made up a pool, of $50 each, on the number of white horses that would be counted on the trip that day. Rothstein's estimate was surprisingly high; Titanic studied the tycoon thoughtfully before he made his own guess, just one horse above Rothstein's. There was an outburst of white horsemeat along the Long Island Rail Road tracks that day—a batch of fifteen animals at one crossing, a batch of twelve at another. The first batch had been planted by Titanic, the second by Rothstein.

"That will teach you not to be close with your money," said Titanic to Rothstein, as he pocketed the pool. "For thirty bucks, you could have had a whole livery stable."

Bear in mind that if Titanic had taken from the rich to give to the poor, as Robin Hood and Jesse James are said to have done, the legend-makers of the gambling world would want no part of him. He would be the wrong kind of hero. But Mr. Thompson has always taken very frankly to give to himself, or to split with the people who stake him. He has seldom made a bet he wasn't sure of winning. He always carries a gimmick—sometimes his hidden athletic skill, sometimes his trained knowledge of percentage, and occasionally a little something extra.

Here are some of the tales they tell:

1. Titanic once bet a peanut vendor $10 he could throw a peanut across Times Square in New York. He took a peanut from the vendor's stack, palmed a loaded one in its place, and pitched the phony goober up against the marquee of the Hotel Astor, across the street.

2. Bill Duffy once backed Titanic in a bet against a powerful golfer, noted for his long drives. Titanic offered to let his opponent make three drives on each hole and play the best drive of the three. It sounded like a big margin to spot a strong hitter, and the party of the second part snapped the bet up. Playing his best drive, he piled up a big lead on the first nine holes. By that time, his arms were so tired from three full swings a hole that he could hardly knock the ball off the tee. Titanic breezed home in the last nine.

3. Titanic once bet $10,000 that Nick (the Greek) Dandalos,

another high operator, would not sink a 25-foot putt. Kissed by the goddess Athena, the Greek holed the ball. Thompson, however, was not one to let $10,000 of his money rest long in someone else's jeans. He bet Nick double or nothing that he could hit a silver dollar with a gun eight times out of eight, from ten feet away. After the ceremony, the Greek gave back the ten grand and kept what was left of the dollar for a souvenir.

4. Titanic's mathematics were as sound as Pascal's. In fact, they were based on the reasoning of that great seventeenth century Frenchman. He once bet a fellow gambler that two of the first thirty persons they met and spoke to would prove to have the same birthday. Strong in the thought that he had 365 days running for him, the second hustler was pleased to accept. Suspecting, not unnaturally, a frame-up, he was careful to approach total strangers and chance passers-by, who could not be known to Titanic. He lost the bet on the twenty-eighth question, when a duplicate birthday turned up.

"To tell the truth," said Titanic afterward, "on each of the last five guys we spoke to, the odds were better than even money in my favor. I'll explain the mathematics to you some time."

Your correspondent will also be glad to explain the mathematics some time, to any reader. He does not quite understand them, but he knows what they are. Titanic's reasoning on the birthday proposition was founded on the fact that the chance against him at first was 364/365th, which, when multiplied by the succeeding chances—363/365th, 362/365th, and so forth—came fairly soon to represent ½, or one chance in two, or even money.

5. Tony Penna, the golf professional, tells of a bet by Titanic that he could throw a pumpkin over a three-story house. The pumpkin, when he produced it, was the size of an orange—but still a pumpkin. Going perhaps into the realm of pure myth, Penna adds that Titanic once bet he could throw a baseball over the Empire State Building. He won it (says Penna) by taking an elevator to the top platform and throwing from there.

Titanic once bet a dice impresario named Nutts Nitti that he could find a hairpin in each block of a stretch of twenty consecutive New York City blocks. He won. The hairpins had been planted in advance.

7. Titanic once bet he could throw a quarter at a potato, from fifteen feet away, and make it stick in the potato at least once in ten tries. Encountering resistance from his opponent, he agreed to settle for seven tries, and scored on the fourth one.

8. Titanic was motoring into Omaha, his temporary base, with a friend one day. As they passed a signpost on the road, Titanic, without looking at it, offered to bet that they would reach the city limits within ten minutes. The signpost made it ten miles to town. The friend, a noticing sort of man, took the bet. He lost. Titanic had moved the signpost five miles closer that morning.

9. There is a standard prop in Titanic's repertory—a two-headed quarter, which he uses with more than standard speed, skill, and acting talent. His opening line, after dinner, is "Let's toss for the check." His next line, while the coin is in the air, is "You cry." If his opponent cries heads, Titanic lets the quarter fall—heads. If the other fellow cries tails, Titanic swings his hand nonchalantly, catches the coin, puts it back in his pocket, and speaks to this effect: "Oh, to hell with gambling for ham and eggs. Let's go Dutch."

10. Titanic is credited with being the man who introduced Rothstein to the art of betting on automobile license plates, at Rothstein's expense. He bet Rothstein, as they stood on a Broadway corner, that the first New Jersey plate to come along would make a better poker hand than the first New York plate. Thirty seconds later, from his parking spot around the corner (there were parking spots in those days), a colleague of Titanic's drove into view in a New Jersey car. His plate number carried three threes.

11. In a Hot Springs, Arkansas, stud-poker game, a player named Burke became justly incensed one evening because he could not win.

"That deck is ice cold, and so is the other one," he bawled. "I ain't had a pair in an hour."

"You ought to know," said Titanic soothingly, "that the odds are against getting a pair in any five-card hand. Now, if you dealt yourself six cards——"

"With these cards," yelled Burke, "I couldn't pair myself if I dealt all night!"—and the way was paved for a Thompson proposition. Titanic offered to let Burke deal himself ten cold hands of six cards each. Before each hand, he offered to bet that there would be a pair in it. They say that the agony of Burke, as he paired himself in eight of the ten hands and thus lost $300 by the sweat of his own fingers, was something to see. Titanic had known that the addition of a sixth card changes the odds on catching a pair from 13 to 10 against to nearly 2 to 1 in favor. And to bet even money on a 2-to-1 favorite, he would walk quite a distance and stay quite awhile.

12. In his early days, Titanic, going through a storeroom in the basement of a sporting club in Ohio on his way to the men's room, spotted a rat and nimbly tipped a barrel over the animal. Later, in the course of the dice game upstairs, he raised the subject of the prevalence of rats in Ohio sporting clubs and made a bet that he could find and shoot one any time. The bet was taken. Titanic returned to the cellar, shot the dead rat, and brought it back to the table with him.

13. Titanic, shooting right-handed, lost a close golf match to an amateur who played in the 90s. Next day, he bet the winner double their first bet that he could beat him playing left-handed. Left-handed, his natural style, Titanic shot an 80. The victim continued to shoot in the 90s.

14. Titanic once bet he could drive a golf ball 500 yards. The bet was popular on all sides, and the interested parties followed Titanic out to the golf course of his choice, on Long Island. He picked a tee on a hill overlooking a lake. It was wintertime. His drive hit the ice and, it seemed to his opponents, never did stop rolling. It went half a mile, if it went a yard.

Titanic, as the district attorney found out in the Rothstein case, does not talk much. All that anyone knows about his origins and early life comes from stray remarks, spaced far apart, that he has let fall to other gamblers on the golf course or at the card table. This writer has seen him only once. It was in the "private" or "upstairs" crap game at the old Chicago Club in Saratoga. Joe Madden, the literary barkeep, pointed him out to me from the sidelines. I saw a slender fellow about six feet tall, his dark hair cut long, wearing a neat gabardine suit and two fair-sized diamond rings. When Titanic left the game a little later, Madden said, "He's going down to the drugstore to get a load of ice cream. That's his dish."

"That's his dish for breakfast," corrected one of the gamblers at the table. "But he don't eat breakfast till he gets up for the races, maybe two o'clock in the afternoon."

A discussion of Titanic's habits ensued. It reminded me of a session of fight men on Jacobs Beach or in the press room at the Garden, discussing some figure of legend like Stanley Ketchel. I asked where the name Titanic had come from. The answer was one I'd heard before, the only one I've ever heard. It may or may not be true.

In a poker game in New York on Thompson's first tour of the East, one player said to another, "What's that guy's name?"

"It ought to be Titanic," said the second player. "He sinks everybody."

The logic here was a little unsound—if I remember the S.S. *Titanic* story, "Iceberg" would have been the right name. But gamblers are seldom good on names. Thompson, for instance, is an easy garbling of Titanic's real name, Thomas. There seems to be no doubt, judging by police files, that he was born Alvin Clarence Thomas, in the state of Arkansas, about 1893. He still talks with a slight Southwestern accent. As a boy, he once said, he acquired the throwing skill that served him handsomely later by killing quail with rocks. He was a good horseshoe pitcher and an expert shot.

Athletic talent is a rare thing in a professional gambler, but what surprised the golf pros of the Pacific Coast and the Southwest, who knew him in his early days and accepted him as an athlete to begin with, was his lightning speed of mind at gambling. He would make twelve to fifteen bets on a single hole, keeping track of them in his head while others took time to make notes. He would lose one bet and make another on the next shot that would bring his stake back doubled. Penna and others noticed that his bets during the match often were bigger than his bet on the match as a whole.

"Yeah, that's right," said Titanic, when someone spoke of this.

"I like to bet 'em when they're out there on the course with me. Especially on the greens. Why? Figure it out for yourself."

It was not hard to figure. When a golfer is out there on the course, any new bet he makes is probably made with his own money, without the help of a backer. When he bets his own money, he gets nervous. Especially on the greens.

In Titanic's youth, they say, he was impatient with mental slowness of any kind, but it could not have been long before he came to recognize that quality, in the people around him, as so much bread and jam for him. Among the money golfers who knew him at one time and another were Penna, Dick Metz, Len Dodson and Ben Hogan. He always told them, as he often told the cops when they picked him up on the curious charge of shooting golf too well, that he was "a former pro." It may have been so, but the chances are that he was a former caddy who, on discovering his own skill at the game, almost immediately became a professional gambler rather than a professional golfer. It was a nice economic choice. The best professional golfers in the country, even in these days of rich prizes, do well to earn $30,000 in a year from tournaments. Titanic has sometimes made $50,000 in a few weeks of well-timed chipping and putting at golf resorts.

"I've been broke," he told a Coast newspaperman once, "but never for more than six hours at a time. When I tap out, somebody I once helped loans me a stake, and I'm back in action again."

Titanic Thompson broke into the Rothstein game, as a young man, because he was good company and a good player—though the state of New York tried to prove, a little later, that trained fingers had something to do with it. The fateful game that led to Rothstein's death and to Titanic's first appearance in print took place on the night of September 7-8, 1928. It was held at the apartment of Jimmy Meehan, a regular member of the circle, on the West Side of New York. Rothstein, because he was rumored to have a finger in every branch of organized crime in the city, was the best-known player in the game, but all the others were noted figures in the gambling, bookmaking, and horse-playing worlds. They included Martin "Red" Bowe, Nigger Nate Raymond, Sam and Meyer Boston, Abe Silverman, George A. Mc-

135

Manus, and Titanic Thompson. The game was stud poker, but as it went along it took on a pattern familiar in that group—it became a "high-card" game, with the biggest money being bet on the size of the first-up card in the stud hand.

There were rumors along Broadway in the following week that Rothstein had lost a packet. There were also rumors that the winners had not been paid in full. It took a gunshot, however, to make the story public property. On November 4, 1928, someone put a revolver slug into Rothstein's body in Room 349 of the Park Central Hotel. Rothstein staggered from the room and died just outside it. The killer pushed aside a screen and threw the gun into the street below. The New York newspapers went to town. It became the biggest crime story since the murder of Herman Rosenthal by Whitey Lewis, Dago Frank, Lefty Louie, and Gyp the Blood.

The overcoat of George McManus, a smiling gambler, brother of a police lieutenant, had been found in Room 349. Soon afterward McManus was indicted for murder, along with three gunmen who never did show up for trial. On November 26, the D.A., Joab H. Banton, arrested Jimmy Meehan, Red Bowe, Sidney Stajer (Rothstein's secretary), Nigger Nate Raymond, and Titanic as material witnesses. All of them but Bowe were held in $100,000 bail. For some reason it was Titanic, then and later, who caught the public's fancy—maybe because he was said to be a Westerner, a lone wolf, a romantic and single-duke gambler of the old school.

It turned out that Titanic had a wife, Mrs. Alice Thomas, who had been living with him at the Mayflower Hotel. A few days after his arrest, she paid him a tearful visit at the West Side prison on Fifty-fourth Street. Titanic then sent for the D.A.'s men, made "important disclosures" (the papers said), and was released in $10,000 bail. What kind of minstrel show he gave to win his freedom is not known. Unofficially it was reported that he had admitted to being in Room 349 just before the murder, leaving when he saw that there might be trouble. Whatever he said, it was plain that the D.A. thought he had laid hold of a fine, friendly witness. The D.A. was very wrong.

When the McManus murder case came to trial, in November

1929, Titanic was running a night club and gambling spot in Milwaukee. He was also running a fever in a Milwaukee hospital. So important was his evidence considered by the prosecution that the trial was delayed for a week. Titanic, in Milwaukee, showed for the first time that he was in no mood to blow whistles.

"I don't know what they want me as a witness for," he told reporters, whom he received in scarlet pajamas in the hospital. "I wasn't with Rothstein on the night of the murder and hadn't seen him or McManus for two months previously. We played cards at that time, and McManus lost a lot of money. That's all I know about the case."

When he did get to New York to testify, the courtroom was packed. Titanic sat in the rear of the room, twisting his fingers nervously, till he was called. The crowd buzzed as he took the stand. McManus, in the dock, sat up and smiled at Titanic. Titanic nodded to McManus. Ferdinand Pecora, later a famous judge, then an assistant D.A. and a strong trial lawyer, moved in on Titanic confidently. It had been established that McManus had lost $51,000 to Rothstein in the celebrated high-card game while Rothstein was losing about $219,000 to some of the others. Pecora's pitch was obvious. He implied that Rothstein, possibly with Titanic's help, had fleeced McManus of the fifty-one grand. Titanic would have no part of this hypothesis. After identifying himself by saying that he gambled on everything from golf to horse races, and referring to McManus as "a square and honest guy," he began to spar Pecora to a standstill.

"Was the game on the level?" asked the prosecutor.

"It couldn't be any other way on high cards," said Titanic with a deeply scornful gesture. "A man who never dealt in his life was peddling the papers. We had to show him how to shuffle."

To "peddle the papers" is to deal. The crowd was delighted with this local color.

"Now, think," said Pecora angrily, after a while. "Wasn't this game crooked?"

"Anyone ought to know," said Titanic, still scornful, "that that's impossible."

"Couldn't a clever dealer give the high card to any man he chose?"

"Certainly not," said Titanic. "It ain't being done."

On other questions, his memory failed.

"You see," he told Pecora patiently, "I just don't remember things. If I bet on a horse today and won ten grand, I probably would not be able to recall the horse's name tomorrow."

While the public gasped at this spacious statement, the defense took over for cross-examination. At once, Titanic's memory improved, and his attitude got friendlier. He said that McManus had shown no ill will after the game.

"He's a swell loser," said Titanic tenderly. "Win or lose, he always smiles."

In short, he probably gave the state less change for its money than any state's witness in recent memory. And it's a matter of record that George A. McManus was acquitted of the murder of Arnold Rothstein.

It's a matter of record, too, that Titanic was annoyed by his notoriety during the trial. For several months afterward, he complained that he could no longer get a "good" game of golf, by which he meant a game with gravy on the side. He may have misstated the case a little. Recently I asked Oswald Jacoby, the card wizard, about a story in the newspapers that said John R. Crawford, an ex-G.I. and a spectacular newcomer to card-playing circles, resented the publicity he got in a big Canasta game for charity because no one wanted to play cards with him any more.

"Don't you believe it," said Mr. Jacoby. "People always want to play with a man with a big reputation. The more money they have, the more they like it."

Be that as it may, Titanic, in Tulsa soon after the trial, was bothered by the galleries that followed him—but he did find one man who wanted to play golf with him just to be able to say he'd done it. Titanic fixed up "a little proposition" for him and won $2,000. There must have been other men with the same ambition, or else Ti's celebrity began to fade, for we cross his trail again in Little Rock, Arkansas, soon afterward, playing golf for $2,000 and $3,000 a round.

True, even a roving gambler likes to stop and run a "store" now and then, but since the time of his first fame, Titanic has found it more comfortable to keep on the move. He and a large restaurant operator and racketeer, whom we will call Tony Rizzo, were moving by train not long ago from California to Tony's base at Hot Springs.

"Tony," said Titanic, "do you ever regret being illiterate?"

"Whaddya mean?" said Tony, hurt. "I ain't so dumb."

"I'm going to teach you to spell two ten-letter words," said Titanic. "The words are 'rhinoceros' and 'anthropoid.' If you can still spell them when we get off the train, I'll pick up the checks for this trip. But take a tip from me—keep spelling them or you'll forget them."

For the rest of the trip, Rizzo kept spelling out, in order, the letters r-h-i-n-o-c-e-r-o-s and a-n-t-h-r-o-p-o-i-d. He still knew them at the Hot Springs station. Titanic paid off.

The gambler set the second stage of the proposition for Tony's restaurant. He first brought an unknown partner, a respectable-looking fellow as shills go, into the act. He rehearsed the shill in the spelling of ten ten-letter words, including "rhinoceros" and "anthropoid." The next night he sat down in Rizzo's restaurant, as usual, with Owney Madden and other lovable tourists. Rizzo himself, as usual, was sitting at a table by himself, wolfing his pizza in solitary grandeur.

"Do you know," said Titanic confidentially, "that that Rizzo just pretends to be ignorant? He puts on a dumb front for business. The guy has got diplomas from two colleges."

This speech aroused great skepticism at Titanic's table, which in turn aroused bets. Titanic covered a thousand dollars' worth, his argument being that Tony could spell any ten-letter word, any one at all, that Mr. Madden and the boys chose to mention. As Titanic expected, a pause followed, while the boys tried to think of a ten-letter word to give Tony. They were somewhat embarrassed. At this point, Titanic's partner hove into view, and Titanic hailed him.

"Excuse me, sir," he said, "but you look as though you might be able to help us. May I ask your business? A lawyer? Fine. Would you mind writing down ten ten-letter words on a piece of paper here, for these gentlemen to choose from?"

The stranger obliged. Looking around, he wrote the word "restaurant," which appeared on Tony's window. He wrote down several others he found on the bill of fare, such as "cacciatore." In and among the rest he inserted the words "rhinoceros" and "anthropoid." He turned the paper over to the boys, who immediately set to work making scratches in the morning line, to protect their bets. They scratched "restaurant"—Tony saw it on the window all day, he might know it. They scratched "cacciatore." "He's Eyetalian," said Mr. Madden, "and he might know all that kind of stuff." This left them, in the end, with "rhinoceros" and "anthropoid." At random, they scratched "rhinoceros." They summoned Mr. Rizzo and desired him to spell the word "anthropoid."

"Sure," said Tony, taking a deep breath. "R-h-i-n-o-c-e-r-o-s."

Titanic paid off the $1,000. The bet belongs to his legend partly because he lost it and partly because he won the money back, with galloping dominoes, the same night. As I said before, he is prosperous just now. A fellow gambler who ran across him in Evansville, Indiana—you are apt find him anywhere—says that Titanic's pajamas and dressing gowns, always brilliant, are more brilliant than ever. His supply of jewels, rings, and stickpins is at high tide. A man like Ti, my informant explains, buys jewels whenever he is in the money, to sell or hock when times are hard.

The Titanic legend would not be so solidly honored in the gambling world, it would not be complete, if the quiet Mr. Thompson had never used the gun he always carries, in defense of the money he takes from the rich to give to himself. The police of Little Rock, years ago, found a letter in Titanic's room which demanded "2 thousand cash or you will be sorry." The police of St. Louis, more recently, found him ready to draw at the sound of a door being opened.

And in Tyler, Texas, a few years back, it was proved clearly that in matters involving Titanic Thompson and his money there is very little kidding. Titanic had had a good day on the golf course. His caddy noticed it. The caddy was sixteen years old, but he had grown-up ideas. At a late hour the same evening, a shot was fired in Tyler, and the police arrived to find the caddy with a bullet in him, while Titanic stood in attendance.

"I shot him," said the gambler. "It was self-defense. He tried to stick me up for my roll."

The young man died the next day. A mask and an unfired gun were found on his person, and the plea of self-defense was allowed. Titanic moved along, with a stronger toehold on history than ever.

FROM The World of John Lardner

KEEP YOUR EYE ON THE BALL

Boy, if the phone should ring
    Or anyone should call;
Whisper that this is Spring,
    To come again next Fall.
Say I have a date on a certain tee,
    Where my friends the sand traps wait in glee;
Tell them the "Doc" has ordered me
    To keep my eye on the ball.

Boy, if they wish to know
    Where I shall haunt the scene;
Tell them to leave and go
    Out by the ancient green.
Tell them to look where the traps are deep
    And the sand flies up in a powdered heap,
And out of the depths loud curses creep
    To the flash of a niblick sheen.

Then if the boss should sigh,
    Or for my presence seek,
Tell him the truth, don't lie;
    Say that my will was weak.

For what is a job to a brassie shot
  That whistles away to an untrapped spot?
Or the thrill of a well cut mashie shot
  Or the sweep of a burnished cleek?

BY GRANTLAND RICE
FROM *Fifty Years of American Golf*

Surely we must account old Tom Morris as one of the wonders
of the sporting world, as he is indubitably in that relation to the
world of golf. How many times have we heard that the light of
that long and happy life was flickering towards its extinction, but
the rumour has no sooner been spread than Tom comes forward in
some activity to give it full denial. Long may he continue to do
so; every time that we hear he is sick upon his bed may a telegram come to us from St. Andrews to say that again he is sitting
in the chair outside his shop, watching the couples as they come
forward in their turn to hole out on that beloved eighteenth putting green, which, with the clubhouse of the Royal and Ancient
beyond it, has during recent times comprised almost the entire
circle of his daily vision. Each time I go to St. Andrews I find him
still cheery, and indeed it seems to me a little cheerier than the
last time that I saw him taking the sun in his chair. There is the
cheery respectful greeting and the felicitous remark that it is "a
gran' day for a roond," and in the next moment he turns his head
to mutter a grumble towards those "boys," who are idling away a
few spare minutes outside Forgan's shop, and are giving evidence
of the freshness of the life that is in them, to which Tom, a
stickler for decorum in all connected with golf, however humbly
or indirectly, demurs. Like most others who are running up the
score of their life's round towards the ninety mark, he is prone to

142

tell you that times have much changed, and that the boys were more sedate in the days when he was one of them. That is as it may be. But despite all the antics of the boys, and the little irritations that they give to old Tom, he remains a cheery Tom to the last, just as he has always been. His life throughout has been imbued with an optimism which has always been the most attractive feature of his character. Every good golfer is an optimist. I deny that it is possible to be a good golfer in the best sense and not be an out-and-out optimist.

Another fine thing about Tom, and one that has always endeared him to the golfing world, is the fact that there has never been anything in the least niggardly in the gratitude which he extends towards the game with which his life has been bound up. Suggest to Tom that there is anything better in life than golf, and you have done the first thing towards raising up a barrier of reserve between him and you. Listen to how he spoke of the game of his heart on a New Year's Day twenty-one years back from now, when even then he was by way of becoming an old man. "An' it hadna been for gowff," he said to the patron who greeted him in the customary form for the first day of the year, "I'm no sure that at this day, sir, I wad hae been a leevin' man. I've had ma troubles an' ma trials, like the lave; an' whiles I thocht they wad hae clean wauved me, sae that to 'lay me doun an' dee'—as the song says—lookit about a' that was left in life for puir Tam. It was like as if ma vera sowle was a'thegither gane oot o' me. But there's naething like a ticht gude gowing mautch to soop yer brain clear o' that kin' o' thing; and wi' the help o' ma God an' o' gowff, I've aye gotten warsled through somehow or ither. The tae thing ta'en wi' the tither, I haena had an ill time o't. I dinna mind that iver I had an unpleasant word frae ony o' the many gentlemen I've played wi'. I've aye tried—as ma business was, sir—to mak' masel' pleesant to them; an' they've aye been awfu' pleesant to me. An' noo, sir, to end a long and maybe a silly crack—bein' maistly about masel'—ye'll just come wi' me, an' ye'll hae a glass o' gude brandy, and I'll have ma pint o' black strap, an' we'll drink a gude New Year to ane anither, an' the like to a' gude gowffers."

Sportsman, in the best sense, Tom has always been, and he

was a worthy predecessor of the men who are to-day at the head of the ranks of the professional golfers. That is a pretty story that is told of Captain Broughton's challenge to Tom to hole a putt for 50 pounds. As everybody knows, Tom was once famous as the man who missed the very shortest putts, to whom there was duly delivered, when he was at Prestwick, a letter which was addressed only to the "Misser of Short Putts, Prestwick." On the occasion under notice Tom was playing to the High Hole on the old course at St. Andrews, and had got into sore trouble, so that he was playing two or three more when Captain Broughton happened to pass by and became a witness of what was happening. Tom, be it noted, always belonged to golfers of that fine and sportsmanlike persistency, who would never give up a hole while there was a single spark of hope remaining alight. "Oh, pick up your ball, Tom, it's no use!" said the Captain half chidingly. "Na, na," answered Tom, "I might hole it!" "If you do I'll give you 50 pounds," retorted the Captain, and it seemed a very safe retort too. "Done!" responded Tom, and thereupon made one more stroke with his iron club, and lo! the ball hopped on to the green, and glided on and on towards the hole, hesitated as it came nearer to it, curled round towards it, crept nearer and nearer until it was on the lip—and down! He had holed! Then said the triumphant Tom, "That will make a nice little nest-egg for me to put in the bank," and the Captain looked very serious and went his way. A few days later the Captain came along with the 50 pounds, and with a smile and a compliment offered it to Tom as the fruits of his achievement; but Tom declined absolutely to take a penny of it. "I thank ye, Captain, and I'm grateful to ye all the same; but I canna tak' the money, because, ye see, ye wisna really meaning it, and it wisna a real wager." And to that he stuck.

BY HENRY LEACH

FROM *The Spirit of the Links*

THE GOLFOMANIAC

We ride in and out pretty often together, he and I, on a suburban train.

That's how I came to talk to him. "Fine morning," I said as I sat down beside him yesterday and opened a newspaper.

"Great!" he answered, "the grass is drying out fast now and the greens will soon be all right to play."

"Yes," I said, "the sun is getting higher and the days are decidedly lengthening."

"For the matter of that," said my friend, "a man could begin to play at six in the morning easily. In fact, I've often wondered that there's so little golf played before breakfast. We happened to be talking about golf, a few of us last night—I don't know how it came up—and we were saying that it seems a pity that some of the best part of the day, say, from five o'clock to seven-thirty, is never used."

"That's true," I answered, and then, to shift the subject, I said, looking out of the window:

"It's a pretty bit of country just here, isn't it?"

"It is," he replied, "but it seems a shame they make no use of it—just a few market gardens and things like that. Why, I noticed along here acres and acres of just glass—some kind of houses for plants or something—and whole fields full of lettuce and things like that. It's a pity they don't make something of it. I was remarking only the other day as I came along in the train with a friend of mine, that you could easily lay out an eighteen-hole course anywhere here."

"Could you?" I said.

"Oh, yes. This ground, you know, is an excellent light soil to shovel up into bunkers. You could drive some big ditches through it and make one or two deep holes—the kind they have on some of the French links. In fact, improve it to any extent."

I glanced at my morning paper. "I see," I said, "that it is again rumored that Lloyd George is at last definitely to retire."

"Funny thing about Lloyd George," answered my friend. "He never played, you know; most extraordinary thing—don't you think?—for a man in his position. Balfour, of course, was very different: I remember when I was over in Scotland last summer I had the honor of going around the course at Dumfries just after Lord Balfour. Pretty interesting experience, don't you think?"

"Were you over on business?" I asked.

"No, not exactly. I went to get a golf ball, a particular golf ball. Of course, I didn't go merely for that. I wanted to get a mashie as well. The only way, you know, to get just what you want is to go to Scotland for it."

"Did you see much of Scotland?"

"I saw it all. I was on the links at St. Andrews and I visited the Loch Lomond course and the course at Inverness. In fact, I saw everything."

"An interesting country, isn't it, historically?"

"It certainly is. Do you know they have played there for over five hundred years! Think of it! They showed me at Loch Lomond the place where they said Robert the Bruce played the Red Douglas (I think that was the other party—at any rate, Bruce was one of them), and I saw where Bonnie Prince Charlie disguised himself as a caddie when the Duke of Cumberland's soldiers were looking for him. Oh, it's a wonderful country historically."

After that I let a silence intervene so as to get a new start. Then I looked up again from my newspaper.

"Look at this," I said, pointing to a headline, *United States Navy Ordered Again to Nicaragua.* "Looks like more trouble, doesn't it?"

"Did you see in the paper a while back," said my companion, "that the United States Navy Department is now making golf compulsory at the training school at Annapolis? That's progressive, isn't it? I suppose it will have to mean shorter cruises at sea;

in fact, probably lessen the use of the navy for sea purposes. But it will raise the standard."

"I suppose so," I answered. "Did you read about this extraordinary murder case on Long Island?"

"No," he said. "I never read murder cases. They don't interest me. In fact, I think this whole continent is getting over-preoccupied with them—"

"Yes, but this case had such odd features—"

"Oh, they all have," he replied, with an air of weariness. "Each one is just boomed by the papers to make a sensation—"

"I know, but in this case it seems that the man was killed with a blow from a golf club."

"What's that? Eh, what's that? Killed him with a blow from a golf club!!"

"Yes, some kind of club—"

"I wonder if it was an iron—let me see the paper—though, for the matter of that, I imagine that a blow with even a driver, let alone one of the steel-handled drivers—where does it say it?— pshaw, it only just says 'a blow with a golf club.' It's a pity the papers don't write these things up with more detail, isn't it? But perhaps it will be better in the afternoon paper . . ."

"Have you played golf much?" I inquired. I saw it was no use to talk of anything else.

"No," answered my companion, "I am sorry to say I haven't. You see, I began late. I've only played twenty years, twenty-one if you count the year that's beginning in May. I don't know what I was doing. I wasted about half my life. In fact, it wasn't till I was well over thirty that I caught on to the game. I suppose a lot of us look back over our lives that way and realize what we have lost.

"And even as it is," he continued, "I don't get much chance to play. At the best I can only manage about four afternoons a week, though of course I get most of Saturday and all Sunday. I get my holiday in the summer, but it's only a month, and that's nothing. In the winter I manage to take a run South for a game once or twice and perhaps a little swack at it around Easter, but only a week at a time. I'm too busy—that's the plain truth of it." He sighed. "It's hard to leave the office before two," he said. "Something always turns up."

And after that he went on to tell me something of the technique of the game, illustrate it with a golf ball on the seat of the car, and the peculiar mental poise needed for driving, and the neat, quick action of the wrist (he showed me how it worked) that is needed to undercut a ball so that it flies straight up in the air. He explained to me how you can do practically anything with a golf ball, provided that you keep your mind absolutely poised and your eye in shape, and your body a trained machine. It appears that even Bobby Jones of Atlanta and people like that fall short very often from the high standard set up by my golfing friend in the surburban car.

So, later in the day, meeting someone in my club who was a person of authority on such things, I made inquiry about my friend. "I rode into town with Llewellyn Smith," I said. "I think he belongs to your golf club. He's a great player, isn't he?"

"A great player!" laughed the expert. "Llewellyn Smith? Why, he can hardly hit a ball! And anyway, he's only played about twenty years!"

BY STEPHEN LEACOCK

FROM *Laugh with Leacock*

A REMARKABLE WOMAN

The team championship at the National Athletic Union track and field meet in 1932 was won by the Employers Casualty Company of Dallas. Those points were achieved through the winning of five individual championships and the tying for a sixth. The entire "team" consisted of one 18-year-old girl, Babe Didrikson.

Implausible is the adjective which best befits the Babe. As far as sport is concerned she had the golden touch of a Midas. When she was only 16 she was named to the All-America Women's Basketball team. She once hit thirteen home runs in a softball double-header. Her top bowling score was 237. In the 1932 Olympics she won two events, setting world records in each, and placed second in the third test although again breaking the world record.

But it was as a golfer in her later years that she gained most renown, dominating the distaff side of the divot-digging pastime with awesome efficiency. Best remembered is the rueful flippancy Bob Hope tossed over his shoulder after pairing with her in a charity match.

"I hit the ball like a girl and she hits it like a man," he said. Hope was at least half-correct. The Babe hit the ball like a man.

But behind that steel-sinewed, square-jawed façade was feminine softness and gushy sentimentality. The first time the Babe ever had any extra money, she took her mother to a department store in her native Beaumont, Texas.

"Momma, pick you out a dress," drawled the Babe, pridefully. Momma did.

"Pick you out another one," urged the Babe, glowing with satisfaction at the astonished look on her mother's face. The Babe kept urging until eight dresses were selected.

"Momma," said the Babe triumphantly, "now you got a dress for every day in the week and two for Sunday." Her devotion to her beloved Momma and Poppa was heart-warming.

There was a tender awkwardness to her romance with George Zaharias, the massive wrestler. They were mutually attracted the moment they met and their love story was a rich and rewarding one through courtship, matrimony and beyond.

Babe Didrikson Zaharias made a strange confession in her autobiography *This Life I've Led*, a wonderfully human character exposition that she wrote with the aid of Harry Paxton.

"Before I was even in my teens," she declared, "I knew exactly what I wanted to be when I grew up. My goal was to be the greatest athlete that ever lived."

This was an odd ambition because the best woman athlete in almost any sport is about on a par with a schoolboy champion. Yet the Babe became the greatest of her sex beyond question and her golf frequently attained unbelievable proficiency. It was no accident, no reliance on natural ability alone. She worked at it with the same indomitable ability with which she fought against the cancer that was to take her life.

Before she started out in the first golf tournament of her career, a reporter asked how well she expected to score.

"I think I'll shoot a 77," she said nonchalantly. This was a bit of bombast which she airily characterized as "Texas talk."

So the gal from Texas shot a 77. It was a freak, of course, and she did not linger long in the match play rounds which followed. But this experience impressed on her the need for giving polish to her game. She did it in typical fashion.

The Babe practiced sixteen hours a day each weekend. On weekdays she was on the course at 5:30 a.m. for a three-hour session. Then she went to her regular job. Most of her lunch hour was spent chipping balls onto a leather chair in her boss's office. After work she took lessons for an hour and practiced until dark.

"I'd hit golf balls until my hands were bloody and sore," she once grimly explained. "Then I'd have tape all over my hands and blood all over the tape."

The price for perfection was high but she paid it willingly. The rewards were high, too. Yet there never were any short cuts for the Babe in anything, either in getting to the top or staying there. Once she was leading a tournament when she discovered that she had played the wrong ball out of the rough. She alone knew it.

"That's it," she said resignedly to the officials. "I've been playing the wrong ball and I have to disqualify myself."

"But no one would have known the difference," remarked some unthinking spectator.

"I'd have known the difference," said the Babe sharply, "and I wouldn't have felt right in my mind. You have to play by the rules of golf just as you have to live by the rules of life. There's no other way."

This was no mere muscle girl who died the other day. The greatness of her athletic achievements permeated the entire character of Babe Didrikson Zaharias until the strength and splendor shone through. She was a remarkable personality.

BY ARTHUR DALEY

FROM *Sports of* The Times

SLAMMING SUKI SUKIYUKI

There was a Japanese golf professional at the swank Hamilton Country Club in Bombay, India, who caused more of a furor in international golfing circles, until his untimely death in 1924, than Bobby Jones or Walter Hagen ever did.

Suki Sukiyuki, Jr., known to his fans as "Slamming Suki," was probably the only golfer in history to win a major golf championship right-handed one year, and left-handed the next. He accomplished this remarkable feat in capturing the British Open in 1919 and 1920.

The bright star of Suki's fame faded, however, when his unparalleled triumphs were disallowed by the sacrosanct Royal and Ancient Golf Club on the grounds that he had employed a type of follow-through not sanctioned in British play. This follow-through, not uncommon among Asiatic golfers, consisted of striking the ball twice in a single swing, but with such great speed that to the unaided eye it appeared to be but a single stroke. Slow motion movies brought the fact to light, however, and thus Suki's record-smashing 275 in 1920, his left-handed year, was actually 550.

Born the son of well-to-do parents in the Honshu province of Japan, Suki spent his early childhood in the Honshu tradition— breeding goldfish and skiing the slopes of Mt. Fujiyama. Suki, Sr., however, soon realized that his young son was in need of schooling of a more formal nature than was then available in Honshu, and sent him post-haste to a private school in Tokyo. One day a group of boys from the school went out to the Imperial Links to see a golfing exhibition by the famous Duncan MacPhee, who was then on a world-wide barnstorming tour. From that day forward Suki was a slave to gutta-percha and hickory. His wealthy parents had him outfitted and arranged to have him take instruction from Tama Shanti, the dour Japanese champion. This was unfortunate in that Shanti was an exponent of the aforementioned illegal follow-through. Suki, for his part, was an apt pupil and within nine months had officially taken Shanti to the cleaners, becoming the new champion of all Japan—a title he never relinquished.

Seeking new fields to conquer, Suki entered the Chinese Closed, at Hong Kong, in 1910. It was there that he inadvertently discovered his amazing ambidexterity. On the eighteenth hole of the final round, and needing but a triple bogey to cop, Suki was in trouble. He had hooked his drive into a rice paddy, blasted out into a small forest of yew trees, and, on his third shot, rolled up tight against the right side of a small ornamental pagoda. His cushion was fast deflating. The hot Chinese sun was pouring down. Suki took off his pith helmet and mopped his sloping brow. What to do?

He assayed the impossible lie, his grinning opponent, and the green some 290 yards away. Smiling thoughtfully, he drew from his bag an adjustable club which some admirer had given him after the Japanese Open the year before. He had never used it, but had carried it in his bag as a kind of good luck piece. Now was certainly the time for it! Setting it for a left-handed driving-iron position, he wound up and struck. The shot was one of those low screamers, straight as a chopstick, that begins to rise slowly and then almost ascends to the heavens. The direction was true, the distance was perfect, and Suki had holed out, left-handed, from almost 300 yards away This became the famous "Pagoda Shot" and heralded a new era for "Slamming Suki" Sukiyuki.

After Hong Kong, Suki dropped out of competition for six weeks, bought himself a set of left-handed clubs and practiced intently. He found that left-handed he was just as proficient as right-handed, if not more so. He decided to enter the Shanghai Open and play strictly left-handed. He won, going away, by sixteen strokes.

For the next two years Suki dominated the Far Eastern scene. He swept through the Opens at Peiping and Peking, won the Specialists at Vladivostodk, and the World Wide at Bangkok. He played sometimes right-handed, sometimes left-handed, sometimes a combination of the two. His unique skill came in particularly handy when he was up against a fence or a tree.

After garnering every conceivable Far Eastern trophy, Slamming Suki made plans to sail for England where competition was stiffer. This project, however, was postponed by World War I. Suki volunteered for the Imperial Navy but was rejected for triple jointedness. Heartbroken, he returned to his home in the Honshu province. There he remained, out of the public eye, for several months. Then, returning to Tokyo, he joined the J.S.O., Japanese equivalent of the U.S.O., and spent the war years entertaining troops with his amazing ambidextrous tap dancing. He would dance sometimes on his right foot, and sometimes on his left.

With the close of the War, Slamming Suki made good on his plan for a tour of the British Isles. He arrived in England early in 1919, just in time for the Ulster Open. Suki immediately became the darling of the galleries. He was physically unprepossessing, but his toothy grin, owl eyes behind thick, black horn-rimmed glasses, and of course his booming shots with either hand, captivated the golfing public. This tournament saw him nosed out by his old idol, MacPhee, but since it was Suki's first golf competition in over four years he was not discouraged.

The year 1919 will not soon be forgotten by those who know golf. It was, of course, the year of Suki's "Big Sweep" of British golf. He won the British Open right-handed, the Irish Sweepstakes left-handed, the Scotch Lowball right-handed, and, to cap everything, the Welsh P.G.A. Championship alternating left- and right-handed strokes.

Suki's fame was unparalleled. He was feted in all of the golfing capitals of the British Isles. The King himself paid him a visit in the lawnmower shed of the famous Royal Portrush course.

Suki was using this as a locker room, following his win in the British Open, since at that time professionals were still denied the use of clubhouse facilities at British courses.

Soon after the 1920 Open, however, the shocking truth of the "double hit" technique that had led to Slamming Suki's amazing successes was bared to the world via the slow motion camera. After returning his many laurels to assorted second place winners, Suki packed his bag, took his two sets of clubs, and set sail for Bombay, India, and the Hamilton Country Club. He was disillusioned and vowed never again to set foot in the Western World.

Suki remained at Hamilton, as professional in residence, until one sad day in 1924. He was in the Bombay station waiting for a train to Karachi, where he was to defend his Indian Invitational title. Becoming impatient, he stepped on to the track to see if the train was coming. He was instantly struck on the left side by the incoming express and hurled to the next track, where he was struck on the right side by an outgoing local. Thus Slamming Suki Sukiyuki died as he had lived—ambidextrously.

BY JACK BARNETT
"Fun in the Rough" FROM *Golf Digest*

A lady pupil once said to me: "Mr. Kirkaldy, they tell me you are a very plain-speaking man, who calls a spade a spade. I am glad of it. I want to know all my faults—my golfing faults, I mean—so don't spare me, please."

I said to her, "My lady, I could not spare you if I tried, but before starting out just drop that 'Mr. Kirkaldy' if you please. Plain Andra for me, leddie."

She laughed heartily. It was a very cold day, just like eating snowballs all the way round. The lady was a poor golfer, but a good sport. When we were out of everybody's sight she produced from the pocket of her golf bag a neat little silver flask with something in it that was just what the doctor ordered. They told me afterwards that the lady was a play-actress from Glasgow. She never came to St. Andrews again, so far as I know, and if my story should come into her hands, she'll remember how I smacked my lips that very cold day.

BY ANDRA KIRKALDY
FROM *My Fifty Years of Golf: Memories*

When Herd and I were in America, I played with an amateur who gripped the club with his left hand down the shaft under the right hand—as lassies usually take hold of the club for the first time. But that American played a clinking game. I gave him four strokes, and just scrambled home in front of him.

"What do you think of my grip?" he asked me afterwards.

"D——d madness!" I said. "I'd as soon think of playing golf on my heid or with my legs crossed."

The American laughed and drawled: "Guess, Kirkaldy, I do nothing like anybody else. It's my only chance in life. I pay for everything before I get it, dine in the morning and breakfast at night. You notice that I paid you my bet on this match before I lost it."

I thought the man was daft, but he must have had brains to play golf as he did. He challenged me to another round, I to adopt his grip and he to adopt mine.

"No, sir," I said. "There's nae fools come frae Fife."

BY ANDRA KIRKALDY
FROM *My Fifty Years of Golf: Memories*

At the time I'm speaking about, Lord Dudley was Lord-Lieu-tenant of Ireland, and he very often had me to play with him. I suppose it was quite right to call him "His Excellency," though I am not much up in such things. He wired to me from London, saying he was coming to St. Andrews, and asking me to give him some games. I was only too pleased, for Lord Dudley was a grand master.

I got a licensed caddie for him and me. After a day or two his lordship was joined by some friends, and he said he would like me to caddie for him, as he was not much taken with the caddie I got for him.

He gave me a sovereign to pay him off in full, and the caddie was quite pleased, like the rest of us, to get money without having to work for it.

Then all the fat was in the fire. There never was such a fuss and fizzle about nothing. I went to the caddie-master, Mr. Alec Taylor, and says I, "Lord Dudley wants me to carry his clubs."

The caddie-master said: "If you carry the clubs, you will be took up to the coort and fined, because you have not any licence as a caddie."

"Gae awa'," says I, "I'm going to carry his lordship's clubs, and you and your bye-laws can do your worst."

"I'll report ye," said the caddie-master. "Your trouble be on your own head, Andra!"

Next morning a policeman made his appearance near the teeing ground. The man in blue said: "Are you going to carry for Lord Dudley?"

"That I am," says I, "at a' risks. He's my master."

The policeman said: "Well, you'll be taken up, because you are not licensed as a caddie, although you're a professional gowffer."

"Dinna talk such balderdash tae me," says I. "There's Lord

156

Dudley over there. Why don't you speak to him about it? A policeman needna be feart tae do his duty. Do you know who Lord Dudley is? He's the Lord-Lieutenant of Ireland. That's like being the King of Ireland. If you have any complaint, go over and tell him."

The policeman said, "I'll watch that," or something of the sort. Anyway he did not go over to Lord Dudley, and I marched away with his lordship's clubs on my shoulder as an unlicensed caddie, telling him nothing about what the policeman said.

A week later I got a summons to appear at the court, charged with carrying clubs for hire without a licence. Never in my life did I feel more affronted. Fancy a professional golfer being disgraced in that way. I tell you it went against the grain to obey that summons.

But what else could I do? I could not run away and have judgment against me for not turning up. The court was crowded as if it had been a murder trial, instead of only being a test case about caddying.

When the Fiscal read out the charge, the Bailie—that is the presiding magistrate—looked over at me as I sat there scowling in the dock, and he says, "Andrew, what have you to say to this charge? Are you guilty or not guilty?"

"Not guilty, of course," says I. "What wrang have I done?"

The caddie-master then came into the witness-box and swore that I carried clubs on such and such a date for hire without the badge that caddies were now required to wear. He also told the court that I had been properly warned and that I committed the offence with my eyes wide open. Just as if I would carry clubs with my eyes shut.

It looked as if I had not a leg to stand on. But I let the court know something different before I was done with them. Mr. Taylor was leaving the building when I hollered to him: "Here, Mr. Taylor, just a word with you. It's my turn now. This is a court of justice, and there's never any justice about a one-sided story. I want the court to let me ask you some questions."

"No, no, no," said one of the three or four magistrates on the Bench.

"Yes, yes, yes," says I. "There's nobody here to defend me but myself, and I claim the right to do so."

The Fiscal agreed that I had a perfect right to question the witness. "But your questions must be proper ones, Andrew," he said.

"They'll be proper enough and to the point," I said. "I'm not going to waste the time of the court either."

The caddie-master was put back in the box, and says I to him, "You are the caddie-master at St. Andrews, are you not, Mr. Taylor?"

"I suppose so," says he.

"That's no answer," says I. "My question was a proper one and I want a proper answer." The Fiscal bore me out.

"Yes," says Mr. Taylor, "I am the caddie-master."

"Right!" says I. "Now will you tell the court whether you saw Lord Dudley take out a ticket for me?"

"I did not," said the caddie-master.

"You say I was caddying for hire," says I. "Did you see Lord Dudley pay me?"

"I did not," says the caddie-master.

"Then what's this case all about," says I, sitting down in a fine temper.

"Tut, tut," says the Bailie. "There is no case at all. Go away, Andrew."

"Not just yet," says I. "Let me say this. Lord Dudley is like the King in Ireland. Now suppose the very King of England was to wire me to caddie for him at St. Andrews, would you be bringing me up here, at my time of life, with all my experience as a professional golfer, to charge me with breaking the law because I didna lower my dignity by taking out a caddie's licence for the job?"

The court just laughed and the folk at the back clapped their hands and rummaged with their feet. I'm telling you it was a great morning in St. Andrews, and everybody I met for days laughed to me. I had a letter from Lord Dudley, in which he jokingly said, "Andrew, you beat them by a few holes that time."

On the way home an old friend who had been at the court came across the street to me, and says he:

158

"Man, Andrew, you've mista'en your calling. You ocht to have been a lawyer. That was a grand cross-examination of yours."

"Did ye think so?" said I.

"That I did," said he, "and I am sure the Fiscal was of the same opeenyun."

"I just gaed to the point by the shortest cut," said I.

"Not a word was wasted," said he. "But, Andra, atween you and me, did you caddie for a fee that time?"

"Good day," says I. "I'm muckle obleeged to you. Did you never try caddyin' for the good of your health?"

BY ANDRA KIRKALDY
FROM *My Fifty Years of Golf: Memories*

Once the doctor advised me to go away for a change to a watering place. "L——d, doctor," said I to him, "d'ye want to put me clean oot of my mind? There's nae golf there that ever I've heard of, and ye never kenned a professional golfer yet that could tak' a holiday withoot golf."

"Busman's holiday!" said the doctor, laughing at me.

"May be so," I said, "but it canna be helpit. Cricketers, footballers and the like may be glad of a rest in their off season, but there's no off season for golfers, the Lord be thankit. We're like fish oot o' the water when the snow or the frost or the fog pits a stop to golf."

BY ANDRA KIRKALDY
FROM *My Fifty Years of Golf: Memories*

Maybe a man is known by the funeral he gets. Tom's was the biggest funeral I ever saw in St. Andrews. The whole of South Street, from the Port to the Cathedral, was a cloud of people, and there were many wet eyes among us, for Old Tom was beloved by everybody. Shopkeepers shut their shops and every house had drawn blinds. The coffin was followed by Professors of the University, members of the Royal and Ancient and of other golf clubs from far and near. Old caddies came too. I helped to carry the coffin from the Cathedral gates to the grave. The Earl of Stair, who was Captain that year, was one of the pall-bearers. The green-keeper carried the silver club and balls. Sandy Herd and his wife came all the way from Huddersfield to pay their respects to Old Tom's memory.

Flags flew at half-mast. The greens were deserted. Not a golf-ball was struck on the links that day, except in the very early morning.

It was a sad day in St. Andrews. School children got a holiday to see Old Tom pass to his everlasting rest in the Cathedral burial-grounds beside his son, Young Tommy, and not far from the grave of the golfing cronie of his youth, Allan Robertson, the feather-ball Champion of Scotland.

It was said of Allan when he died in 1859, "They may toll the bells and shut up the shops at St. Andrews, for their greatest is gone." The same words could well have been spoken of Old Tom Morris sixty years afterward.

BY ANDRA KIRKALDY
FROM *My Fifty Years of Golf: Memories*

HOLE EIGHT ON THE DEVIL IN GOLF

If the devil is perfectly at home on a golf-course it is doubtless because that place is so thoroughly well paved with good intentions. There can be no question as to his presence there. How, otherwise, are you to account for certain things that happen to golfers? Surely it is not "the spirits of the wise" that do "sit in the clouds and mock us." It is a dark and sinister force, and, so far from being content to perch upon a cloud, it comes right down to earth, infests every turn of the course, and even lurks in the locker-room. If you do not believe this, accept an invitation to play in a foursome at a club you have never visited before. Let it be on a Saturday, when the crowd is thickest and the time-card is as adamant. Linger a little longer over luncheon than you should and then hurry home to dress. Look out of the window and observe the throng at the first tee. Look at your watch and bend to tie your shoe with the realization that you have just two minutes in which to take your place in the game. And then have your shoe-lace snap, close to the eyelet. I will not repeat your gloss upon this pretty situation.

> " 'Tis not mine to record
> What Angels shrink from: even the very Devil
> On this occasion his own work abhorred."

And no wonder. I would not make a mountain out of a mole-hill, a life-line out of a shoe-lace. Goodness knows that though men have died and the worms have eaten them it has not been because they were late at the first tee. But it is the kind of mischance that makes you "dancing mad" and it is unthinkable without diabolical intervention.

There is a whole catalogue of these little pinpricks which are to be credited to his majesty. Take your short-sighted man, who can't play without his golf glasses. Let him discover, on some such visit as I have indicated, that he has remembered to bring everything else but has left the one indispensable aid at home. Reader, did you ever try playing golf with a pair of bifocals on your nose? If not, try it, and then say whether your predicament is devilish or not. I know of only one other posture of affairs to beat it. That is to reach, say, the tenth hole, well out on the course, remote from the club-house, a good "twelve miles from a lemon," and to take out on that sequestered spot the cigar you have been saving up for about the middle of the game. Everybody in the foursome is in the same blissful case. Pipes come out, and cigarettes. Everybody is ready to light up. And there isn't a match in the house! Not one of the players has a match. Not one of the caddies has a match. There isn't a man with a match anywhere in sight, for miles around. For once Lucifer belies his name. You call upon it in vain. He has gone up a tree to mock at you. Positively, at a moment like that, I have heard his derisive chuckle.

It is when the game moves on that he comes down and moves with it. You can almost see him. His gloomy features,

> "Like a midnight dial,
> Scowl the dark index of a fearful hour."

It is the hour, known to every golfer, in which you try to repeat. Then ensues diabolism of an uncannily high order. You made the hole, a day earlier in the week, in par. You know just how you did it. So much distance is to be assigned to your drive. The second shot will leave you, inevitably, with an easy approach. You have hopes of a four. You are certain of a five. The devil is most like himself at such a juncture. He lets you have your drive, thereby increasing your certitude. He is good to your second shot. But although you know all about the approach, just why you should "go easy" with it, just why you should avoid running over, he comes nimbly to the front and takes you into the pit beyond. O pit, pit, how aptly art thou named! Art thou not his designated dwelling-place? It is there, above all other hazards, that you are "as helpless as the Devil can wish."

You land there never so decisively, never so snugly ensconced in an unplayable lie, as when, having won the hole once, you try to repeat. I can't believe that it is pure error that accounts for this special brand of humiliation. Some analysts lay it to self-consciousness. It is just because you are thinking of repeating, they say, that you lose your grip on concentration and fetch up on toast. It is the demon, rather, who works the evil. One of my fellow golfers is a particularly good driver, straight and far. In a recent game I saw him slice his ball out of bounds from nearly every tee, sometimes two balls from the same tee. He knew better and there were several players present quite willing to tell him the reason for it if he needed light. But he couldn't help going on slicing. He kept at it with the devotion of a train-despatcher. He knew nothing about my theory of demoniacal possession, yet I was not in the least surprised when he laid it all on the devil.

Some students of the game, strangers to the delights of mystical speculation, are prone to explain away the more fantastic of golfing collapses by what they call, with scientific simplicity and aplomb, physical condition. It is all a matter of nerves, they tell you, a matter of co-ordination. As a friend of mine remarked the other day, "the character of the drive is determined by the synchronization of the pathway of the hands and the pathway of the club-head at the moment of impact," and this in turn depends upon your bodily state. Can't you hear that chuckle coming up from the pit? As a matter of fact there is nothing like the complete disequilibration of all your corporeal faculties to assure you one of the best of your games. It is when you are outrageously fit that you fall by the wayside. Get up in the morning feeling like a king, all set for a game that you have long been anticipating. Go to the course in the most luxurious of cars. Drive off in cloudless weather, with a cherished friend, having a clear field ahead and no one to press you. It is a million dollars to a tin doughnut that you will flub your drive. It is when all these conditions are reversed and you are made aware, with the upward swing of your club, that you've got a nail in your shoe, that you really hit the ball. Look at the champions, with their not infrequent "slumps." Is it physical condition that betrays them? Why, they haven't any nerves. It is a subtler enemy that lays them low. The devil, after all, is more respectable to cite than an alibi, the most hateful pest in golf. When a great golfer misses a fifteen-inch putt let him repeat for his consolation the words of Cassio: "Every inordinate cup is unbless'd, and the ingredient is a devil."

BY ROYAL CORTISSOZ

FROM *Nine Holes of Golf*

THE RIVERCLIFF GOLF KILLINGS

The district attorney has given me the following certified copy of my sworn testimony, and I am telling the story of this golf game to the public just as I told it in the grand jury room.

THE CASE OF SILAS W. AMHERST, BANKER

QUESTION: Professor Waddems, will you tell the jury just when it was that you first noted evidences of the criminal tendencies, amounting to total depravity, in the late Silas W. Amherst?

ANSWER: It was on the 30th of September, 1936, at 4:17 p.m.

QUESTION: Where were you when you first began to suspect that the man had such an evil nature?

ANSWER: On the Rivercliff golf course, sir, at the second hole.

QUESTION: A par-four hole, Professor?

ANSWER: It is called that, yes, sir; but it is unfairly trapped.

QUESTION: What is your usual score on this hole, Professor Waddems? Remember, you are on oath, and you have waived immunity in this inquiry.

ANSWER: I have never yet received fair treatment with regard to this hole. My normal score on this hole is five, with an occasional par four and sometimes a birdie three. But disgraceful tactics have always been employed against me on this hole to prevent me from playing my normal game.

164

QUESTION: Is it a water hole?

ANSWER: Yes, sir.

QUESTION: Is it the same water hole from which the body of Silas W. Amherst was removed on October 3, 1936, a few days after he was last seen alone with you?

ANSWER: No, sir. That was the fifteenth hole. The water at the fifteenth hole is much deeper than the water at the second hole or the seventh hole. In the water at the fifteenth hole there are now several other bod——

QUESTION: Be careful, Professor! This inquiry is devoted entirely to Silas W. Amherst, and you are not compelled to incriminate or degrade yourself. Professor, are you a nervous, irritable, testy, violent person?

ANSWER: No, sir! No, sir! No, sir! And the man that dares to call me that is . . . (*A portion of Prof. Waddems' reply is stricken from the record.*)

QUESTION: Quietly, Professor, quietly! Tell these gentlemen how you gained the unruffled patience and philosophic calm that have made you the great golfer that you are.

ANSWER: For twenty-five years I lectured on philosophy and psychology at various universities. And I apply these principles to my golf game.

QUESTION: In spite of your thorough scientific knowledge of the game, have you ever broken a hundred?

ANSWER: Yes, sir, many times.

QUESTION: Think, Professor!

ANSWER: Yes, sir; yes, sir; yes, sir!

QUESTION: Mildly, please, Professor! Quietly! I will put the question in a different way. Professor, has any opponent with whom you played ever *admitted* that you broke a hundred, or has any card that you turned in after playing around alone been credited, if it showed you *had* broken a hundred?

ANSWER: I don't remember, sir. My game has been misrepresented and persecuted for years at Rivercliff.

QUESTION: To return to Mr. Amherst. Tell the jury exactly what happened at the second hole which revealed the man's irreclaimable blackness of character.

ANSWER: Well, sir, I teed up for my drive and addressed the

ball. And just as I brought my club back, and it was poised for the down stroke, he said to me:

"Professor, you're driving with a brassie, aren't you?"

I gave him a look of mild expostulation, checked the drive, and stood in front of the ball again.

"I don't think your stance is right, Professor," he said. "Let me show you the proper stance—you don't mind my showing you, do you, Professor?"

Then he proceeded to show me—and I may say in passing that his theories were entirely faulty.

"I noticed on the first tee," he went on, "that you didn't understand how to pivot. You want to get your body into it, Professor. Like this," and he made a swing in demonstration.

"Your instruction, Mr. Amherst," I said politely, "is entirely gratuitous and all wrong."

"I thought you'd be glad to have me show you, Professor," he said. "And if I were you, I wouldn't play that new ball on this water hole. Here, I'll lend you a floater."

And the man actually took from his bag a floater, removed my ball, and teed up the one he had lent me.

"Now, Professor," he said, "a little more freedom in your swing. Keep your eye on the ball and don't let your hands come through ahead of the club. I noticed you had a tendency that way. I think your grip is wrong. Professor. Oh yes, certainly wrong! Here, let me show you the correct grip. And keep your head down, keep your head down!"

QUESTION: Was it then, Professor, that the tragedy occurred?

ANSWER: No, sir! No, sir! No, sir!

QUESTION: Quietly, Professor, quietly! You remained calm?

ANSWER: I am always calm! I never lose my temper! I am always patient! Self-contained! Restrained! Philosophical! Unperturbed! Nothing excites me! Nothing, I say, nothing! Nothing! Nothing! Nothing!

QUESTION: There, there, Professor, easily, easily now! What happened next?

ANSWER: I took a driving-iron from my bag and addressed the ball again. I—

QUESTION: Just a moment, Professor. Why did you not continue with the brassie?

ANSWER: It was broken, sir.

QUESTION: Broken? How? I do not understand. How did it become broken?

ANSWER: I do not remember.

QUESTION: Between Mr. Amherst's instruction with the brassie and your taking the driving iron from the bag, as I understand it, the brassie was somehow broken. Please fill up this interval for the jury. What happened?

ANSWER: I can't recall, sir.

QUESTION: Come, come, Professor! How was the brassie broken?

ANSWER: It hit the sandbox, sir.

QUESTION: How could it hit the sandbox?

ANSWER: Well, it was an old brassie, and after I had made a few practice swings with it, I decided that it was poorly balanced and that I had better get rid of it once and for all. I did not wish to give it to a caddie, for I do not think it is fair to give poor clubs to these boys who are earnestly striving to educate themselves to be professionals; they are poor boys, for the most part, and we who are in better circumstances should see that they have a fair start in life. So I broke the brassie against the sandbox and took my driving iron, and—

QUESTION: Just a minute, Professor! These practice strokes that you made with the brassie, were there five or six of them?

ANSWER: I don't recollect, sir.

QUESTION: Did any one of them hit the ball?

ANSWER: No, sir! No, sir! No, sir! The brassie never touched the ball! The ball moved because there was a bent twig under it—this man Amherst had teed up his floater for me with a pat of sand upon a bent twig—and the twig straightened up and moved the sand, and the ball rolled off it.

QUESTION (*by the foreman of the jury*): Professor Waddems, how far did the ball roll when the twig straightened up?

ANSWER: Well, sir, it had been teed up at the very edge of the driving green, and the ground is pretty high there, and the ball rolled down the slope, and it gained a great deal of momentum as it rolled down the slope, like an avalanche as it comes rolling down a mountainside, and at the bottom of the slope it struck a rut in the road the work-and-upkeep wagons use on the course,

167

and that rut connects with the asphalt drive that leads in to the clubhouse, and when the ball struck the asphalt road it had already gained so much momentum that it rolled for some distance along the asphalt road, and then it crashed into the underbrush near the road and hit a sapling and bounded over onto the first fairway, all on account of the slope of the ground, for it had never been touched with the brassie at all.

QUESTION: Professor, did this happen to the ball five or six times before you discarded the brassie and took the driving iron?

ANSWER: No, sir. I only recall three times.

QUESTION: Go on, Professor. After your breaking of the brassie, you took the driving iron. What happened then?

ANSWER: Then Mr. Amherst stepped up and said to me, "Professor, let me give you a few tips about iron play. And you must keep your head down, keep your head down!"

QUESTION: Did you lose your temper then?

ANSWER: I never lose my temper! Never! Never! Never!

QUESTION: Quietly, now, Professor, quietly! Go on.

ANSWER: I made a magnificent drive, which cleared the water jump, and my second shot was on the green. I holed out with two putts. "A par four," I said, marking it on my card.

"You mean nine," said this man Amherst. Gentlemen, he had the effrontery to claim that the five practice swings I had made with the brassie, just simply to humor him in his demonstrations, were actual golf strokes!

(*Sensation in the grand jury room. Cries of "Outrageous!" "Impossible!" "The Dastard!" from various grand jurymen. The outburst quelled with difficulty by the district attorney.*)

QUESTION (*by the foreman of the jury*): Professor Waddems, did you end it all then?

ANSWER: No, sir. I kept my self-control. Gentlemen, I am always for peace! I am a meek person. I am mild. I will endure persecution to a point beyond anything that is possible to a man who has not had my years of training in philosophy and applied psychology. I merely got another caddie and proceeded with the game, yielding the point to Mr. Amherst for the sake of peace.

QUESTION: Got another caddie?

ANSWER: Yes, sir. The one I started out with was injured.

QUESTION: How, Professor?

ANSWER: I don't remember.

QUESTION: Think Professor! Was it by a fall?

ANSWER: Oh yes, now I recollect! It *was* by a fall. The caddie fell from a tree just beyond the second green and broke his shoulder.

QUESTION: What was he doing in the tree?

ANSWER: He had retired to the top of the tree under a peculiar misapprehension, sir. He had agreed with Mr. Amherst with regard to the question as to whether I should take nine strokes or a par four; and I think he misinterpreted some sudden motion of mine as a threat.

QUESTION: A motion with a golf club?

ANSWER: It may have been, sir. I had a club in my hand, and I remember that my mind at the moment was engrossed with a problem connected with the underlying psychology of the full swing with wooden clubs.

QUESTION: Well, Professor, the caddie is now at the top of the tree, laboring under a misapprehension. What caused his fall?

ANSWER: I think the wooden club must have slipped somehow from my hands, sir. It flew to the top of the tree and disturbed his balance, causing him to fall.

QUESTION: Was he a good caddie?

ANSWER: There are no good caddies, sir.

(*Ripple of acquiescent laughter round the grand jury room.*)

QUESTION: Then, Professor, you went on to the next driving green. Tell what happened from this point on to the fifteenth hole, where the body of Silas W. Amherst was found four days later.

ANSWER: Advice, sir, advice! That's what happened! Advice! One long, intolerable gehenna of gratuitous advice! Gentlemen, I don't know whether any of you ever have had the misfortune to play golf with the late Silas W. Amherst, but if you have—

(*Cries from various grand jurors: "Yes, yes, I played with him!" "Attaboy, Professor!" "I knew him, Prof!" etc., etc. District attorney begs for order; witness continues.*)

ANSWER: Advice! Advice! Advice! And always from fiendish malignity of the man concealed under a cloak of helpful friendliness! Advice! Advice! Advice! And to me! I, who have studied the basic principles of the game more thoroughly than any other man in America today! Gentlemen, if I were not the most patient man in the world, Silas W. Amherst would have bit the dust twenty times between the second and the fifteenth holes that day! His explanations—to me! His continual babble and chatter! His demonstrations! Every club I took from my bag, he *explained* to me! Gentlemen, some of them were clubs that I had designed myself and had had manufactured to fit my own original theories with regard to golf! But I kept my temper! I never lose my temper! Never! Never! Never!

QUESTION: Does any particularly insulting phrase of advice stand out in your memory, Professor?

ANSWER: Yes, sir! A dozen times on every hole he would cry to me as I addressed the ball, "Keep your head down, Professor, keep your head down!"

THE DISTRICT ATTORNEY: Please sit down, Professor; and do not bang on the chairs with your walking stick as you talk. We cannot hear your testimony.

THE PROFESSOR: Yes, sir. Well, at the fifteenth hole, while he was standing on the edge of the water, looking for a ball—

QUESTION: Professor, is it true that the fifteenth hole at Rivercliff is really a pool, fed by subterranean springs, and so deep that no plummet has ever sounded its bottom?

ANSWER: Exactly, sir. As Silas W. Amherst stood on the edge of it, it occurred to me that perhaps the man's conscience had awakened and that he was going to commit suicide for the good of the human race, gentlemen. And so I gave him a little pat of approval —on the back; and he fell in. Gentlemen, he judged himself and executed himself, and I still approve.

QUESTION: Would you mind telling the jurors, Professor, just what Mr. Amherst said immediately before you patted him approvingly on the back?

ANSWER: He said, "You just stick to me, Professor, and do as I show you, and I'll make some kind of golfer out of you yet."

QUESTION: Did he try to struggle to land, and did you hold his head under water?

ANSWER: Yes, sir, I generously assisted him in his purpose to that extent.

QUESTION: What did you say while you were assisting him?

ANSWER: I said, "Keep your head down, Mr. Amherst, keep your head down!"

THE FOREMAN OF THE JURY: Mr. District Attorney, speaking for the other members of this jury as well as for myself, it is ridiculous to consider the matter of finding any true bill or indictment of any sort against Professor Waddems in the case of the late Mr. Amherst. The pat of approval was more than justified, and we consider Professor Waddems a public benefactor.

THE DISTRICT ATTORNEY: Tomorrow we will take up the case of Willie, alias "Freckled," Briggs, the caddie who met his death on October 4, 1936, at the Rivercliff Country Club. I suggest that the slight rain we have had today, which is happily over with, should contribute greatly to what is known as a good brassie lie on the fairways. You are dismissed for the day.

BY DON MARQUIS

FROM *Sun Dial Time*

ST. ANDREWS: THE CRADLE OF GOLF

This piece was written in 1950 and was published in *Holiday* the following spring. Since that date some changes have taken place even in that secluded, time-resisting corner of Scotland. Commander Carson has been succeeded as the secretary of the Royal and Ancient by Brigadier Eric Brickman, a crisp and tidy administrator who makes what may be the hardest job in golf look easy. Like the Commander, the Brigadier, it is a pleasure to report, has a penchant for tweed knickers and wears them well. A change of a quite unanticipated nature took place at the R & A in 1955 on the occasion of the Commonwealth Cup matches when,

171

for the first time in history, ladies were invited into the club-house. Aside from a few grumbles from the invariable rear guard, most of the members found that cocktail party not only surprisingly painless but actually a good sort of thing, you know, and another such mixed affair was held with equal success on the eve of the first World Amateur Team Championship in 1958. This championship brought back to the old gray town the golfer it loves the most, Bobby Jones, who had returned to captain the American team. Jones was made an honorary freeman of St. Andrews and was presented with the freedom of the borough by his old and adoring friends in a ceremony so full of deep-felt emotion, on both sides, and so moving that many who attended were unable to voice their thoughts for many minutes afterward. I shall always remember what Billy Joe Patton, from North Carolina, said about Jones when he finally spoke up on the way home, his voice charged with feeling and sectional chauvinism: "He's the greatest Southerner who ever lived."

There is one other change that might be mentioned. The official record for the Old Course has now been lowered to 66. This occurred in the 1960 British Open in which Arnold Palmer, a most popular visitor, made his gallant and driving bid to add the British Open to his previous victories that year in our Open and the Masters, and ultimately failed by only one shot.

* * *

The hold that St. Andrews has over the world's 10,000,000 golfers has not yet reached that point where, at five regular intervals each day, the game's devotees abruptly drop the cares of the hour, kneel, and face the old gray town on the North Sea where the game was nurtured. There is, however, little to choose between St. Andrews and Mecca in the frenetic fidelity they extract from their followers. Every pious golfer dreams of making a pilgrimage to St. Andrews, and a considerable number realize this ambition. Since the war an average of 8,000 visitors has journeyed to St. Andrews each year. For a few of them, the attraction is a tourist's sight of the house on South Street where Mary Queen of Scots slept, uneasily; the Church of the Holy Trinity, where a local boy, John Knox, cut loose with one of his most inflammatory sermons; and the noble buildings of St. Andrews University, Scotland's oldest, which dates back to 1413. But, by and large, the thousands who make their way annually to St. Andrews come to worship at the Old Course, the most famous links in the world.

Considering that it is only thirty-three miles northeast of Edinburgh, St. Andrews is not an easy place to get to. The sacred town lies on the eastern tip of Fifeshire, a peninsula which noses into the North Sea between the Firth of Tay on the north and the Firth of Forth to the south. The train ride from Edinburgh, on the main line north to Aberdeen, offers a fairly spectacular crossing of the Firth of Forth via the high, gaunt railroad bridge on which Robert Donat performed his acrobatics in *The Thirty-Nine Steps*, but passengers for St. Andrews must descend at Leuchars, five miles distant, and there change to a spur line which operates on a capricious schedule. Most golfers choose to close in on the old town by auto. The road from Edinburgh, once the ferry across the Forth has been negotiated, plods through somber coastal towns, each with its links and its "golf hotel." The approach from Glasgow, on the West Coast, a drive of three hours, is far more rural and relaxing and would be altogether preferable were it not that *leaving* Glasgow necessarily presupposes *being in* Glasgow. Whatever road he travels, the pilgrim, because of the ambivalence of the route markers at all key intersections, will lose his way on the average of once every twenty minutes, and he will learn from asking directions that the proper Scottish pronunciation of his goal is *Sintandrooz*.

St. Andrews makes a stirring first impression. Perched on a rocky plateau fifty feet above the Firth of Tay, not a smoke-stack in view, its medieval towers gleaming gray-white in the sun, it looms solemnly before the pilgrim, completely unrelated to the countryside through which he has passed. St. Andrews was named for the patron saint of Scotland, and while it is legend and not history that the relics of St. Andrew were carried there in 735 by St. Regulus, the town is old enough to have run through several full careers: Pictish stronghold, headquarters of the Roman Catholic Church in Scotland, storm center of the Reformation, prosperous trading port, plague-struck and all but deserted village—all this before the spread of golf throughout the world, beginning just about a century ago, gave the old town something new to live for.

In this town the only native who hurries to snatch the minute is the golfer. His small canvas bag is over his shoulder, he strides briskly past the golf hotels lining the seaside strip called the Scores, quickening his pace as he nears the Old Course at the foot of the town in order not to be late for his assigned starting time on the first tee. The rest of the 9,000 regular inhabitants operate less by the watch than by the more luxurious chronometer of chimes and church bells. The milkman chugs his truck from house to house, resting at the wheel while his wife makes the deliveries. In the cafés the university students talk easily over coffee between classes, the girls wearing their bright-red college gowns, as they do on many occasions when they are not required, because the gown "does more" for them than any other number in their wardrobes. The slow pace and good air of St. Andrews have made it a favorite retreat of superannuated military and naval officers. It is also a fine place for thinking as well as retiring. Carlyle, Froude, Thomas Hughes, Trollope, Mrs. Oliphant, Kingsley, Millais, and Landseer are just a few of the prominent artists and writers who found they flourished in St. Andrews in summer.

It is a salutary circumstance that the town of St. Andrews is charming beyond expectation for, at first meeting, the Old Course —the shrine itself—is a majestic letdown. To an American accustomed to mounting a raised tee and squinting down a tree-lined fairway, the Old Course, a billowing sea of grass-covered dunes, doesn't even look like a golf course. Bobby Jones, who ended up thinking the Old Course the finest he had ever played, was sure it was the worst after his first round. A decade later, Gene Sarazen, on his first visit, walked off the eighteenth green indignantly demanding to know how a pasture which had traps smack in the middle of its fairways could presume to be considered a peerless test of golf. Sam Snead flew to St. Andrews expressly for the 1946 British Open, took one look at the course, asked if he were in the right town, and, finding that he was, wanted to fly right back again. Sam stayed on and proceeded to win that championship, aided in no small way by the conviction,

174

acquired after he and the Old Course had got better acquainted, that if he honestly played better golf shots than anyone else in the field, the course would see to it that no one beat him.

It is familiarity which breeds respect and love for the Old Course. It is like no other. In the United States, for example, our courses are *constructed*—fairways blasted through hillsides, streams diverted to fit the strategy of the approach shots, greens built to order by bulldozers. The Old Course wasn't made. It was always there. Today the word *links* is used indiscriminately by most golfers as if it were simply a synonym for *course*. Actually a links, or linksland, is a stretch of sandy soil deposited by the receding ocean. Linksland fringes the eastern coast of Scotland, and it was the logical place for playing golf, a game which may have been imported in germ from Holland but which was developed by the Scots into its present sublimely contagious form.

In a strange and wonderful way, the inhabitants of St. Andrews from the earliest days sensed that nature had blessed them with the best of all links for golf. Nature alone has been permitted to alter the topography. The incredible result is that the links, in general contour, probably looks much the same today as it did in 1100, the round year that historians have fixed on as the date when the natives of St. Andrews first began to put their links to its historic use.

Until late in the nineteenth century, the Old Course, hemmed in by the Firth of Tay and the estuary of the Eden River, was the only course on the thumb-shaped spit of linksland below the town. Two other eighteen-hole courses, the New and Jubilee, laid out in 1894 and 1946 respectively, now occupy the reclaimed land between the northern boundary of the Old Course and the Firth; a fourth eighteen holes, called the Eden, was wedged in between the southern boundary of the Old Course and the Eden estuary in 1914. The ocean has receded about one hundred feet during the last seventy-five years, and assuming that this has been its customary pace of retreat over the centuries, its waters must have at one time washed up to the very edges of the Old Course and determined its singular snakelike design. It is as narrow as a course can be. The first seven holes march in an almost straight line away from the town; the eighth, ninth, tenth, and eleventh perform a small clockwise loop around the tip of the promontory; then holes twelve through eighteen march straight back to town alongside the first seven. The adjoining fairways are not separated by rough, and there is always ample room to the left, except on the loop holes. They are tightly flanked on the right by out-of-bounds or by heavy rough composed of gorselike whins and heather, presenting the slicer with far less latitude for error than the hooker. Not only are the parallel fairways fused into one wide fairway but, save on the first, ninth, seventeenth, and eighteenth, an outgoing hole and an incoming hole share the same green, the second with the sixteenth, the third with the fifteenth, and so on. The cups for the two holes are at opposite ends of the huge double greens. The largest of these, servicing the fifth and thirteenth holes, is over an acre; putts 140 feet long are often a nerve-racking reality.

The contours of the green are treacherous, their surface is slippery, and the earth itself so hard and resilient that a player cannot stroke his approach for the pin and hope to have the ball sit down abruptly, as it does on our soft, watered greens. Instead, he must resort to a pitch-and-run approach, landing his shot a calculated distance from his target so that the ball, after its bound and roll, will stop in the neighborhood of the pin. An equal accuracy is demanded on the tee-shots to avoid the mélange of fairway bunkers, those celebrated pits which were burrowed, long before the invention of golf, by sheep nestling behind the dunes to keep out of the bitter wind. On the direct line from tee to green on the fourteenth or Long Hole, for example, the golfer is first menaced by a formidable group of bunkers, the Beardies, lying in wait for him at the 200-mark. A hundred yards farther down the fairway stands Benty Bunker, backed up by Kitchen, and at the 400-yard mark he must deal with Hell, most feared of all the bunkers on the Old Course. To attempt the straight-line route to the green is folly on the fourteenth, and, for that matter, on nearly every hole of the eighteen. A golfer must tack back and forth among the hazards like a sailor. He must study the immediate mood of each hole each time he mounts the tee, for the slightest change in the wind requires new strategy. It takes brains as well as technical skill to meet the challenge of St. Andrews, and therein lies its enduring greatness.

The Old Course is moderately long, measuring 6,572 yards from the regular tees, 6,883 yards from the back or "Tiger" tees, created in 1946. From both sets of tees, par is 73, and the record for the extended course, held by Dai Rees, the Welsh professional, is 67. No man has ever played a round without taking at least one 5, though Bobby Jones once got as far as the seventeenth with nothing above a 4 on his card and missed his 4 there only because he muffed a two-foot putt. This seventeenth—called the Road Hole because of the road which runs directly behind the green—is, along with the fourteenth and the eleventh (the Eden), the best known and most frequently copied of the individual holes. About 466 yards long, a most difficult par four, the seventeenth is an easy hole to collapse on. The ideal drive involves a risky carry over the roofs of Auchterlonie's drying sheds, and the knowledge that the road lurks behind the green inflicts overcautiousness on even the seasoned golfer as he plays the long second shot. The eleventh, one of the two par 3's on the course, can be reached some days with an easy seven-iron; on other days a full spoon is not too much club, so drastically does the direction and force of the wind influence the playing character of its 164 yards. The slanting green is protected by deep, high-walled bunkers, and two finalists in one amateur championship, after frolicking in these pits, halved the hole in eighteen.

Men who have golfed on the Old Course all their lives are startled to find that they keep on uncovering new and hidden ways to play the holes. The most notable case is that of Ted Blackwell, the game's longest driver at the turn of the century, who swore up and down for thirty-five years that the sixteenth hole didn't belong on the same course with the other seventeen. No matter where you hit your drive, the contours around the green were such that you couldn't get your approach shot to sit down within birdie distance of the pin. In his thirty-sixth year of playing the Old Course, Blackwell stumbled upon the secret to the sixteenth. Left of the bunker called the Principal's Nose, Blackwell reported, there was an all but imperceptible hollow in the fairway. If you placed your drive in that hollow instead of

177

swatting it for distance, when you looked toward the green, you saw a perfect channel down the fairway and over the apron to the pin. After this discovery, Blackwell actually was able to birdie the sixteenth on an average of once every three rounds.

The natives of St. Andrews have been reared from the cradle to regard golf as a part of living only a little less basic than eating. Seventy-five per cent of the population plays the game, and the nongolfers know the Old Course intimately from their Sunday walks when golfing is prohibited (except on the Eden) and the links become the village green. In the evenings there is usually a group of townsfolk gathered behind the eighteenth green, smoking pipes and chatting as they watch a pilgrim struggle home, chuckling among themselves as he lines up his putt, since they know he will fail to notice that the green slopes, almost invisibly, down from the back right-hand corner.

St. Andrews astonishes itself, and those who know it, with the wanton way it loses its characteristic dignity and turns into a Glendale of bobby-soxers when a famous pilgrim, such as General Eisenhower or General Bradley, shows up for a round of golf. The town's most fantastic performance in recent years came on Monday, May 22, 1950, when the first round of the British Amateur got under way. This was the first time since the war that St. Andrews was the scene of that tournament, and the lure of the Old Course attracted a record number of entries (324) which included a record invasion of Americans (35) which in turn included Bing Crosby. For the Scots, Crosby stands forth as the consummate American personality. When the word was released that Bing had mailed in his entry for the Amateur, St. Andrews began to seethe with an excitement it had not known since John Knox inflamed his parishioners to sack the cathedral. Crosby teed off at nine fifty-five that memorable Monday morning against his first-round opponent, a local carpenter and hillbilly singer named Wilson. A cold wind was snarling off the sea and a disagreeably wet rain was falling, but over 7,000 spectators, many of them transported by special bus from other corners of Fifeshire, were happily squashed along the roped-off perimeter of the course straining for a glimpse of the glamorous pilgrim. Bing came through magnificently. He drew spontaneous applause from his vast gallery by scoring two beautiful birdies on the first three holes. Though he ultimately lost the match, 3 and 2, he demonstrated that he was a bona fide golfer. On top of this, he did not play *too* well. He didn't avoid the Old Course's pitfalls. That would have been sacrilegious. Bing left town almost immediately after his match, and St. Andrews gradually regained its composure.

St. Andrews is extremely susceptible to love affairs with certain types of Americans and never forgets the deeds of its heroes. It is twenty-four years since Bobby Jones won the British Open on the Old Course and twenty-one years since he won the British Amateur there, but Bobby's miracles are as fresh in the minds and hearts of St. Andrews as if they were accomplished yesterday. It is impossible for a caddie who is toting for an American to walk down the fourth fairway without pointing out Cottage Bunker from which Bobby holed a full spade-mashie shot. Whenever Jones played, all of St. Andrews streamed down to the links to admire its adopted son. On the afternoon that Bobby opposed Cyril Tolley in the 1930 British Amateur, the town was completely deserted, a fact that did not escape the attention of Gerald Fairlie, a novelist. In plotting his next mystery, Fairlie selected that afternoon as the time when the villain committed the murder in downtown St. Andrews and, though covered with the stains of his crime, was able to make his escape undetected in broad daylight down the empty streets.

Any visitor can play the Old Course by paying a green fee of three shillings and sixpence (about fifty cents). The Old Course is a public course, owned by the "ratepayers" of St. Andrews and regulated by the Town Council. Until 1946, when a Provisional Order was passed permitting the Council to charge ratepayers thirty shillings a year for their golf privileges, a green fee had never been levied on legitimate St. Andresans. It was their links and they could prove it in writing, going back to the parchment covenant of January 25, 1552, when the provost and bailies of the town, in granting to Archbishop Hamilton permission to raise rabbits on the north part of the links, made certain that he clearly recognized the townsfolks' right to use the links for drying their fishing nets and bleaching their linen and for enjoying their "golf, futball, schuting, at all gamis, and with all uther maner of pastime."

One of his successors, Archbishop Gladstanes, went a step further and issued a charter in 1614 which stated that title to the links was vested in the town. Towards the end of the eighteenth century, however, St. Andrews, to rescue itself from the debt, sold the links to Mr. Erskine of Cambo. No one stopped playing golf, but titularly the town had lost possession of the links. In 1894, when the Royal and Ancient Golf Club of St. Andrews was attempting to buy the land back from the Cheapes of Strathyrum, into whose hands it had passed, the town was roused to action. If anyone had a right to purchase the links, the Town Council argued, it was the citizens of St. Andrews and not a private club. The issue was debated in Parliament, and two months later, in June, 1894, St. Andrews formally regained its links by paying the Cheape family 5,000 pounds.

Most of the ratepayers of St. Andrews live so close to the links that a locker room is a superfluity, but for the golfer who likes to play his extra holes in sympathetic company, there are three clubs he can join. The New Club, founded in 1902, is the one to which businessmen and professional men belong. It has close to 800 members who pay annual dues of thirty shillings if they live within the town limits or twenty-one shillings if they live in the country. The New Club's modest clubhouse fronts on Links Road beside the eighteenth fairway. Close by stands the St. Andrews Club, the tradesman's and the artisan's club, established in 1843. Since its members, who presently number about 900, must cough up all of fifteen shillings (or $2.10) a year, it is easy to understand the sudden paralysis that overtakes Scottish emigrants after they have innocently asked the cost of joining an American club. The Royal and Ancient, the third club, is an entirely different type of organization and a story in itself.

The Royal and Ancient is the most important institution in the world of golf, an eminence which its members have come to accept with equanimity. The R & A is not the world's oldest golf club—it is just about everything else—for the Honorable Company of Edinburgh Golfers had banded together a few years before the "twenty-two noblemen and gentlemen" of St. Andrews formed their club in May, 1754. At this first meeting, certain articles and laws, thirteen in number, were drafted to govern the members' play—the oldest surviving code in golf. A century later, when the R & A issued a revised codification of twenty-two rules, the club's prestige as a legislative authority had reached the point where all the other golf clubs in Britain willingly accepted the R & A's codification. (The most significant innovation was that eighteen holes constituted one round of golf.) Today, golf clubs throughout the world, with the exception of those in the United States and its outlying possessions, adhere to the rules promulgated by the R & A.

The prestige of membership in the club is enormous. The dues are not. Local members are charged ten guineas annually; English members, eight guineas; and foreign or "supernumerary" members, one guinea. The entrance fee for all is twenty guineas, and the total number of members is limited to 1,000, a figure that has seldom been approached. Earl Mountbatten, Field Marshal Montgomery, General Eisenhower, and the Aga Khan are a few of the front-line personalities who presently belong to the R & A. Winston Churchill was invited to become an honorary member but begged off on the grounds that he had no interest in golf. The supernumerary list includes about sixty Americans, headed by Bobby Jones and Francis Ouimet.

The R & A and the United States Golf Association, the official governing body for American golf, see eye to eye on most important issues, but there are a few interesting deviations. The official British and American golf balls, for example, weigh the same ("not more than 1.62 ounces avoirdupois"), but whereas the American ball must not be less than 1.68 inches in diameter, the R & A specifies a minimum of 1.62 inches. That six-hundredths of an inch makes a surprisingly great difference, especially on gusty days when the "heavier" British ball bores through winds which blow the American ball right back into the golfer's face. The American ball putts a little better. The R & A regulation which our golfers criticize most frequently is the one barring the Schenectady putter. This ruling, which was apparently conceived in a petulance uncharacteristic of the R & A, went on the books a few years after Walter J. Travis, a choleric but skillful American golfer, had putted his way with his Schenectady model to the British Amateur title in 1904, delivering a terrific blow to British pride, since no foreigner had ever before captured that championship. In this country we define a Schenectady as a putter in which the shaft is joined to the center of the blade. In the British interpretation, however, any putter in which the minutest fraction of the heel extends beyond the intersection of the shaft and the blade is outlawed.

The home of the Royal and Ancient is a stately sandstone clubhouse, approximately a century old and suitably weather-stained, poised directly behind the first tee of the Old Course. Through its corridors of Canadian yellow pine have passed a succession of members whose main object in life was the advancement of their club, but it is doubtful if any single individual contributed as much as Maj. Murray Belshes of Buttergash. Up to 1834, when Major Belshes swung into action, the club was called the Society of St. Andrews Golfers. In Major Belshes' mind, that wasn't good enough. Nothing short of royal endorsement would do. In a letter to Sir Herbert Taylor, the private secretary of King William IV, Major Belshes retailed his club's glorious history and requested that the king honor the club by becoming its patron. Sir Herbert replied that he was sorry, but consent was out of the question. If the king agreed to be the patron of one golf club, every other golf club in the realm would kick up a fuss. This flat refusal did not perturb Major Murray Belshes. Perhaps he hadn't made things clear, the major wrote; St. Andrews merited a privileged rating and he couldn't see how granting it would be at all indiscreet, especially since the king happened to be Duke of St. Andrews. In 1836, King William agreed to become the club's patron and to permit the club to style itself the Royal and Ancient. In addition, the king sent along a gold medal which became the first prize at the annual autumn tournament.

Most men would have rested on their laurels, but not Maj. Murray Belshes. He next went after Queen Adelaide. She should really become the club's patroness, he argued nicely. After all, *she* was the *Duchess* of St. Andrews. Queen Adelaide gave in. In 1838 the new patroness presented the R & A with a silver medal which, since that date, has been worn by the club captain on all public appearances.

The captaincy of the R & A is held to be the highest honor a British golfer can receive. Originally, the member who turned in the lowest score at the autumn tournament automatically acceded to the captaincy, but this formula was scrapped in 1806 and a rotation set up whereby the captain for one year would be a Scot who was a prominent golfer, to be followed the next year by a distinguished member of Scottish life, to be followed in turn by a local laird, a commoner who held office—then back to a prominent Scottish golfer to start a new three-year cycle. Toward the close of the nineteenth century, after a tremendous fervor for golf had swept over England, this rotation was amended so that the captain every fourth year should be an outstanding English golfer. From time to time the sequence has been interrupted and members of the royal family have been invited to head the club that King William IV made royal as well as ancient. Edward VII accepted the captaincy in 1863, when he was Prince of Wales, and the line has been continued by Prince Leopold in 1876, the Duke of Windsor (the Prince of Wales) in 1922, King George VI (then Duke of York) in 1930, and the late Duke of Kent in 1937. The next member of the royal family slated for the captaincy is the Duke of Edinburgh. The incoming captain inherits, among other things, the locker used by Allan Robertson, the greatest golfer of the first half of the nineteenth century and the R & A's first noteworthy custodian.

One of the many traditional ceremonies which the R & A nourishes calls for the incoming captain to "drive himself into office." On the third Wednesday in September, during the autumn meeting, he steps onto the first tee, the Queen Adelaide medal around his neck. Spread down the fairway before him stand the caddies. Since the caddie who retrieves the captain's ball receives a gold sovereign, each caddie takes up the position where he thinks he has the best chance of fielding the drive. This makes for a delicate situation. When the Duke of Windsor drove himself into office, some of the caddies, in the words of Sir Guy Campbell, "stood disloyally close to the tee." Gold sovereigns are all but extinct nowadays, but rather than default on any part of this ceremony, the R & A has used its influence with the Bank of England to have a small supply of these coins struck specifically for the club. As for the captain's golf ball, it is traditional to cast a facsimile in silver (or in gold when the captain is a member of the royal house) and to fasten it to a silver golf club. All space on the original Silver Golf Club was filled before the nineteenth century had been long under way, and a replacement was then procured by subscription.

At the annual autumn dinner, the silver golf clubs, each dripping heavily with silver golf balls, are displayed in front of the head table where sit the former captains in their pink coats. After the toasts and speeches have been concluded and the new captain installed, the members file past and kiss the silver clubs and golf balls. These visible symbols of the club's continuity are draped in blue and white, the club's colors, and carried in front of the R & A contingent on national occasions such as the abdication of King Edward VIII and the proclamation of the present king when the club participates in the procession through the streets of the town. The balls and clubs are draped in black for R & A funerals, the most exotic of the club's continuing rituals. To qualify for an R & A funeral, a member must be buried within the city boundaries, for the clubs and balls cannot be taken beyond those limits.

There is at the Royal and Ancient, as in every august British club, a small but articulate coterie of members who have acquired the deep grain of stuffiness invariably produced by life in a leather chair. This ultraconservative element regards the R & A as its private preserve and is daily on the prowl to discover some new grounds for outrage. An inexhaustible subject of discussion among this set is the financial beating the club has been subjected to as a reward for developing the golf links. This point of view is shared by the other members. The R & A, up to 1894, voluntarily supplied the funds for keeping up the Old Course in the style it thought the old girl deserved. Then under the provisions of the Links Act and subsequent governmental ordinances, the R & A, almost as if it were being penalized for some wrong-doing, was *directed* to assume the cost of maintaining the Old Course, ordered to build the New and the Eden and the Jubilee courses and to underwrite the maintenance of the New Course. The expense of keeping the Old and the New in top-notch condition now comes to a pretty farthing, 5,800 pounds in 1949, for example. The Town Council, which is required by law only to chip in what it considers a fair amount, has seldom contributed more than 500 pounds in any one year.

During the two centuries it has been operating the Old Course without owning it, the R & A has made many astute moves, but none quite as brilliant as the appointment in 1865 of Old Tom Morris as custodian, a combination of greenkeeper and professional. More than any one other person, Old Tom was responsible for investing golf in St. Andrews with its unique and remarkable charm. As a golfer Old Tom was not quite as proficient as his son, Young Tom, the finest golfer of that century, or Allan Robertson, who was never beaten in a stake match played on level terms. However, it was the man himself and not the golfer who came to be enshrined a good many years before his death as the game's authentic Grand Old Man. His chief traits were an unsticky kindness and courtesy and a love of his fellow golfer that warmed the home-town crony or the eager pilgrim who came within a putt's length of his shop beside the eighteenth green.

Old Tom Morris died in 1908. He was buried in the cathedral yard, alongside Young Tom and Allan Robertson, and the eighteenth hole was named in his honor. The custodianship then devolved on one Andrew Kirkaldy, almost the antithesis of Old Tom, a rough and ready customer who couldn't open his mouth without swearing—or saying something witty. Andra made so many wonderful cracks that countless others he may not have made were attributed to him. He is credited, for instance, with being the first person who, asked how the world was treating him, spat in reply, "Vera seldom, sir, vera seldom." A typical Andraism concerns the time he was playing with a golfer who was unfortunate enough to be trapped in Hell Bunker. Beginning with his mashie and changing to a more lofted club after each failure, the golfer tried vainly to extricate his ball. "What should I do now,

Andra?" he hollered up from the depths after his desperate sequence had taken him through every club in his bag and his ball still remained in the bunker. "If I were ye," Andra answered brusquely, "I'd tak' the nine-forty train."

BY HERBERT WARREN WIND

FROM *The Gilded Age of Sport*

WHEN GOLF WAS A GAME

It was late at night, but the house was ablaze with light. The little ones, who should long since have been abed, were very noisily awake. Plainly, something was going on, but what it was no one would tell me.

I was led into a room and the door was closed. "Prepare yourself for a shock," I was warned. Outside, I could hear voices whispering. Suddenly the door was flung open and in marched the family, singing, "Happy birthday to you!" And on my lap they laid their collective gift—a gorgeous set of golf clubs, matched, numbered, certified and hooded.

It was a shock, as they had promised. I blanched and my hand shook as I fingered the chromium-plated instruments of a renewed servitude. Years ago I had shaken off the yoke of this enslaving pastime and had been a relatively free man thereafter. Now I am back in the galleys, pivoting, pronating and trying once more to solve the unanswerable mystery of the putt.

It is the family's idea that I am to get out of doors, relax, enjoy the beauties of nature and drink the scented air of the greensward. Too young to know what I have been through, they cannot understand that in presenting me with a set of golf clubs they are presenting a runaway slave with a nice new set of chains, a convalescent from mortal illness with a new set of lethal germs, a cured addict of morphine with a bright and shining hypodermic!

The fact is that I was once a devotee of slice and hook. My lips first touched the fatal cup 'way back in the days of the hard ball, when 150 yards was a man's drive and people in red coats played against bogey. I used implements now known only to the archaeologist, such as the cleek and the baffy. In those days clubs had names (as did holes) and science had not invaded sport with a numbering system that made golf as dryly technical as the triangulation of an artillery problem.

In those days the turf was mowed by sheep and one drove from a pinch of sand. There were bunkers to impede the blunderer and they stayed put from season to season. There were no brass-buttoned flunkies fluttering around the locker houses and no such thing as a starting time. Even strong men used floaters on the water holes.

In that consulship of Plancus golf was a *game*. A set of sticks, gathered from here and there and stoutly shafted with hickory, lasted a lifetime and were passed on to posterity. The annual model mania had not appeared, and the ball with a center guaranteed to outdrive all others had not begun to dominate the advertising pages of the magazines. Men did not visit their professional oftener than they visited their dentists, and a round of golf (on what was then called a "links") had not tried to outdo the speculative possibilities of the stock market.

Ah, well, it is a sign of advancing senility when one begins to lament a golden past. One must keep abreast of changing times. I shall yield to the numerology of modern golf and bow to the necessity of getting my right hand through, as with cold and repellent steel I smite a piece of dry ice enveloped in latex. I shall be more or less miserable, but it will be the misery of the mustard plaster. In my anguish at the hopeless task of trying to manage my anatomy in the manner of Bobby Jones, I shall forget my lesser woes.

As I struggle to keep my left hand over, my arm straight, my head down and my courage up, I shall achieve respite from the task of trying to make sense out of politics. In the pain of missed putts I shall forget the gnawing ache that plagues the amateur

187

economist. And when my ball goes soaring off into the bushes, in the old familiar slice, I shall bellow so loud that the reverberations from Washington will echo thinly in my ears.

The more I think of it the happper this choice of birthday gifts becomes. I have had some years of freedom, but I begin to suspect that the domesticated bird is happiest in a cage. Like a recaptured canary I shall thrill contentedly inside the bars of golf, and when, at the end of the day's pleasure, the last torturing putt gurgles in the cup, work will seem like play.

BY HOWARD VINCENT O'BRIEN

FROM *All Things Considered*

CONCERNING CADDIES

The caddie is an indispensable adjunct to the game of golf, and for the most part he fulfils his functions very capably; but there are caddies of every imaginable variety, and their vagaries are such as to cause wonderment on the part of their employers sometimes, amusement at others, and not infrequently exasperation. Some of them know too much about the game, and others far too little, and I hardly know which of these classes is in the long run the worse for the golfers who engage them to carry their clubs.

An incident of which I heard that happened to a well-known player on the North Berwick links, must have been very trying to him. On a busy day all the regular caddies had been engaged, and the fishermen were drafted into the club-carrying service. The player, having asked one of these fishermen if he knew anything about the game, and having been informed that he had only a little knowledge of it, resigned himself calmly to the inevitable, and told the man complacently that he would do. This player happened to be left-handed, and took up his stance on the first tee accordingly, whereupon the son of the sea at once adopted the part of tutor, and with some warmth and show of contempt exclaimed loudly, "I dinna ken much aboot the game, but ye dinna ken a wee bit. Mon, ye're standing on the wrong side of the baw! Awa' to the other side!" Golfers at the beginning of a round are proverbially susceptible to small influences, and when a player is accustomed to lean somewhat upon his caddie, as even some of the best occasionally do, I can well imagine that such a trivial matter as this is enough to mar a tee shot.

There were some strange specimens of the caddie species at Ganton when I was there. "Make a tee, boy," said a golfer to one of them, evidently a novice, one day. The player had been waiting about for something under a minute, while his servant showed no sign of making the usual preparations for the tee shot. The boy did not seem to understand. "Make a tee, boy," exclaimed the player a second time sharply, but still there was no response, and then the man called for some sand, bent down and made the tee himself. At this the boy attributed the failure of his understanding to the player's limited powers of expression, and somewhat scornfully exclaimed, "Why, if you had told me it was a cock-shot that was wanted, I should have known what you meant!" On competition days at Ganton we had often to secure a number of lads who had never seen the game played before, and very interesting specimens of the youth of Yorkshire they often were. One day, I remember, a competitor pulled his ball very very badly, and his caddie, who had gone on a little way in front, received it hard on a very tender part of his head. He was not seriously hurt, but much pained, and forthwith, excusably perhaps, he gave way to tears. To soothe him his employer presented him with half a sovereign. The tears suddenly ceased, the boy's face broke into a happy smile, and a moment later, when the two were trudging away towards the hole, the youngster ingenuously inquired, "Will you be coming out again this week, sir?"

There is a kinship between this story and that of the caddie at North Berwick, son of the greenkeeper there, some years ago, when first he began to carry clubs. He was a very precocious little fellow, and the player for whom he had been engaged to carry for the day was a well-known golfer from the south. When the day's play was far advanced, and the time of reckoning was drawing nigh, the boy seized an opportunity of sidling close up to his patron and asking him, "D'ye ken Bob S——?" the said Bob being one of the notabilities of the links. The player answered that he had not the pleasure of Mr. Robert's acquaintance so far, and inquired of the boy why he asked such a question. "Weel," was the answer, "it's a peety ye dinna ken Bob S—— . He's a rale fine gentleman, for he aye gies twa shillin' a roond for carryin' till'm; no like some that ca' themsels gentlemen, an' only gie a shillin'."

But lest it should be imagined from the recital of these incidents that the caddie is invariably over-greedy, and that he has no soul for anything but the pecuniary reward of his service, let there by way of contrast be told the story of the boy who was willing to carry clubs for nothing—the one solitary instance of such a disposition to self-sacrifice that there is on record. This time the golfer was not a great one. He had his faults, and they were numerous, and for their conquest and suppression he came to the conclusion that it would be better if he went out alone over the links and wrestled with them determinedly. A caddie watched him going out thus solitary, and felt sorry, so he said to him, "I will carry your clubs for a shilling, sir." But the golfer replied, "No, my boy, not to-day, thanks; I will carry them myself." The golfer missed his drive, foozled his second, put his third into a bunker, and endured other agonies. The caddie had been following at a respectful distance, and when the ball had been duly picked up out of the bunker, he made a further appeal. "I will carry for ninepence, sir." "No, I do not want a caddie," was the answer again. "I will carry for sixpence, then." "No, go away." On the next tee the player, overcome by conflicting emotions, missed the ball altogether two or three times, and then was the caddie's opportunity, which he seized without hesitation. "I will carry for the fun of the thing, sir!"

This is a digression, but I fear that digressions are inevitable when one enters upon the subject of caddies, and is persuaded to dip into one's recollection of caddie stories. The ignorant caddie is trying, but not less is the one who knows too much about the

190

game, or thinks he does, and insists upon inflicting his superior knowledge upon you during the whole course of the round. Once when I was playing for the Championship, my clubs were carried by a caddie who swore horribly at me all the time, notwithstanding that from the beginning I was going strongly for the first place. That boy got on my nerves. I was approaching well, but my putting was certainly not so sure and confident as it might have been. "What the ——— is the good of shooting at the flag if you can't putt worth a d——!" he exclaimed in great disgust on one occasion when I had the misfortune to miss holing out a somewhat short putt. He has begged to be allowed to carry for me many times since then, but I have steadfastly refused his offer, for I would not be handicapped with him upon any consideration. The caddie I like best of all, and he who I am convinced is the best servant for the average golfer, is he who thoroughly understands the game, has a deep knowledge of the course that is being played over, knows exactly what club to give you upon any and every occasion, and limits his functions to giving you a club without being asked for it. This caddie is a silent caddie, who knows that words of his are out of place, and that they would only tend to upset his master's game. It will generally be found that he, above all others, is the one who takes a deep and sympathetic interest in the game. He never upon any consideration gives advice without being asked for it. On the other hand, he takes care that no act or omission of his shall ever cause his man the most momentary irritation, for he has sufficient knowledge of the golfer's temperament to know that these trifles are a constant source of bad holes. When the player is preparing for his shot, and his eye is wandering anxiously between the ball and the hole, he puts out his hand whilst still continuing his survey of the ground, and as he puts it out he feels it grasp the handle of the exact club that is wanted. There is little need to look at it. The caddie knew and acted. The stance is taken while the player is still in his thoughtful mood, the shot is made while his mind is still concentrated to the utmost extent on the difficult task in hand, and then, after a happy result, the player and this faithful, truly sympathetic caddie go quietly on their way. When you are on the green he never needs to be told to go to the pin. He is always there, standing at the hole as soon as the time has come to putt; and while, if the putt is a poor thing, he has nothing to say (for silence is more than ever welcome at such a time of sorrow and disappointment), he permits himself a few courteous words of congratulation if a great success has been achieved at the last stroke at the hole, and the crown been placed upon an effort that has been truly praiseworthy throughout. This is my ideal caddie, and I am prepared to make some concessions to have him always at my side during the most trying rounds that I have to play. If he always performs the duties I have named, promptly and quietly, I do not care whether he really knows much about the game or not. If a caddie does the round of a course often enough in the company of good golfers, he knows the club to use for every particular stroke, even though he may have no practical knowledge of the game, and I ask nothing more of him than that he should always hand that club to me without keeping me waiting for a single moment. These caddies are a rarer species than the others.

I am no advocate of female labour, but I have often, after an experience of the girl caddie, been tempted to wish that there were more of them in the land, for they are uncommonly good. The little girl of humble lot seems, nine times out of ten, to possess all those qualities which go to the making of a good caddie—according to my standard of a good caddie—in a remarkable degree. Unlike some of her elder sisters, she never talks; but she always watches the game very closely and takes a deep interest in it. She is most anxious—if anything too anxious—to do her service properly and well, and to the most complete satisfaction of the gentleman who will reward her for it at the finish. She never keeps you waiting for your bag. The clubs are always there at your hand. If it is obvious to this little girl's simple intelligence that you want your brassy, she has it ready for you. If there is a doubt about the club, she does not make the mistake of offering you one on chance, as it were. She is too timid for that. She holds the bag before you and lets you choose yourself and carry all the responsibility on your own shoulders. The good boy caddie, whom I have referred to as my ideal, does that also. I said he was always waiting with the club ready, but if it is evident to him, as to the player, that it is a difficult question of judgment as to which particular club should be taken in somewhat puzzling circumstances, he allows the golfer to make his choice from the whole collection in the bag, making no suggestion of his own either by word or movement, unless invited to do so. Cannot every golfer recall numberless instances of bad shots and holes lost because in one of these moments of doubt, when his own inclination was leaning to the employment of one particular club, his caddie thrust another before him? Feeling that there must be something good in the caddie's recommendation, he has been tempted in spite of himself to use it. How frequently are the consequences disastrous in such circumstances as these, and how unenviable are the golfer's after reflections upon his own weakness! Yes, decidedly the girl caddie excels. I have seen her on many links up and down the country, and she is always good. In one of my last matches last season—at Luton—I had one to carry for me, and she was as good as any. Perhaps it may be urged by some players that it is not a good thing for girls to do this work. About that I have nothing to say. I only know that they do their duty well.

A peculiarly caustic but half-unconscious humour is the characteristic of caddies everywhere, but particularly in the north, and while golfers continue to lack absolute perfection, and their ministering attendants to expect it from them every time, it will probably remain a characteristic. A fair specimen was the remark of his caddie to a player whose handicap was several strokes removed from scratch, and who, having become badly bunkered on one occasion, tried nearly every iron club in his bag in a vain endeavor to get out. The case was heartbreaking, and he turned despairingly to his caddie with the question, "What on earth shall I take now?" There was little encouragement in the answer, "Take the 4.5 train." There is a good story also of a certain Welshman of title who became enthusiastic over the game, though he did not excel at it. He conceived that it would be a good thing to make a tour of the famous Scottish courses with the object of improving his play, and in due season he arrived at a certain famous green, where he employed as his caddie an individual who had a considerable reputation for blunt candour. The turf suffered severely every time this player made use of his irons, and the caddie shook his head gloomily and sadly as he witnessed the destructive work that went on daily. At last there came a day when he could stand it no longer, and when the Welshman had taken a mighty swipe at the ball with a heavy iron and made a deep excavation for several inches behind it, the club carrier moaned painfully, "O lord, man, hae mercy on puir auld Scotland!" It is said that the golfer played no more on those links. It was on this same course that two players went out one morning to play, and found a friend waiting alone on the first tee, who said that he had fixed up a match with a certain Captain Blank, who would be coming along presently. The possibility of a foursome was considered, and a question was asked as to what kind of a player the Captain was, his partner replying, "Oh, he is excellent. He drives a good ball, plays his irons well, and is exceedingly useful at the short game; in fact, he is a first-rate all-round man." Expecting confirmation of this eulogium, he turned to his caddie and said, "You know the Captain's play well enough. Now, what sort of a player would you say he is?" The caddie replied scornfully, "Captain Blank! He canna play a shot worth a d——. He's nae better than yoursel'!"

The fact is that no player is great in the eyes of his caddie, for on one occasion when two gentlemen who were very fair hands at the game were doing a round and being closely pressed by a couple behind, who seemed to be driving inordinately long balls, one of them observed that perhaps they had better let them go through as they seemed to be playing both well and quickly. "Na, na, naething o' the kind," interposed one of the caddies. "They're just twa duffers like yersels!" And great eminence in other fields counts for nothing with the caddie if his man cannot golf in good style. There is the story told by Mr. A. J. Balfour* of the distinguished general, hero of many battles, who, having duly found his way into his twentieth bunker, was startled by a cry of irritation from his caddie, "Come, come, old gentleman, this will never do!" This great statesman-golfer relates another anecdote showing that caddies are much the same the whole world over. An English golfer was playing at Pau and had a French caddie

* Mr. A. J. Balfour, later Earl Balfour, English prime minister and elder statesman.

attending upon him. He made one particularly fine approach shot, and, as golfers will at such times, he turned round to the boy with excusable vanity for applause. But the boy's English vocabulary so far comprised only two words which he had heard uttered on several occasions, but the sense of which he did not understand. Feeling sure, however, that they must be appropriate to this occasion, and desiring to be appreciative, he smiled pleasantly into the golfer's face and murmured, "Beastly fluke!" Mr. Balfour, by the way, has a particular and decided taste in caddies, for he has written that he can gladly endure severe or even contemptuous criticism from them; can bear to have it pointed out to him that all his misfortunes are the direct and inevitable result of his own folly; can listen with equanimity when failure is prophesied of some stroke he is attempting, and can note unmoved the self-satisfied smile with which the fulfilment of the prophecy is accentuated; but ignorant and stupid indifference is intolerable to him. The caddie, in the statesman's opinion, is not, and ought not, to be regarded as a machine for carrying clubs at a shilling a round, but rather occupies, or ought to occupy, the position of competent adviser or interested spectator. The caddie ought to be as anxious for the success of his side as if he were one of the players, and should watch each move in the game with benevolent if critical interest, being always ready with the appropriate club, and, if need be, with the appropriate comment.

But I don't like to see this anxiety for the success of one's fortunes upon the links carried to excess. It is then a disturbing factor, and its humorous aspect does not always appeal to one as it should. Some golfers might be flattered when they come to know that their caddies have backed them to the extent of half the remuneration they will receive for carrying the clubs for the round. It is a touching expression of the caddie's belief in them. But after all this kind of thing does not help to make a good caddie. Apart from other considerations, it does not make the boy carry any the better because he is over-anxious about the result of the match, and, though some golfers might be inclined to ridicule the suggestion, it nevertheless is a disturbing element in one's game if one knows that even the caddie will be very deeply concerned if every stroke does not come off just as well as it ought to.

The caddie is not above letting you know of his wager; sometimes he will even tell you of it. Two golfers of some Highland celebrity were playing a match one day at Luffness, and after a hard round they came to the eighteenth tee all square and but this one hole to play. At this critical stage of the game the caddie of one of them approached his master and nervously whispered to him, "Please, sir, wad ye do your very best here, for there's money on this match." And the golfer did try to do his very best indeed, but he pressed and he foozled, and he lost the hole and the match. Sympathetically he turned to his caddie to ask him what was the amount of the lost wager that he might pay it for him and soften his disappointment. "It was a penny, sir," said the boy. . . .

Golfers should, I think, sometimes be on their guard lest a too kind-hearted caddie, in an excess of zeal for his employer, should be tempted to transgress the laws of the game, or depart from strict truthfulness in his behalf. Sometimes it is done with a wonderful air of innocence and simplicity. Caddies have been known, when their employers have been in doubt as to exactly how many strokes they have played at certain holes, to give an emphatic, but none the less untruthful declaration, on the side of fewness. They mean well, but mistakenly, and it is better for everybody concerned, but particularly for the caddies, that they should be severely reprimanded when there is reason to doubt their good faith.

And who shall say that another, and for our purposes the final characteristic of the average caddie of experience, is not a wonderful amount of solid wordly common-sense of a variety specially adapted to golf? And what golfer is there who has not at one time or another had the advantage of it? But he may at the time have been unconscious of the assistance. There is the historic case of the caddie on the Scottish links who warned a beginner, dallying too much on the tee, that he "maunna address the ba' saw muckle." Forthwith the southern tyro, greatly exasperated at his own failure, burst out, "So far as I know I haven't said a word to the infernal thing, but the irritation of this beastly game is enough, and if I have any more of your confounded tongue you may repent it!" Then the caddie murmured to himself, "I dinna like 'is look. I'll better get 'm roond as pleesant as possible." Could any advice have been more delicately worded than that of the caddie to the stout clergyman who with all his strength made a most mighty swing at his ball on the tee with the usual result—a foozle? "It'll nae do, sir; ye ken ye canna drive as far as that." "Wha—wha—what do you mean by such a remark? As far as what?" gasped the reverend but irate gentleman. "I jist mean, sir, that ye canna drive as far as ye wad like."

Perhaps we shall never hear the best caddie stories, for is it not likely that a great abundance of them are made and told in the sheds after the day's play is over, and when the golfer's tools are being wiped and cleaned, and his irons burnished to a beautiful brightness? It is then that the caddie is in his happiest vein, his tongue and disposition untrammelled by the presence of the club members. "What're ye doin' cleanin' them clubs so grand?" asked one caddie of another, who was evidently bestowing unusual pains on the polishing of the set that were in his keeping. The caddie was in a thoughtful mood. He was the regular attendant of an old golfer who had had a most disastrous day. "I'm to clean 'em better than ever," he answered. "And when I've cleaned 'em I've got to break 'em across my knee. And then I've got to chuck 'em in the bloomin' river." Sometimes, we see, if he is a simple-hearted, faithful caddie, his lot is not a happy one.

BY HARRY VARDON

FROM *The Complete Golfer*

IS GOLF FUNNY?

No. But golfers are. Also, amusing things often happen while the game is played. On those occasions, if you have any sense of humour, your concentration is knocked for six, and then some dullard who hasn't learnt how to laugh wins, and bang goes half-a-crown. . . .

At Pine Valley, that challenging course in the United States, one of our opponents in a four-ball found his ball lodged in a clump of honeysuckle. There is no such thing as an unplayable lie at Pine Valley. You must have a go. My partner and I stood by, trying not to smirk. The unfortunate player examined his ball, turned to partner John Arthur Brown (who happens to be President of the Club) and muttered: "We don't have problems like this at the office." Except for a tut-tut from John there was dead silence.

When a man laughs aloud on a golf course it is bad. Golf is no joke. The chap who fluffs a shot and then guffaws is depraved. This is not the stuff from which real addicts are made. Laughter comes later—sometimes not until days have passed.

A friend of mine played a round at Letchworth with his wife one summer Saturday evening. They were the last couple out and my pal was cracking the ball long and straight. At the 13th his drive carried the hill and the ball went bounding downwards out of sight. You cannot see the pin from the tee on this hole for it is in the hollow, but my friend's drive was a peach and there was a reasonable chance of the ball finishing on the green, or very close.

To the couple's surprise, when they got to the top of the hill, the ball was not in sight. They went towards the green and searched for about ten minutes, then proceeded to the next tee muttering about yet another golf mystery. . . .

That night, my friend slept badly. Suddenly, he shook his wife and shouted: "Did you look in the hole?" The poor girl became conscious and, realising that her addicted husband was still fretting about the drive on the 13th, had to admit that she had not looked in the hole. Each had thought the other had checked on the remote possibility of an ace!

My friend came to life, tugged on his trousers, bounded down the stairs, and slammed the door. His wife heard the car starting up. Before settling down again she glanced at the clock. It was half-past five and a pleasant dawn suffused the room in pink light. She closed her eyes peacefully but not for long.

The front door opened again and the husband called upstairs: "You'll have to come. *If this is a hole in one, I need a witness.*"

His sleepy lady in a dressing gown, my friend in a coma . . . they arrived at the club. Hurried across country to the 13th.

It would have been nice to record in this way the story of a perfect hole. But I cannot. When the couple reached the green they found the cup was empty. Deeply disconsolate they made for home.

A workman at the entrance to the course threw over a suspicious glance. My friend's face reddened. "We've been looking for a golf ball," he said.

Some people might say that very few golfing laughs have anything to do with women. Here is an exception. Freddy has a wife who is golf-addicted. I don't know whether her passion had anything to do with it, but one morning they had a terrific row. My friend stamped from the house, slammed the door and started his day at the office with a scowl like thunder. During the forenoon he met a near-neighbour who asked him if he was moving house.

Freddy shook his head and looked surprised. "I only wondered," said his friend, "seeing your furniture out in the garden . . ."

"Heavens!" thought Freddy, "she's gone home to her mother —and taken the furniture!"

The poor man hurried home. What did he find? Trouble? Not a bit of it. Odd items of dining-room furniture were certainly in the garden. The big carpet was hanging from the clothes-line and into it, with great gusto, his golfing wife was driving practice balls!

The nice thing about golf humour is that it can be enjoyed when courses are enshrouded in the tragedy of deep snow or impenetrable fog. I mean when play is impossible. I used to travel in the train with an addict who, behind his newspaper, chuckled quietly to himself nearly every time we passed Potters Bar golf course. I never asked, but it was obvious that a glimpse of the fairways jogged a pleasant memory. . . .

BY GEORGE HOUGHTON

FROM *Golf Addicts on Parade*

THE FABULOUS COMMODORE HEARD

Twenty-nine years ago a stocky Texan came from the club-house at Houston to the first tee. He was looking for a foursome—needed four more to make up a poker game. He was quite indignant when the four golfers refused to give up golf for a game of poker.

His name was Commodore Bryan Heard of Houston and Dallas, Texas. He was then 45 years old and he had never seen a game of golf. Twenty years later at the age of 65, he started shooting his age. That means at the age of 65 he shot a 65—at the age of 66 he shot a 66—a 67 when he was 67—a 68 when he was 68—a 69 when he was 69—and a 70 when he was 70—all over standard length course. He is now 75 and despite cataract trouble with both eyes, with his vision badly blurred—in spite of having a leg and arm broken when a taxicab knocked him down—at the age of 75 he has turned in a 74—shooting under his age.

In many respects Commodore Bryan Heard, now of Dallas, is the most remarkable golfer in the history of the game.

In the first place you must visualize a player who started golf at 45, and who, after he was 60, has broken 70 more than a hundred times. I first heard of the stocky little Commodore in 1915. He was then 56 years old. That was the year when a famous 14-year-old phenom, named Bobby Jones, was starting his unforgettable rampage. The kid of 14 collided with the veteran of 56 in a southern championship—and took a trimming. The Commodore stalked around in 71—too fast a pace for the 14-year-old Georgian, for almost anybody.

"How did you get started?" I once asked the Commodore.

And it developed that it all dated back to the day he tried to get up the poker game. He tried using a little derision to pry his friends away from a "sissy" pastime and was lured into showing what *he* could do in the way of hitting a little white ball. Then it was the four friends who put on the deriding act.

"I swung three times and missed," the Commodore relates, "and so I went back to town and asked at the store for a sack of sticks. 'You mean a bag of golf clubs,' the clerk said. I bought one of every kind of club he had and three dozen balls. On the way home, I saw what I think was the first Ford car that ever came to Texas—at least, it was the first I ever saw. Well, I thought while I was learning golf I would just learn to drive a car, too. So I bought the Ford. Next morning I went down and got the engineer off my boat and told him I wanted him to work the engine of the car while I steered it. With him working the levers and me steering was the way we got out to the golf course. As soon as we could get the car stopped, I got out and teed off. Then we got back in and drove off down the fairway after the ball, and ran round and round it till we could get the car stopped again. The drivin' was specially good on the greens and we would go around two or three times before I'd putt.

"And that was how I played my first game of golf. . . . We got mighty near halfway around before the greens committee came and put us off.

"Then I began practicing and playing, regular. It took me two years to get to an 80 and some time longer to reach and break 70. I've always used the old fashioned two-handed grip. That's about all the grip they knew about when I started—and I still like it best. It gives my hands and wrists more power and more freedom of action—feels more natural.

"It didn't take me long," the Commodore said, "to find that it wasn't so hard to get somewhere within thirty or forty yards of the average green in two strokes. So I began working on my short game—the short pitches, the chip shots, and the putting. I kept this up until I'd bet even money that from forty yards I'd get down in two strokes."

And he'd break you at this bet. The Commodore has always had control of a low pitch-and-run or chip-and-run—also of a low cut shot where he could stop the ball within a foot of the landing spot. That shows the marvelous use he always had of his hands, getting so much backspin.

He decided the best putting method was to place the forefinger of his right hand down the shaft and then putt as if he were waving that finger on the desired line. Golf has known no better putter. Even at the age of 75 with impaired eyesight he is still deadly within ten feet of the cup. He didn't adopt his peculiar putting grip until he was 67.

By the time Commodore Heard had passed 60, he became poison to the leading amateurs and even the best professionals who came through Texas. Through past years more than one crack pro has told me of meeting a stocky Texan, giving him six or eight strokes, and taking a good beating on level terms. He took into camp such crack golfers as George Rotan and Frank Godchaux, among the best of the amateurs, and fed them 69's or 70's in various tournaments. One of the leading amateurs in Memphis once gave him eight strokes for a bet. The Commodore beat him 17 up without using a stroke in eighteen holes—breaking 70 that day—and leaving behind the most astonished golfer in the whole world.

He played Pine Valley when it was first opened—when only fourteen holes were finished. He shot every hole in par that round —and those who have played Pine Valley know what that means. He came North and they made bets against him at Lido—the old Lido. The bets were that he couldn't break 80. On his first trip around he shot a 73.

There was another remarkable exhibition of skill and stamina at Asheville, N.C. At the age of 69 he played thirty-six holes daily for thirty-one successive days, leaving that community almost bankrupt when he departed. One reason for this is the Commodore's smooth, simple, easy swing. He hits almost every shot on a straight line to the right spot. He seldom has a hook or slice. They travel like an arrow. This applies to both wood and iron.

Commodore Heard's body action is a trifle limited, but relaxed, never tightened. He gives you the impression of a great pair of hands at work swinging the head of the club. His freedom from tension is remarkable. This somewhat limited body action responds perfectly to live hands and live wrists. One of the strongest features of his game is the fine control he has on a No.1

or No.2 iron, even through a cross wind. This is the big test of the real golfer.

The Southwest knows all about Commodore Heard. He had been a golfing marvel for twenty years—from fifty-five to seventy five—in addition to being one of the most popular citizens of that great commonwealth. Texas has turned out more than its share of fine golfers—but the Commodore's record still heads the parade.

BY GRANTLAND RICE

FROM *American Golfer*

I was playing golf that day
   When the Germans landed.
All our soldiers ran away,
   All our ships were stranded.
Such were my surprise and shame
They almost put me off my game.

BY ANONYMOUS

FROM *The Fireside Book of Humorous Poetry*

AFFORESTATION

A waggish friend of the writer's suggested the other day how interesting it would be if, on any ordinary golf links, a tree could be made to spring up by magic on the spot where somebody had cheated.

Colonel B.
Drove from the tee;
Fell in a bunker—play'd two and play'd three;
Four, and then out.
Then, with a clout,
(Due to impatience and chagrin, no doubt)
Sent the ball speeding far over the green,
Into a drain.—
At it again!
Four to recover, and two to lie dead,
Two to putt out, making total Thirteen.
"How many, Colonel?" —Scratching his head,
"Eight—no, no, wait a bit—seven," he said.
Ev'n as he spoke
Straightway an oak!
O, what a beautiful, beautiful tree!
Fifty-two feet,
Foliage complete—
And it grows on the edge of the Seventeenth Tee.

Stout Mrs. Y.,
Playing a tie,
Had a most difficult, difficult lie.
What to be done?
Lift and lose one?
Clearly impossible—match to be won!
Far to the right
Chanc'd to catch sight
Of her rival, with back turn'd, addressing a shot—
Knew what to do;
Pointed a shoe;
And the ball trickled out to a *much* better spot.
O, Mrs. Y.,
Look at the sky!
See, what a beautiful, beautiful pine!
With its far-spreading shade
What a *difference* it's made
To the look of the fairway of bare Number Nine!

But alas and alack!
It was eighteen months back
That the trees 'gan to spring this curious way.
Now our Holg Club is shut
Not a drive or a putt,
Not a chip makes the echoes in P . . . na today;
Not a Kroflite leaps now o'er those well-wooded lands—
But the Forest Department are rubbing their hands.

BY E. A. WODEHOUSE
FROM *The Fireside Book of Humorous Poetry*

Burns and I were constant golfing companions in those days. I could always beat George. He made me feel like a pro. George found it impossible to take golf seriously, and he could always get a laugh out of me. I made him feel like a great comedian. We were an ideal twosome.

The Hillcrest didn't regard us as ideal members, however. We had too little respect for Club regulations. One summer when the weather got unbearably hot, George and I took our shirts off on the course, which was against the rules. The Board of Governors wrote us a letter requesting that we desist from this flagrant violation. The day after we got the letter it was still hot, and we went back on the course and took off our shirts again.

We were called on the carpet and warned that if we did it again we'd be suspended. We did it again. We were suspended from the club for two weeks.

The day the suspension was up, we gave our word we'd never break the rule about shirts again. This time we kept our word and kept our shirts on. But on reaching the third tee, we took off our pants. We had checked and found there was no rule against this.

So we played eighteen holes in shirts and undershorts and nobody stopped us. Fortunately for all concerned the weather turned cool before the next meeting of the Board of Governors.

Only once did I have a serious fight with the club. That was when I led a campaign to revoke the by-law that only persons of the Jewish faith could be members. I am proud to say I won the fight, and Hillcrest ceased being a restricted club.

BY HARPO MARX

FROM *Harpo Speaks!*

A lady once played a nice approach to a high plateau green, and her opponent, a man, was bunkered in a deep pit-like hazard to one side of it. Her caddie went to the flag, and they both stood there waiting for the other player, who had disappeared into the pit. Chunks of turf flew up, showers of sand, odd pebbles and so forth—but of the other player or his ball there was no sign.

The lady's caddie, beside himself at last, turned to her and said:

"Gawd, miss, he must be comin' underground!"

BY CHARLES GRAVES AND HENRY LONGHURST

FROM *Candid Caddies*

THE CHARM OF GOLF

When he reads of the notable doings of famous golfers, the eighteen-handicap man has no envy in his heart. For by this time he has discovered the great secret of golf. Before he began to play it he wondered wherein lay the fascination of it; now he knows. Golf is so popular simply because it is the best game in the world at which to be bad.

Consider what it is to be bad at cricket. You have bought a new bat, perfect in balance; a new pair of pads, white as the driven snow; gloves of the very latest design. Do they let you use them? No. After one ball, in the negotiation of which neither your bat, nor your pads, nor your gloves came into play, they send you back into the pavilion to spend the rest of the afternoon listening to fatuous stories of some old gentleman who knew Fuller Pilch. And when your side takes the field, where are you? Probably at long leg both ends, exposed to the public gaze as the worst fieldsman in London. How devastating are your emotions. Remorse, anger, mortification, fill your heart; above all, envy—envy of the lucky immortals who disport themselves on the green level of Lord's.

Consider what it is to be bad at lawn tennis. True, you are allowed to hold on to your new racket all through the game, but how often are you allowed to employ it usefully? How often does your partner cry "Mine!" and bundle you out of the way? Is there pleasure in playing football badly? You may spend the full eighty minutes in your new boots, but your relations with the ball may be distant. They do not give you a ball to yourself at football.

But how different a game is golf. At golf it is the bad player who gets the most strokes. However good his opponent, the bad player has the right to play out each hole to the end; he will get more than his share of the game. He need have no fears that his new driver will not be employed. He will have as many swings with it as the scratch man; more, if he misses the ball altogether upon one or two tees. If he buys a new niblick he is certain to get fun out of it on the very first day.

And, above all, there is this to be said for golfing mediocrity—the bad player can make the strokes of the good player. The poor cricketer has perhaps never made fifty in his life; as soon as he stands at the wickets he knows that he is not going to make fifty to-day. But the eighteen-handicap man has some time or other played every hole on the course to perfection. He has driven a ball 250 yards; he has made superb approaches; he has run down the long putt. Any of these things may suddenly happen to him again. And therefore it is not his fate to have to sit in the club smoking-room after his second round and listen to the wonderful deeds of others. He can join in too. He can say with perfect truth, "I once carried the ditch at the fourth with my second," or "I remember when I drove into the bunker guarding the eighth green," or even "I did a three at the eleventh this afternoon"— bogey being five. But if the bad cricketer says, "I remember when I took a century in forty minutes off Lockwood and Richardson," he is nothing but a liar.

For these and other reasons golf is the best game in the world for the bad player. And sometimes I am tempted to go further and say that it is a better game for the bad player than for the good player. The joy of driving a ball straight after a week of slicing, the joy of putting a mashie shot dead, the joy of even a moderate stroke with a brassie; best of all, the joy of the perfect cleek shot—these things the good player will never know. Every stroke we bad players make we make in hope. It is never so bad but it might have been worse; it is never so bad but we are confident of doing better next time. And if the next stroke is good, what happiness fills our soul. How eagerly we tell ourselves that in a little while all our strokes will be as good.

What does Vardon know of this? If he does a five hole in four he blames himself that he did not do it in three; if he does it in five he is miserable. He will never experience that happy surprise with which we hail our best strokes. Only his bad strokes surprise him, and then we may suppose that he is not happy. His length and accuracy are mechanical; they are not the result, as so often in our case, of some suddenly applied maxim or some suddenly discovered innovation. The only thing which can vary in his game is his putting, and putting is not golf but croquet.

But of course we, too, are going to be as good as Vardon one day. We are only postponing the day because meanwhile it is so pleasant to be bad. And it is part of the charm of being bad at golf that in a moment, in a single night, we may become good. If the bad cricketer said to a good cricketer, "What am I doing wrong?" the only possible answer would be, "Nothing particular, except that you can't play cricket." But if you or I were to say to our scratch friend, "What am I doing wrong?" he would reply at once, "Moving the head," or "Dropping the right knee," or "Not getting the wrists in soon enough," and by to-morrow we should be different players. Upon such a little depends, or seems to the eighteen-handicap to depend, excellence in golf.

And so, perfectly happy in our present badness and confident of our future goodness, we long-handicap men remain. Perhaps it would be pleasanter to be a little more certain of getting the ball safely off the first tee; perhaps at the fourteenth hole, where there is a right of way and the public encroach, we should like to feel that we have done with topping; perhaps—

Well, perhaps we might get our handicap down to fifteen this summer. But no lower; certainly no lower.

BY A. A. MILNE

FROM *Not That It Matters*

ANYONE FOR GOLF?

The last time I was in Israel was many years ago, and I must admit there have been quite a few changes. The first thing people asked me in those days was: "Have you seen our Huleh project?" The Huleh project was a valley which the Israelis had drained, thus adding thousands of acres of arable land, and the Israelis were quite proud of it.

But times have changed even in Israel, and this time the first question almost everyone has asked me is: "Have you seen our new golf course?" Israel hasn't had a golf course for two thousand years (there is a theory the Romans used to play a similar game, but with IX instead of XVIII holes), and they are bursting with pride in spite of the fact not too many people here know exactly what golf is.

They say that three years ago an American newspaperman got up at a press conference given by Premier David Ben-Gurion and said: "Mr. Prime Minister, is it true you are building a golf course so you can invite President Eisenhower to Israel?"

The Prime Minister looked startled and whispered to his aid: "What is golf?"

"It's a game," the aid whispered back.

The Prime Minister said to the American newspaperman: "No, I don't play games."

Israel's first golf course is located at Caesarea, ancient port of the Roman legions. The land and the course belong to the Rothschild family and it's a private club with about 250 members.

The course is bordered on one side by the sea and on the other side by Jordan. If you slice the ball, you go in the ocean. If you hook it, you can start a war. If you hit an Arab, the United Nations penalizes you two strokes.

The other problem of Caesarea is the sand traps. Since Caesarea has so many ruins, somebody who finds himself in a sand trap might dig up an entire Phoenician city with his niblick, in which case he's not allowed to blast out until a member of the Israeli archaeological society arrives. Something like this can hold up a game for days.

In discussing golf with our Israeli friends, I discovered they had varied opinions on it. One said: "We only had room for nine holes, and since we wanted eighteen we had to launch the Sinai campaign. The Gaza Strip would have made a wonderful parking lot."

There are no books in Hebrew on golf, and some of the members still haven't got the hang of the game. I met one member who never played, and another who had been a member for ten months and went seven holes before he gave up. A lady member, Miss Sharona Aron, an Israeli singer of fame, told me she was taking lessons.

"What's par for the course?" I asked.

Miss Aron shrugged her shoulders: "Who knows?"

The favorite day for golf in Israel is Saturday, the day of rest, just as the favorite day in the Christian world is Sunday. This has caused a certain amount of consternation in religious circles down here, but the Israeli golf players answer the criticism like true golfers anywhere: "When else can we play?"

BY ART BUCHWALD
FROM *How Much Is That in Dollars?*

It is odd how some headliners pass on and are forgotten at once, except in the casual sense. Others die and years later you still half expect them to come strolling around the next corner, smiling a greeting. Mildred (Babe) Zaharias was one of these.

You know the Babe has vanished forever around the final dogleg, but you can't quite believe it. The Babe is a legend like old Tom Morris and Admiral Nelson and Paul Bunyan, and legends never die. During her eight years as a professional golfer, in good health and bad, the Babe won almost 60 tournaments. From 1948 through 1951 she earned the world title at Tam O'Shanter, and when she returned for another try in 1952, although she should have been resting from a recent operation, she readily admitted she was there "because I don't want nobody to win this thing but me!"

Golf was her life and she always turned in a memorable performance. During exhibitions she would rifle a drive far down the fairway, with graceful power, then turn to the male portion of the gallery and ask with polite mockery, "Don't you wish you could hit 'em like that?" The Babe was a showboat, but in the colorful, not the temperamental, way. Once at Tam her approach to the second green stopped atop a hastily abandoned raincoat. The Babe walked up, surveyed the situation with pretended but impressive concern (she must have known she was entitled to remove the coat), then chipped off the wrinkled surface for one putt and a birdie as the spectators roared in approval.

The Babe wasn't around last season. She spent her favorite time of year dying of cancer in a Texas hospital. You knew you wouldn't see her this summer, either. But there were moments when the shimmer of the sun played tricks. You would have sworn that was the Babe, striding along two fairways over, or disappearing through some distant door. Or if there was a huge crowd following some feminine foursome, it was easy to imagine the Babe was there, at home and happy in the middle of the fuss and excitement. The Babe loved crowds. And the crowds loved the Babe.

BY ROBERT CROMIE
in "The Wake of the News,"
FROM *Chicago* Tribune

ANY GOLF CHAMPIONSHIP

(An official statement—with apologies)

I'm driving straight and my irons are good;
I'm getting home as a winner should;
I'm down the middle every sock,
And I ought to win by a city block.
I'm on the pin when I see the green,
Moving on like a young machine;
You orter see my half-iron pokes,
I orter lead by a dozen strokes—
ButthehellofitisIain'tputtin.

BY GRANTLAND RICE

FROM *Wake Up the Echoes*

THE FABLE OF THE CADDY WHO
HURT HIS HEAD WHILE THINKING

One day a Caddy sat in the Long Grass near the Ninth Hole
and wondered if he had a Soul. His Number was 27, and he
almost had forgotten his Real Name.

As he sat and Meditated, two Players passed him. They were
going the Long Round, and the Frenzy was upon them.

They followed the Gutta Percha Balls with the intent swift-

213

ness of trained Bird Dogs, and each talked feverishly of Brassy Lies, and getting past the Bunker, and Lofting to the Green, and Slicing into the Bramble—each telling his own Game to the Ambient Air, and ignoring what the other Fellow had to say.

As they did the St. Andrews Full Swing for eighty Yards apiece and then Followed Through with the usual Explanations of how it Happened, the Caddy looked at them and Reflected that they were much inferior to his Father.

His Father was too Serious a Man to get out in Mardi Gras Clothes and hammer a Ball from one Red Flag to another.

His Father worked in a Lumber Yard.

He was an Earnest Citizen, who seldom Smiled, and he knew all about the Silver Question and how J. Pierpont Morgan done up a Free People on the Bond Issue.

The Caddy wondered why it was that his Father, a really Great Man, had to shove Lumber all day and could seldom get one Dollar to rub against another, while these superficial Johnnies who played Golf all the Time had Money to Throw at the Birds. The more he Thought the more his Head ached.

MORAL: *Don't try to Account for Anything.*

BY GEORGE ADE

FROM *Fables in Slang*

THE HAWK THEY COULDN'T KILL

"I won't know until I play whether I can get back the edge I had before. I don't know if I'll start favoring a shoulder or an ankle that's paining me and then throw my game off. But there's one thing I'm sure of. There's nothing about death that will ever frighten me now."

Pain had torn at the little man for months and death had

made a run at him and the hard lines in his face had been etched there as if by acid. The Texas sun had tanned him, but his gaunt, still-handsome face reflected his ordeal just as surely as did the scars on his body. His jacket hung slackly on him, making him look like a small boy in a big brother's coat and underscoring his frailness. The laces of his G.I. boots were loosened at the tops to ease the pressure on his swollen ankles. Yet in his eyes there was neither despair nor desperation. There was the same icy stare which was the outward manifestation of the most indomitable spirit golf has known, the look which had chilled his competitors as he drove himself to the top of his profession and had helped to earn him that scarcely endearing nickname, "The Hawk."

It was the summer of 1949 and Ben Hogan sat in the living room of his home in Fort Worth. The friend who had come expecting to see a hopeless invalid—to view, as it were, the mortal remains of the greatest golfer of his time—abruptly lost the feeling that he was there to offer Ben or anyone else his condolences. As Hogan talked of his hopes and his plan for the future in the same intense way he approached a ball in a difficult lie, taking nothing for granted yet determined not to fail because of anything over which he had control, the visitor began to absorb his confidence. When the man left he took with him, as did others who visited Hogan at that time, a conviction that he might yet live to see a miracle.

If only men of superior faith can believe in miracles, it must be said that, where Hogan was concerned, most of the country's sports fans were infidels. The terrible highway accident which shattered the little golf champion's body and the even more ravaging complications which followed a month later must surely have put an end to his career. Most of his friends were grateful that he was still alive. They looked forward to the day when he could join them on the veranda of one of the country clubs he had once conquered and, perhaps, at some distant date, even hit a few balls in a friendly foursome. They remembered the reports from the scene of the accident, how a giant bus had roared down on the Hogan car, plowed into it head-on and squashed it as a stampeding elephant would mangle a small animal that had wandered into its path.

Yet, even as they consigned him to the graveyard of champions and debated the identity of his successor as the country's finest golfer, Hogan was slowly conditioning himself for what was to be the most incredible comeback in the history of American sports. The doctors had mended his shattered bones and tied up his torn veins; now it was up to him to strengthen his muscles, regain his co-ordination and bring under control the nerves which had carried him to the top in the most nerve-wracking of all games. At the age of thirty-seven he was faced with the task of rebuilding what had been a nearly flawless golfing machine. To understand the magnitude of that task, remember that Bobby Jones, the sport's most famous player before Hogan, had retired from competitive golf at twenty-eight.

But William Benjamin Hogan seemed to have been put on this earth for the purpose of hurdling obstacles. Looking back now on his career, it can be said that Hogan first overcame the greatest handicap any athlete can have—no talent. That deficiency alone was enough to endear him to millions of duffers. Though born in Dublin, Texas, a son of the village blacksmith, on August 13, 1912, Ben spent most of his boyhood in Fort Worth, where his mother had moved the family after his father's death. In common with so many other great athletes, he lived his early years in poverty. When he grew up the memory of those lean days still haunted him and added its weight to the desperate hunger for victory which we associate with him. He sold papers for a time but, hearing that caddies were paid sixty-five cents an hour, plus tips, he applied for a job at one of the city's finest golf courses, the Glen Garden Country Club.

The skinny, underfed little Hogan, only twelve years old, had his first battle on his hands. He was a natural mark for the older, bigger boys. He had only been at work a day or two when his "colleagues" stuffed him into a frail barrel and rolled him down a hill. Having survived that ordeal with little damage except to his dignity, he was forced to fight one of the other caddies. Hogan, who even today looks as if he would have made a champion boxer, sailed into his unlucky opponent and proved himself with his fists.

There was another battle that was not to be won so easily. As they made their living from golf, all of the caddies wanted to be able to play the game, too, and they spent their spare hours practicing driving and putting. And, as all boys do, they made even their practice sessions a form of competition. The boy who hit the shortest drive was forced to retrieve the balls for the other caddies. Ben was small and skinny; he was left-handed and there were only right-handed clubs available for him at the club; and so he became the regular retriever for his colleagues.

It was here that Hogan formulated what has since become his motto, the true secret of his success: "If you can't outplay them, outwork them." Though worn out from hauling heavy bags of clubs over the rolling course all day, he stayed there after the others had gone home and worked long hours at the practice tee. Slowly he began to feel that hitting a ball right-handed was the natural way. Slowly he began to get the distance on his drives that would end his days as a "retriever" for the other caddies. This was the origin of his powerful backswing, the mighty effort which was to propel the longest drives any little man has ever hit on a golf course.

"There is no such thing as a natural swing," Hogan has often said, and the young Ben Hogan was certainly the living proof of that conviction. Veteran golfers who watched the little fellow on the course were impressed by his determination but appalled by his form. One friend from those days still carries a vivid picture in his mind of the clumsy beginner. "He couldn't do one thing right. He sure couldn't putt. Everybody used to laugh at him because he practically ran at the ball to hit it."

But Hogan loved golf and he saw in it a way out of the poverty which had darkened all of his early life. He had neither the size nor the natural talent. Such considerations were as nothing to a man with Ben's fierce singleness of purpose. He worked and worked on his game and soon he was beating most of the other young men around Fort Worth. He stopped growing when he reached five feet, eight and a half inches and 140 pounds. Yet out of such refractory material was evolving a fine golfer—one good enough to leave Fort Worth and hit the tournament trail. Or so he thought.

The few dollars in his pockets couldn't carry him very far. There was little chance to win any real money against the tough

217

veterans of the tournament circuit then, and Ben was usually forced to return to Fort Worth and earn his living with any one of a half-dozen jobs. And, in 1935, he married his childhood sweetheart, Valerie Fox. Knowing how much he loved the game, Valerie urged him to go back to the golf circuit, feeling that he was now ready to compete with the old pros. Ben thought so, too. "When I made the tour before," he told a friend some years later, "I'd have an occasional good round, but I couldn't keep it up. One good shot or one good round doesn't mean a thing in this game. You've got to keep it up for seventy-two holes."

Ben and Valerie set out together in 1937. He had never won a tournament, and there were times when it appeared that he never would. Everything seemed to go against him. In 1938 the Hogans drove their battered jalopy into Oakland for a tournament and, because they couldn't afford a parking lot, left the car in a vacant lot. He played badly in the tournament, winning but a few dollars, and when they got back to the lot they found that the car had been jacked up by thieves and stripped of its tires.

"You might say that that was a break for me," Ben will tell you. "I knew then that things couldn't get much worse for us. And Valerie, who must have figured I was beginning to lose heart, pretended she was more optimistic than ever."

Things did take a turn for the better. There were no tournament victories, but he gave the winner a run for it almost every time. In fact, he was beginning to finish second with such regularity that he earned for himself the nickname, "Runner-Up Hogan." Anyone who has ever met him can tell you how much that name must have rankled him.

Through it all he worked harder than any other man in golf. "I never heard of a harder worker in golf or any other sport," Bobby Jones once said of him. He had mastered nearly every shot now except the putt, and that was costing him tournaments.

"I used to feel sorry for the little guy," Jimmy Demaret, the colorful pro, says. "Imagine anybody feeling sorry for Hogan now! I get tired of seeing his rear end and his elbows when he bends down to pick the ball out of the cup. But then it just seemed that he *never* was going to learn to putt."

Nineteen forty was his year. He finished second in his first six tournaments, meanwhile keeping Valerie awake at night as he practiced putting on the rug in their hotel rooms. It had been eight years since he first set out on the tour in 1932. When he finally broke through, winning the Pinehurst North & South Open, he was on his way to greatness. He just kept winning. By the end of the year he was golf's biggest money winner. Again in 1941 and 1942 he was the leading money winner in the country and he was acclaimed the finest golfer in the world.

And then, when he had perfected his marvelous style, the bottom dropped out of his world, just as it did for so many other people. World War II had reached America and Ben was off to join the Air Corps. He returned after the war and regained his peak much more quickly than most of his colleagues did. He was working as hard as ever. At the top of his game in 1947 he was audacious enough to alter his golfing style, having learned to control his hook by fading the ball. And in 1948 he accomplished the unprecedented feat of sweeping the U.S. Open (his first), the Western Open and the PGA tournament.

To win the U.S. Open he had to top a magnificent performance by his old friend Demaret. Jimmy had finished with a score of 278, an all-time low for the Open. "But I knew I didn't have this tournament won," Demaret recalls. "I knew that Hogan was going great, too, and so I sat on the clubhouse veranda to watch him come in. Then I saw him walking down the eighteenth fairway and I knew my goose was cooked. His head was so low he looked like a gopher climbing out of a hole. When Ben walks like that you know there's nothing going to stop him. I just began figuring what I was going to do with my second-place money."

Demaret knew what he was talking about. Ben finished with a new record of 276 and captured the Open title.

He was in a class by himself, but there was always his obsession to improve on perfection. "It takes him three hours to play nine holes in practice," one of his caddies said. "He'll make me drop a dozen or so balls in a sand trap and then he'll go down there and blast every darn one of them out. Then, like as not, he'll knock another dozen out of there."

A reporter once asked Hogan if he ever relaxed on the course. A look of genuine astonishment crossed his face. "Relax? How can anybody relax and play golf? You have to grip the club, don't you?"

Every other golfer in the business realized what Demaret meant when he said that he knew, after one look at Hogan, that he had no chance to win the 1948 Open. A group stood around the fifteenth green at a tournament one day and watched another famous golfer line up a putt. It was a tournament which Hogan had not entered. "Look at that fellow," one of the group said. "He's as cool as can be out there. I even saw him grinning a few minutes ago. But if Hogan was in this tournament you'd see this guy shake when he lit his cigarette. He's got ulcers, and do you know who gave them to him? Ben Hogan."

There was something menacing about Hogan in his prime. He chose his club and strode toward the ball with all the grim purposefulness of an executioner approaching his grisly job. Standing over the ball, his knees loose, his butt out, his toes pointing outward, at a slight angle, he was an extraordinary symbol of the great athlete about to spring into action. That stance foretold the powerful, beautifully coordinated swing and the graceful follow-through. It sprang out inevitably, like the bright spectacular patterns from a Chinese firecracker.

Nineteen forty-nine promised to be another brilliant year for Ben. He began by winning the Bing Crosby Invitational and the Long Beach Open, then lost in a play-off to Demaret at Phoenix. Most of the golfers were pushing on to Tucson, but Ben decided to pass up the tournament there and go home for a brief rest before setting out again in quest of the season's more important prizes. Many of his friends urged him to reconsider and go to Tucson.

"No, I want the rest," he told them. "It isn't the golf that wears you out, it's the traveling. I want to die an old man, not a young one."

Less than twenty-four hours later he lay near death in an El Paso hospital.

It was early in the morning of February 2. Ben and Valerie were driving toward Fort Worth on Highway 80, a straight, flat road which stretched interminably across the desolate west Texas prairie. They drove through an early-morning brightness and frequent patches of thick fog which had descended on them. Then they drove for miles wrapped in the fog, the climbing sun only occasionally showing wanly through the murky wall. Ben switched on his headlights. Sometimes the ghost of a car would take form ahead, become palpable only as it reached them, and then fade again into the fog behind. Ben slowed his car to thirty miles an hour. Peering through the windshield he detected two luminous circles coming toward him. He crept closer to the right side of the road. And then the two circles became four and were right on top of him. Out of the fog rushed a mountain of a bus, passing a six-wheeler truck, and Hogan, kept on the road by the culvert on his right, didn't have a chance in the world.

"I put my head down and dived across Valerie like I was diving into a pool of water."

That reflexive action saved both of their lives. The shuddering impact hurled part of the engine back into the driver's seat and demolished the car. Valerie, suffering cuts and bruises, had been saved by her husband's protecting body. She pulled the crushed little champion from his car. Hogan lay there by the roadside for well over an hour as, in the confusion, each bystander thought the other had called an ambulance.

"I thought he was dying," one witness said later. "He just got grayer and grayer."

Finally an ambulance arrived from the nearby town of Van Horn and carried Hogan to a hospital in El Paso, 119 miles away. There the doctors recorded his more serious injuries: a fractured pelvis, a broken left collarbone, a broken left ankle and a chipped rib. The extent of his internal injuries was not to be realized until a month later.

The blood clot that threatened to choke off his life suddenly developed early in March. It came just at a time when the doctors believed Ben was on the way back to health. Moving up his left leg, the clot appeared headed for his heart. The doctors in El Paso thinned Ben's blood and sent for Dr. Alton S. Ochsner, a famous New Orleans surgeon. Because there was difficulty in arranging the surgeon's air passage from New Orleans to El Paso, Hogan's friends finally had him picked up in an Air Force bomber.

When Ochsner arrived, he found the golfer in critical condition. Hogan's blood count was dangerously low, and the clot seemed deadly. He was immediately given a blood transfusion. In a two-hour abdominal operation, Ochsner tied off the vena cava, a large vein which feeds blood into the right auricle of the heart. There were serious doubts about Ben's survival and one major news service sent out an up-to-date obituary of him, ready to be put into type when the reporters keeping the "death watch" at the hospital flashed the signal.

The obituary's only possible use came a little over a year later when it might have been valuable in throwing together a biography of Hogan in his hour of triumph. From the moment he began to shake off the dulling effects of the operation, Ben was on the road back to the top of the golf world. He seemed not to care, or even be aware, that so many knowledgeable people were saying that he would never again play tournament golf.

Two weeks later he was being wheeled about the hospital's grounds to soak up the warm Texas sun. Soon he was out of the hospital and back in his own home in Fort Worth. There were long hours of massage and then the first halting steps as he learned to walk again. When this obstacle was past, he began taking short walks around his bedroom. Later he jogged up and down on the living-room rug, strengthening the muscles in his legs and at the same time squeezing in his hand a rubber ball in an effort to regain his powerful grip. Finally there were long walks around the block, walks that sometimes stretched out so that a worried Valerie drove through the neighborhood looking for him. And almost everywhere he went he carried with him a golf club, partly because he wanted to get the feel of it in his hands again and partly because he often needed it to rest on. Friends who feared that he was pushing himself too fast invariably got this answer:

"There's no point in just getting up and standing," Ben would tell them. "I've got to walk to get back in shape. I just walk as far as I can and then I lie down and rest."

Nemesis itself must grow weary of pursuing a man like that.

There came inevitably the day when Hogan took his clubs and went out to the golf course. He could play only a few holes and he brought a chair with him so that he could occasionally stop to rest. The damage to his veins had affected the circulation of his blood, and his legs and feet were badly swollen after even the least exertion. And then a curious thing happened. As Ben's strength and stamina returned, so did his marvelous co-ordination. He was amazed to find that, after an eight-month break, his golf game was rapidly returning to what it had been before the accident.

When asked if he planned to go back to competitive golf, Hogan gave his interviewers an honest answer. "There's a good possibility," he said, "but right now I can't say for sure. I'll just have to wait and see how I'm feeling and how my game shapes up. But there's one thing I can say for sure: I'm not going out there and shoot in the eighties."

By then Hogan must have felt fairly certain that he could play golf as well as he ever had. What worried him was the condition of his legs. Would they stand up for a grueling eighteen holes? Or, even worse, the thirty-six holes that he would sometimes have to play in one day? He didn't wait very long to put himself to a test. In January, 1950, less than a year after his accident, Hogan entered the Los Angeles Open. Nobody, of course, expected him to make any kind of a showing. This was just a warmup, a dress rehearsal for the big tournaments of the future. Many of the onlookers believed that Hogan wouldn't even be able to finish the seventy-two-hole tournament over the rugged Riviera Club course.

Then Hogan began to play and it suddenly seemed that he had never been away at all. He almost dominated the field and, on the verge of winning off by himself, he was overhauled on the final day when Slammin' Sammy Snead turned in one of the most brilliant rounds of his career. The two old rivals had finished in a tie. Hogan (or, more accurately, Hogan's legs) weren't quite ready for the extra round of golf required for the play-off, and Snead walked off with the title. Yet this had been a minor miracle. Hogan was back on the tour and he was a threat to every golfer in the land.

"Losing that play-off was one of the best breaks I ever got," Ben said later. "My game had rounded into shape so easily that I was getting cocky about it. I might have begun taking my come-back less seriously. I might have let down."

No one who knows Hogan could take that last remark seri-ously. Whenever he picked up a golf club, the little champion became all business, an attitude which led him into many mis-understandings throughout the great days of his career. Re-porters, fans, even his colleagues in professional golf, were fre-quently irritated by what they considered Hogan's rudeness, aloofness or insatiable greed. In each case the "misunderstanding" could be traced directly to Ben's almost demonic craving for victory—a craving which made him so intent on the course that he often neglected the niceties which the public expects from its heroes.

As the 1950 U.S. Open, the year's biggest tournament, drew closer, Hogan was on better terms with the press than ever before. The writers, aware of the awesome demands he was making on himself, were openly rooting for him to make a suc-cessful comeback and were more than willing to forget their past differences with him. Hogan, too, was ready to bury the hatchet. He had only one complaint. With the Open approaching, he wanted the newspapermen to treat him as a golfer, not as a cripple; he wanted them to write about the tournament, not his aching legs. In reply to one question he snapped:

"It doesn't make any difference how my legs are doing. I'm hurting all over and, damn it, these legs have got to take it just the same as I'm doing."

But whether Ben liked it or not, people were talking about his legs and his courageous attempt to win back the Open title. Add-ing spice to his quest was his impressive showing in the tour-nament at Los Angeles. Though it hardly seemed likely that he could make a serious run at the Open title, his earlier perform-ance had created the notion in people's minds that he would cause some excitement at Ardmore, Pennsylvania, where the Open was to be played. It was a wonderful thought.

The greatest golfers in the country descended on the Merion Country Club at Ardmore on Thursday, June 8, for the start of the 1950 Open. The course was one of the toughest on the entire circuit, with treacherous stretches of rough bordering its narrow fairways. To these natural hazards was added the huge gallery which followed Hogan and clogged the fairways. The weather was unseasonably hot at Ardmore and fans who trouped the entire eighteen holes were weary and soaked with perspiration when they finally made their way back to the clubhouse.

Most of the excitement that first day centered around Lee Mackey, Jr., an obscure young pro from Birmingham, Alabama, who fired an astounding 64. Hogan shot a 72, two over par and good enough to place him well up among the leaders. On Friday Hogan came back with a brilliant 69 to move within two strokes of Dutch Harrison, who had taken over the lead from Mackey. That unfortunate young man, whose record-breaking performance had made him a hero only the day before, shot a dismal 81 and dropped completely out of the running.

Hogan could not be overlooked now, but the odds were against him. The tournament was scheduled to end on Saturday with thirty-six holes of golf, eighteen in the morning and eighteen in the afternoon, to be played under the most excruciating pressure. The murderous par 70 course had already taken its toll of many of the finest golfers in the 165-man field, including Demaret, Snead and Cary Middlecoff. "I'm putting like my doggoned arms is broke," muttered Snead as he walked off the course after one particularly upsetting round.

Nothing seemed to be upsetting Hogan. He played his first eighteen holes that day in 72; another such round would undoubtedly win the title for him. But it had been two years since he had played 36 holes in one day and the heat out there on the course was enough to melt legs that were younger and sounder than his. He started well enough but the thousands of fans who made up his gallery saw that he was wilting. Sixteen months was not time enough to repair the frightful damage. He went one over par on both the fifteenth and the seventeenth holes. By then the word had reached him: Lloyd Mangrum and George Fazio had each finished with a final total of 287. Ben needed a par four on the last hole to tie the two leaders and join them in a play-off on Sunday.

Hogan bowed his neck for a tremendous effort. He drove down the middle of the fairway, a good drive which put him in a favorable position on this dangerous 458-yard hole. His next shot went on the green, and then he was in the cup in two putts for his par four. There would be a play-off on Sunday and Ben Hogan would be in it.

He trudged painfully back to the clubhouse. Mangrum, winner of the 1946 Open, grinned at him. "See you tomorrow, Ben," he said.

Hogan let himself down into a chair. Then he settled back and a faint smile crossed his sweat-streaked face. "Yep, see you tomorrow."

"Tomorrow" was another hot day. Hogan was convinced that he could win the play-off by carding a par. Fazio was not a first-rate golfer and did not figure to offer him the competition he could expect from Mangrum. Lloyd was a gambler, and when his shots were falling right he was as good as anybody. Refreshed by a good night's sleep, the swelling in his legs down again, Hogan was bolstered by the confidence that is part of the make-up of every great champion. At the end of nine holes Hogan and Mangrum were tied with 36 each, while Fazio clung doggedly on with 37.

Now they were on the last nine holes. Hogan took a stroke lead over Mangrum on the tenth, but Lloyd got it back on the eleventh. Then Ben moved ahead again. Fazio finally dropped out of serious contention on the fourteenth and, after fifteen holes, Ben still had his one-stroke lead. And then came an incredible break. On the sixteenth, Mangrum lifted his ball to blow an insect from it. This was a stupendous blunder, a clear violation of the professional golfing rules against picking up a ball. He was penalized two strokes.

When Hogan learned of the incident his face, for the first time during the tournament, broke into a wide grin. Victory, he felt, was now assured, but victory in this tournament meant so much to him that he wanted it without the slightest taint. He wanted to win by more than the two penalty strokes. On the short seventeenth hole he drove his first shot to within fifty feet of the cup. He did not have a clear shot at it, though, for he had to putt over a rise. This was certainly a moment for caution. But Ben refused to "back in" to his title. The long putt, confidently stroked, rolled true to the cup and dropped in. As the spectators roared their approval, the usually stolid Hogan took off his cap, twirled it in his fingers and bowed low to acknowledge their tribute.

That was it. Ben shot a par four on the last hole to finish with a spectacular final round score of 69, four strokes ahead of Mangrum. The little man had come all the way back. As columnist Red Smith wrote the next day: "This was a spiritual victory, an absolute triumph of will."

And who won the *1951* Open? Why, Ben Hogan won that one, too.

BY MEL ALLEN
WITH FRANK GRAHAM, JR.
FROM *It Takes Heart*

THE FREEMASONRY OF GOLF

Golf may be, and is, used by people of every colour, race, creed and temperament, in every climate and all the year round. No recreation, apart from the simplest contests of the river and field, has been so universal since the world began, with the single exception of chess. And wherever and whenever it is played, it extends its benign influence towards the promotion of fast friendship among the players. There is no freemasonry like the freemasonry of golf. To its temples in every land are always welcomed the faithful and earnest craftsman from where'er he came, and he is passed on the signs of the bag and the stance and the little pimpled ball. For it is one of the articles of belief that no man can be a good and enthusiastic golfer of experience and at the same time a thoroughly bad fellow, for at the outset of his

227

career the bad fellow would never be happy in his game. . . . Thus has our happy game of golf wound a bright cordon round the world, and so does she play her part in the great evolution of general contentment.

BY HENRY LEACH

FROM *In Praise of Golf*

THE CHOICE

Hand me that bag in the corner, give me my brassy stout,
For things are running crosswise, and Betty and I are out.

For Betty will brook no rival, and Golf was the love of my youth;
That Betty is madly jealous is the sad and sordid truth.

And my weekly round of the links is the rift within our lute,
And I know she is exacting, and she thinks I am a brute.

Betty is pretty to look on, Betty's a dear and a pet—
But I know I can go round better than ever I've gone round yet.

Betty's a maid of a thousand, and deeply in love am I—
But I'll drive the Dyke from the tee, or ever I come to die.

And Betty has written a letter, to say that our match is off,
Unless I can give to her wholly the love which belongs to Golf.

Now I have been servant to Love for barely a twelvemonth clear,
But Golf has been my mistress a matter of fifteen year.

There is joy in a stolen putt, in the ball picked clean away
From a heavy lie—but the game is dead ere dusk of day;—

Yet the thought of that leary putt is a treasure I always keep,
And the clean-hit second remains to sweeten the hours of sleep.

Give me that club on the sofa, let me consider a while;—
Here is my Favourite Mashie; there is a Wifely Smile.

Betty my wife at fifty, dour and old and grey—
And a thousand new links opened between the Thames and the
    Spey.

Here is my dearest Driver, let me consider anew,
Old Friend—and who is Betty, that I should abandon you?

The sweetest maiden Betty may turn to a shrew or a minx;
And heavy the bonds of Wedlock, but light is the chain of the
    Links.

BY ROBERT K. RISK

FROM Songs of the Links

GOLF IN THE DARK

There is at least one instance of a golf match being played in
the dark. This was on Montrose links, and the players were Lord
Kennedy and a Mr. Cruickshanks. The match, which was one of
three holes, was got up at ten o'clock at night, and one of the

conditions was that it should be played off immediately. Each man's caddie carried a lantern, and a light was placed at the hole, otherwise the match was fought out in the dark. In order that the balls when driven should not be lost, a string of caddies covered the course and traced the balls by the whizzing sound they made in their flight overhead.

BY ROBERT K. RISK

FROM *Songs of the Links*

THE SCRATCH MAN

He stood at the Bar. When in the clubhouse he was never far away—from the Bar. Other members, indifferent players of 10 handicap and over, stood him drinks. Which he drank. He was their good player. Their Pride. Junior members looked on him with awe, and told each other of his feats. And records. The Pro, who, of course, was an Ass, sold them clubs which had belonged to their idol. At fancy prices. They thinking, in their ignorance, that his science had been imparted to the club. Which, as a matter of fact, he had never seen. This being business on the part of the Pro. Who must needs live.

He stood at the Bar. And gave his judgment on problems submitted to him by those below him in handicap. He gave his opinion as to the best ball. Mentioning a make that he knew the Pro was anxious to sell. He having had them in stock a long time. The Pro had given him one to try. And mentioned in an off-hand manner that he wished he could get rid of them. They understood each other. The Scratch Man. And the Pro.

And on the notice-board was the Amateur record for the course. It was his. Signed by the Pro. And beside it was the Pro's record. One stroke less. Signed by a beginner. Who, intent on keeping his eye on the ball, forgot to keep it on the Pro.

The club, like other clubs, played club matches. In their last match, they were handicapped. Their idol sent back word. "Touch of flu, sorry." The best player of the other team was a well-known Amateur. The Scratch Man had never lost a club match. His percentage was 100. He was careful of his average. But he kept the result of one match locked away in his memory. And told no one. But the Pro knew. It happened thus. The links were deserted, save for the Scratch Man. And the Stranger, who was staying in the district. He was sitting in the clubroom when the Scratch Man entered. And, with visions of half-a-crown, invited him to play. But the Stranger had not his clubs. So borrowed some from the Pro. Who looked at him with interest, after he had selected some. And even followed him round, so interested was he. The Scratch Man offered him a handicap, which the Stranger refused. And justified his audacity by smashing him by seven up and six. With borrowed clubs. After he had gone the Scratch Man drank with the Pro. And swore him to silence. And the Pro sold him a club. On the spur of the moment. They never knew the Stranger's name, but *Golfing* was taken in at the clubhouse. Some time afterwards, there, on the front page, was the Stranger. It was the week after the Amateur Championship. And the Pro stuck it up in his shop. This match the Scratch Man never spoke of. But when he came into the shop, and cursed the state of the course, the Pro looked at the Photo. And said nothing. On this occasion Silence was Golden.

The Scratch Man had been Captain, President, and had filled all the offices. When he played, other matches stood aside to let him pass. None dare keep him waiting. But he never thanked them. It was his right as their idol. He stood at the Bar. The Scratch Man.

BY HARRY FULFORD

FROM *Golf's Little Ironies*

231

GALLERY-SHY

He came out from the showers feeling like an old man, feeling like fifty. He wouldn't even be forty for three years. But he was too old for the heat and the course he had fought today; too much of his youth and his fire had been left on the fairways of half a hundred courses around the country.

Spade Gregory was combing his wet hair near the lockers, stooping a little to catch his image on the mirror nailed to a post. Spade was tall and lanky and bony. Where he got his marvelous coordination was a mystery to Barney.

Spade said, "You slipping, Barney-boy?"

"If a 74 is slipping, I am. But this course . . . And then, it's the Open. You know—my jinx."

Spade said nothing to this. He had won the Open twice, long ago, and he knew it was Barney's dream to win it.

Barney said, "I'm a stubborn man. Fifteen years ago, I said I wouldn't quit until I won the Open. This stubbornness can be overdone, I'm beginning to believe."

Spade studied his hair critically. "That heat," he said, "is enough to make me quit, as of today. Why do we do it, Barney? Why don't we sign up with some club, some club without ambitions, and get fat and play in State meets once a year, and raise kids and become solid citizens?"

Barney wanted to say, *because we're following the dream, because we want to fight only the best, because we're not satisfied with the minors.* But all he said was, "You got me, Spade. I've never been able to figure that one out."

Then Spade had left, and Barney was there alone in the locker room. For some reason, he felt lonely. Outside, in the parking lot, Jane would be waiting. For ten years, Jane had always been waiting. Thinking of that, some of his loneliness left him.

Ten years ago, the year they were married, had been Barney's big year. On the Coast and through the grapefruit circuit, and into the big summer meets, he had been unbeatable. They had salted plenty, that first year. Enough to carry them through some of the leaner years. But even that year, he had lost the Open. On the last hole, to a crazy kid who had come up from nowhere, and gone back to where he came from, right after the meet. That had been tough, losing that year.

Ten years ago, his gallery had been immense, wherever he appeared. There had been years since when he'd had a one-person gallery—Jane. This was one of those years.

He went out, and up the steps, through the nearly deserted clubhouse to the parking lot. Jane could have waited in the clubhouse, but she preferred the car, for some reason.

There were six or seven cars in the lot, and one of them was the small tan convertible. He saw the flick of her lighter, and knew she had seen him. She always had a cigarette waiting for him; she always lighted two, as soon as she saw him.

When he opened the door of the convertible, she handed him one. She said, "You looked good out there this afternoon. You looked like you might do it."

He found the stuff for a smile. He considered her gravely, her blue-black, short hair, the incredible blue of her eyes, and that impish grin she always managed, especially on the hot days. He tilted up her chin and kissed her.

"What did I ever do?" he asked. "Why were the gods so kind?"

"You looked good that year," she said. "You looked like you were going to be rich. I hope you don't think it was love?"

"Huh," he said. "You couldn't resist me. I was young and full of beans. It was sheer animal attraction."

He thought, *I was twenty-seven and she was twenty-two, and it was magic; it was part of the dream. And now she's thirty-two and looks sixteen and I'm thirty-seven and feel seventy.*

"It's been a long trail, hasn't it?" he asked.

"It's been fun," she said. "You're just getting old, honey." There was a group of houses, all new, all white, overlooking the course. She kept her eyes on them as they moved by. "Nice," she said.

"Better than hotel rooms," he said.

The low music of her laugh was like an echo in the coupe. "Here it comes, and I'll answer you before you ask. No, I'm not sorry I didn't settle down in Newton Falls. Yes, I'm glad I'm married to a tournament pro. And it's all been fun, every minute of it, even when you lost. Because when you lost, you needed me that much more, and a woman wants to be needed."

"Well," he said, "all right. I guess it's just been a hot day."

"And this is the Open," she added, "and you always tighten up when you come to this one. That's why you blow it. But you'll do all right. You'll get the touch. You started to get it on those last two holes, today."

"You saw that," he said marveling. "I wasn't even sure of it myself."

"You're not analytical," she teased him. "You're all muscle."

"Of course," he said. "I owe it all to Charles Atlas, too."

The coupe moved on through the dusk. There was no further conversation, only the noise from the tappets. Those tappets, Barney reflected, had needed adjusting for a month.

The next morning was no better. The sun was concentrating, it seemed, on the rolling fairways of Puckahoe, giving the Open its personal attention.

Medal play, Barney thought, and that's what hurts. That's where you can't make any mistakes, even little ones. In match play, you can blow up, now and then, and still cop. But medal play keeps the heat on you every second.

He was paired with Ned Avery in a morning round. Ned's gallery and his combined wouldn't have made much more than a big family. But Jane was there, wearing her white playsuit, wearing a big smile, wearing her love like a banner. That was really all the gallery he needed.

The first was a slight dogleg to the right, and his drive had just enough fade to take the turn. He played a three-iron from there, a three that went a little more up than out, but had enough overspin to bounce in front of the green, and roll for the pin. It was a clean, crisp shot.

Ned said, "A birdie you'll settle for. For a minute I thought it would be an eagle. You're looking sharp, boy."

234

It was a two-foot putt, and dropped with a rattle.

As they walked to the second tee, someone from the gallery behind said, "What a man." That would be Jane.

The second was a two-hundred-and-fifteen-yard par three, and he settled for a three. The third was uphill all the way, and he felt it in his legs, for some reason. *Lord,* he thought, *I'm not that old!*

He went on through the third and fourth and fifth, settling for par. He didn't go crazy until the sixth. Five hundred yards a dogleg to the left, with the trees on the left too high for any kind of a shortcut. He played it for a hook, and the hook was there, and when they came down around the bend, they saw the ball had rolled and rolled, as a hooked ball will at times.

His caddie was reaching for a number-four wood, but Barney shook his head. He chose, instead, a two-iron, and reached just a little. He reached all the way to the green with a sweet, straight shot. The way it looked from here, it was a one-putter for sure.

The way it looked is the way it was, and he stroked it home with confidence for an eagle three.

Which set the pattern for the rest of the morning. He couldn't go wrong. He holed out a chip shot, and one-putted almost everything that could be called a putt. In the wonder of it he forgot the sun and the lag in his legs. He almost forgot Jane, back there, in her playsuit.

He came home with a 65, low man.

They had lunch at the clubhouse, just he and Jane and Spade Gregory. Spade had a 68 and was justly proud. Spade said, "The sadistic fiend who laid this torture trail out is turning over in his grave. What'd you do, change your breakfast food?"

"My great skill," Barney said by way of explanation, "and my prodigious strength." He smiled at Jane. "And the faith of my fair wife."

Spade said, "That's the first time I ever saw you smile, once the Open was under way."

And Barney realized that was no jest. And he thought, *I've never won this one, never.* A thought which lived with him through lunch.

Spade said, "Harper posted a 66 and Snead blew up—that

back of his. That Harper would be the guy to beat, I suppose he always is."

"Mr. Golf," Barney said with due reverence. And to Jane, "Let's go out and follow him around this afternoon."

Jane shook her head. "You're going to work with your woods this afternoon, especially the two and three. I saw you reach with that iron this morning."

Spade grinned. He said, "She doesn't miss much, does she?"

"Not much," Barney admitted. And thought, *She hasn't missed much but a home and kids and a normal, reasonable life.* He said, in sudden decision, "If I could get a pro's job, in the right place, this would be my last year on the trail. It's getting too rough for me."

"Amen," said Spade. . . . Jane said nothing, but she looked at him curiously.

After an afternoon on the driving range, they went into town for supper, to a little place they had found. It was there Jane asked, "Did you really mean that—what you said at lunch?"

"About settling down at some club?"

She nodded, her eyes grave and watchful.

"I did."

"Well, Tom Danvers is retiring. I got a letter from Mama today, and she says you could have that job. And the Ramsay house is for sale. Do you remember the Ramsay house?"

Tom Danvers was the pro at the Newton Falls Country Club. And Barney remembered the Ramsay house. It was about a block from Jane's home. He asked, "How many bundles of hay do we have in the bank?"

"Not much," she said. "Second or third place would do it, though, with what we have."

He knew what all this meant to her. But he said, "Have you forgotten that 65 I just carded? Are you belittling me?"

"You're second right now," she said. "You could almost bank on coming home in the first three. Winning isn't the only thing, you know."

This sacrilege he couldn't fathom. He said, "Why did you get out the whip, then? Why did you make me work on those woods, this hot day?"

236

"So you could give it all you had. So you could put all your heart and all your skill and all your knowledge into playing your best. That's what's important, not winning."

"You sound like an editorial for *American Youth*," he said.

"I'm right, though, aren't I, honey?"

"Yes," he admitted honestly, "you are. I've enjoyed a lot of tournaments I haven't won. I've enjoyed knowing the boys, and watching them. And I've won my share."

"And this morning," she informed him, "whether you know it or not, you set a new course record."

He stared at her. "I did? Nobody told me that."

"Well, you did. And the rest is a breeze. The rest will be a cinch for a money spot."

Thirty-six holes, he thought, and that sun. Thirty-six holes tomorrow on that heart-breaking layout. A breeze? Figuring just for a money spot, yes. Figuring a home and a pro's job at a friendly club in Jane's home town, sure. Why not? Why beat his brains out for the ego satisfaction of being top dog? Just his best, that's all they were paying for, just all he had.

They went to a movie that night. This was something he had never before been able to do on a night before the last thirty-six holes. It was a funny movie, and he laughed without reservation, and felt about seventeen years old. Just a year older than Jane looked.

He bought a paper after the show, and read about himself and the new course record he had set, and felt warmly happy. On that course, a 65 . . . He'd done that, at his age.

He slept the sleep of the innocent. . . .

In the morning, he and Jane drove out to the club for breakfast. He ate well. He wasn't tight, or nervous or tired. But he was hot. But then, everybody was hot. Even Mr. Golf, Texas man that he was, would be warm today.

Mr. Golf hadn't done so well his first round, but he had beaten Barney by three strokes. So that meant the unbeatable Texan was two strokes up on him right now, at the halfway mark. But the rest of the field had been licked by the sun. Barney held down the second spot with a three-stroke edge.

Barney thought, *If I could really get hot* . . . But, no, the three spot, the two spot. He'd settle for that. He'd settle for the Ramsay home in Newton Falls, and the years ahead with Jane.

Overhead, the glaring sun made its plans for the day. They hadn't seen anything yet, those mortals below, chasing that silly ball over the hills. They hadn't seen *anything*.

Spade came over to their table. He said, "You're lucky. You and I and Ned Avery are going to go around together from here in. You're both going to have the rapture of my wit and wisdom."

"I can hardly wait," Barney said. But he felt happy about it.

"Tell him about our house," Jane said. "Tell him about the back porch, where we're going to sit nights, drinking beer. Tell him about the gleaming kitchen and the picket fence. Tell him about us."

Spade said, "That sounds like it's for me, too. Where is this heaven?"

"In Newton Falls," Jane said. "That's in Ohio. That's a mighty nice town. It's my town."

"It must be a nice town, then."

Little Ben Hogan stopped, on his way by. "You looked like a champ there, yesterday morning, Barney boy."

Barney smiled. "I was—yesterday morning. Every dog has his day, or anyway, his morning."

Ben said, "Next year should be your year, Barney." He walked on.

Spade said, "And those weren't empty words. You'll make a mint next year."

"This is my last year," Barney said, and there was a silence. Spade, for once, had no words. Jane sniffed.

Then they went out into the furnace of the day.

There was a gallery this morning. Spade was always a colorful player, but it wasn't only Spade who brought them. They wanted a look at this young-old man who had shot a 65 on this layout—the trickiest, nastiest course in the country.

Spade said, "Take a bow, miracle man. Give them a smile."

Barney said, "I'll settle for a 75, this round."

"Stay with me," Spade said, "and wear diamonds."

Spade then stepped up, and hit one. He was all bone and four inches more than six feet tall. He looked like a well-dressed scarecrow, and he wound up like a dervish.

But when he unwound, it was all there, all at the moment of impact, and the ball went out low, fast, and climbing only a little. Then it dropped, and it was a drive to end all drives.

The murmur rose in the gallery, and Spade turned and bowed gravely. "Ain't I marvelous?" he whispered to Barney. "How *do* I *do* it?"

Barney chuckled. "You've got me."

Barney didn't try to match it. He wasn't playing for blood today. He smacked a clean one out there, a low ball with a lot of overspin, and it kept rolling. It rolled and rolled and was only about twenty yards short of Spade's, just around the bend.

Ned's matched Barney's.

The sun burned down, working at its job, concentrating, being antisocial.

Barney took a four iron, and laid the ball up on the green, but high. Ned's was short of the green.

Spade took a six iron, and lofted one. It went up and up, reaching. It continued to go, as if it had some power of its own and dropped on the green, only inches from the pin.

Spade said, "My touch must be off. I should have dropped that one."

"You'll probably miss the putt," Barney said.

When they got to the green, they saw it wasn't a putt that could be missed. It was about three inches from the cup. Ned chipped up for an eight-foot putt, and then Barney studied his.

It was downhill. It had a side slope to contend with, and it was a good twenty-five feet. Barney should have tightened up, but Spade was smiling like a cat-eating canary, and Barney couldn't tighten up with Spade around. They'd heckled each other too often.

Barney studied it carefully, then went over and stroked it boldly.

The early speed wasn't much. For a moment, Barney feared it wasn't enough. But the green was fast. The ball hesitated on the edge a split second—then dropped for the birdie.

Ned put his home, in his careful way, for a par. Spade nudged his in and shook his head.

Barney said, "Something wrong?"

"Something wrong? No, no, no—I play perfect golf, and you

239

slop a twenty-five foot putt in. You trying to make me look bad in front of all these people?"

"Slop," Barney said. "Skill like that, iron nerves like that—and you call it slop!"

They went on after the first, halving them all, right up to the sixteenth. Barney felt no pressure; he played each shot the way he thought it should be played, and caution never haunted him. Spade kept up a running fire of comment; Spade helped him to almost forget the sun.

For sixteen holes, they shared sixties. Ned had a 63.

On the seventeenth tee, Barney looked at Spade. "We're playing some golf," he said. "We might be doing all right. You know that?"

"I always play a lot of golf," Spade said, "but I haven't done all right for years."

Barney thought, I can do it, maybe. I can still win this one. Unless somebody's gone crazy, I'm well up there. If Harper should crack, if the heat . . . But Mr. Golf wasn't one to crack, either under heat or the fire of competition.

Barney felt the old Open jitters coming, and he fought it. When he moved up to take his stance, he looked over to see Jane in the forefront of the gallery. Her smile looked a little weak.

His backswing wasn't smooth, and when he brought the club back, it came down on an inside arc. The ball started out in a straight line, but when the slice came, it was horrible. It was something right out of a dub's nightmare.

There was murmur in the gallery as the ball soared into the tangled underbrush to the right of the fairway.

There was no chatter, this time, as they walked down. Barney's caddie was already in the jungle, and he had found the ball by the time Barney got there.

There was a chance; it wasn't completely hopeless. The ball was clear enough, in the center of a glade. But there were saplings all around, to catch a high ball. The underbrush prevented any attempt at a straight shot.

Barney spent some time on it. He would need immediate loft, with a clean shot. He would need a hell of a lot of luck.

He took an eight iron, and played it for the angle, for the

240

maximum distance that would still bring him clear of the rough. He played it like a man making the most of a bad situation, not like a man who was afraid he was going to blow the tournament. It soared, cleared the saplings, and headed greenward.

Barney's tenseness melted a little.

When they came back to civilization, they saw it had stopped right on the edge of the fairway, some two hundred or more yards from the green.

He walked up with Spade. Spade had put two clean shots together, and his ball was reposing gracefully on the green. In two.

"I can still take you on this one," Barney said.

"You should live so long," said Spade.

Barney selected a four wood, and played it well, played it with a small prayer. It went out on a gradual incline and then soared. It dropped on the green, bounced twice, and died.

Both Barney and Spade two-putted that green, Barney for the bogie, and Spade for the par.

Which gave him a 65, with the eighteenth still to go.

The eighteenth was a long par four, but straight. Spade's drive went out in the Spade fashion, looking as if it could conceivably travel around the world, unless something got in the way. Ned's drive was straight and true, but not long.

Now would be the time to hit one, Barney thought, so he went up and hit one. It wasn't as long as Spade's, but it was the longest drive he had hit for years.

Ned's spoon shot was clean and careful and true.

Barney's iron shot was clean and not careful and something more than true. It went up and out, and came to rest a few feet from the cup. Which would give him a 3, which would give him a 68 for this morning's round.

Spade put too much into his second, and the ball disappeared into the underbrush behind the green.

Barney looked at him in dismay, but Spade was laughing. Spade said, "Those damned Wheaties. I knew I shouldn't have taken that second bowl this morning."

"Look," Barney said, "you're still in this tournament. That could be a money shot, right there."

Spade shrugged. "All I've got is my best. That was my best, at the moment."

The ball hadn't, as a matter of fact, gone into the underbrush. It had gone beyond, on the short grass near the drive.

Spade lofted it up, over the brush, and the ball rolled in an arching curve onto the green. It continued to roll to within two feet of the cup. Which gave Spade the par. Ned two-putted for his par, and Barney's birdie was a cinch.

Applause spattered through the gallery, and Jane came out to walk between Spade and Barney.

"Nice golf," Jane said. "I'd say 68 is very fine for a couple of relics like you two."

"I wonder what Harper did," Barney said.

"What difference does it make?" Jane asked. "You're not fighting Harper. Harper's got a home—in Texas. Mr. Golf isn't settling for a 68—you can be sure of that."

"Huh," said Spade. "Will you listen to the girl? You working for the F.H.A. or something? Maybe you think Harper's a spring chicken? Why this fine scorn?"

"I just don't want you boys to break your hearts," Jane said. "Now run and take your showers, and we'll go into town for lunch."

Barney didn't realize how tired he was until he got into a warm shower. He kept thinking of Spade's words about age. And he realized, for the first time, that all of them were old, all the top men were as old as he and Spade. Some were older.

Spade said, "You're looking thoughtful. You're looking unnatural."

"I was thinking," Barney said, "that a man's as old as he feels."

"What a profound and original observation," Spade jeered. "Did you think it up all alone?"

Barney threw his soap at him.

Spade ducked, and said, "Who do you think is in third place?"

"I haven't seen it. Who is?"

"Me," Spade said proudly. "Tied with Hogan, I am. And where do you think I'll be when I blast you out of the picture this afternoon? How do you think I'll look, in the pictures, congratulating Harper?"

"No uglier than usual," Barney said. "I'm glad it's just you I've got to beat. That I can do."

Barney did some rapid computing in his mind. "You took a 74 that first round, too, then. You didn't tell me that, in the locker room that night. You didn't look to me like a guy who'd taken a 74."

"What should I do, wear mourning? It wasn't a funeral, just another game of golf."

Barney stepped out of the shower. Just another game of golf. From the time he was fourteen, he had played lots of games of golf. When he settled down in Newton Falls, in the Ramsay house with the cool back porch, there would still be lots of golf ahead of him. It was a game. He had been making a disease out of it.

He and Spade went up the steps together, presently, and Barney headed for the bulletin board.

But Jane stopped him on the way. She had a sheet of paper in her hand. "I've got it all right here," she said. "Let's get into town. We'll never get a table if we don't hurry."

They could eat here, Barney reflected. There were some vacant tables in the pros' section. But Jane liked that little restaurant in town. The three of them walked to the coupe, as Jane gave them the story.

Harper had carded another 66. That was the first news. That gave him four strokes on Barney. That made it a cinch. With eighteen holes to go, nobody was going to pick up four strokes on Harper.

Hogan was tied with Spade at 210. Barney's 207 looked good for second. With any kind of a break at all, it was a sure second, and Barney said as much.

Spade was grinning. "Wouldn't you settle for third? You won't let it break your heart if I should make a monkey out of you this afternoon?"

Jane reached into her purse. "I've got five dollars that says Barney will beat you by two strokes, for the eighteen."

"Taken," said Spade promptly. "That boy's good, but not *that* good—not today," He handed her a five.

It was cool in the restaurant, and the food was good, and they enjoyed it too much. Spade said finally, "Holy cow! We're overdue, right this minute. Let's get logging."

They went out into the cloudless heat, and piled into the coupe. Barney made it boil, going back. When they came within view of the first tee, they saw the caddies already out there, and Ned Avery waiting. But there had been some delay in the afternoon's schedule, so they were on time. By about two minutes.

"Well," Barney said, "I can't win this one, not any more. But I can win that five dollars for Jane. That'll be some consolation." Fifteen years of tournament golf, and he'd never won the Open. And this was his last year. His decision was final, on that.

"You'll need to work," Spade said. "Five bucks is a lot of hay. I can play some golf, for that kind of money."

Then the first tee was clear, and they walked out. The gallery seemed to be even bigger than this morning's. Barney couldn't figure that out. Harper and Hogan were already on the course. They should have the big gallery.

He saw Jane talking to one of the officials as he went up to tee off. Spade was whispering something to Ned Avery. Then he forgot all that and concentrated on the job at hand.

Barney could feel, at the moment of impact, that this was going to be a drive. That clean click was there, and he was loose and confident. Everything felt right.

It was a drive. It was better than Spade's drive on the same hole this morning. And better than Spade's drive on the same hole that afternoon.

Ned chuckled. "You'll break his heart. Don't beat him at his own game."

Barney didn't beat Spade at his own game. Not after that first drive. Spade went back to his superiority there, and Barney made it up with the fairway woods, with his irons. On the greens, they were evenly matched that afternoon.

They halved hole after hole. They picked up birdies on the first, and fifth and the eighth. The gallery grew and grew, and Barney began to wonder. The sun came back, to make a last gallant stand.

Barney kept his hands dry, and tried to forget the ache in his legs, the perspiration that ran in rivulets down his legs and chest and back. He tried to forget everything but keeping up with Spade.

Spade was making that a job of work. He had never been better than he was that afternoon. They finished the outgoing nine with a very classy pair of 33's.

Ned said, on the tenth tee, "You boys are sweet today. You boys are in there." He shook his head. "If I was your age . . ."

Barney stared at him. "Our age? How old are you?"

"Forty-six," Ned said, "last month. I shouldn't be here on a day like this. But I can't quit . . ."

They were near the clubhouse now, and more fans came over to join the already mammoth gallery.

Barney said to Spade, "What's happening? Did Harper blow up, or something?"

"They come to see me," Spade said. "There might be better golfers on this course, but how many of them have my looks?"

They went on. Through the tenth and eleventh, through the twelfth. And now there was a gallery on the tees, and waiting at the greens, and it looked as if every fan at the meet must be following them.

They picked up a birdie on the thirteenth. On the fourteenth, Spade and Ned were down in par, but Barney had a birdie three.

That advantage he maintained, right up to the last tee. There he said, "You'd better be hot, Spade, my boy, on this one. It's five bucks, if I can take this one."

"A little more than that," Spade said, and his voice was grave. "You're five under par right now. Harper shot a 68 this last round. I just learned that. Harper's got a 275. Par on this one, and the meet's yours."

"With a 66 this morning? You crazy? How could he have a 275?"

"With a 70 this morning," Spade corrected him. "Jane just didn't want you to tighten up. I'm telling you this now, because if you tighten up, you shouldn't win. If you muff this one, you deserve being second best. You and Harper started even this afternoon."

The dream, Barney thought. Just a four—that's all he needed. A four to cop and a bogie to tie. This was the time to play some real golf.

That's why they'd been late coming from lunch. That's why Jane hadn't let him get to the bulletin board and why they hadn't eaten at the clubhouse. That much they'd done for him.

But now the chips were down, and they'd see if he was a champ or not. Now would be the real, the important test.

He looked up and thumbed his nose at the sun, and the gallery tittered. He took his stance, and didn't fuss with it. No waggle, just a hipbreak, and the clubhead moving smoothly back, and the down-swing in the arc, in the groove.

A clean impact, and a clean shot, straight and reaching, with overspin. Combined with the hard fairway, a fine drive.

Spade's was better, but off the tee nobody was going to be able to beat Spade.

Ned played his second, and Barney came up to his. It was far short of his morning's drive. It was a shot for a wood, if he could loft a wood enough. Without the loft, a wood would be too much, and he remembered that there was shrubbery behind that tee.

He took a four wood from the caddie. Again, he didn't fuss with it. He took some turf along, and the ball went soaring, high into the brightness of the sky. It could be short, too short, not . . .

It was the most accurate wood he had played in the last three days. It was a one-putter for sure. It was the tournament.

Spade said, "That's the way to play them, young fellow. You deserve to win this one."

As they moved up to the green, the gallery was noisy, and he was sure he heard Jane's voice. He looked around and saw her. She was trying to hide her excitement, and not doing too well at it. Her fingers were crossed behind her.

The rest he didn't remember too well.

Ned came home in four, and Spade, too, and the one-putt was exactly that.

Then Harper was shaking his hand and grinning, losing the same way he won, with a smile. Hogan said, "You're too much for us, Barney-boy."

Spade had copped third, Hogan fourth.

Then Jane was there, and in his arms, and the gallery applauded mightily.

The shower room was a haven. In the locker room, there was

some hilarity, but the shower room was comparatively quiet. He managed to sneak out after he'd dressed. There'd be a dance tonight. He'd see the rest of them then.

He went out to the parking lot, and the coupe was there. He saw the flare of Jane's lighter.

When he opened the door, she handed him his cigarette. Her voice sounded choked as she said, "Hello. Hello, Champ."

He closed the door, and kissed her. "You lie very well," he said.

"There was some more," she told him. "Some other lies, too."

"About the pro at Newton Falls? About the Ramsay house?"

She nodded humbly, her eyes on his face. "I wanted to take the heat off you. I knew you could do it, if you forgot about winning. Was I cruel, Barney?"

"To yourself," he said. "That's what you've wanted through it all, isn't it? Just a home, and a place to settle down?"

"No," she said, but there was no conviction in her words. "I wanted to be with you, no matter where you were. The rest didn't matter. You'll be all right next year. You'll be back at the top."

"Sure, if I wanted to be. But I'll tell you something. It isn't important enough. I'd rather just be with you. If it isn't Newton Falls, it'll be somewhere else. I guess the Open medalist can get a job at some club. And there are lots of white houses with picket fences and cool back porches and gleaming kitchens."

He could see by the expression in those blue eyes that he was saying what she wanted to hear, what she'd waited to hear. He said, "Let's get something cool to drink. Let's go to town."

The coupe went down the drive, with the tappets clicking. In Newton Falls, or wherever they settled, Barney told himself, he would have those tappets adjusted.

BY WILLIAM CAMPBELL GAULT
FROM *The Argosy Book of Sports Stories*

ADVICE TO BEGINNERS

Do not, as is most often done, begin your first two or three attempts at striking the ball with a cleek. Begin with a short stiff wooden club—for two reasons: the mode of striking the ball is not quite the same with an iron club as with a wooden one, and with an iron club an unskilful player is more likely to cut fids of turf—*golfice,* "divots"—out of the green. This will by no means conduce to your popularity with the other players on that green. If even with your wooden club, you should cut up turf, be careful to replace it. Golf is not agriculture.

BY HORACE HUTCHINSON
FROM *Hints on the Game of Golf*

Golf consists in striking a small ball of some hard material into a series of holes—generally 18 in number—with a variety of wooden and iron-headed clubs, which experience has proved to be the best adapted to the purpose.

BY H. RIDER HAGGARD
"Definition of Golf" FROM *Golf Illustrated*

"To break clubs over one's knees is a sign of weakness," declares a psychologist. The really strong-minded golfer breaks them over his caddie's back.

FROM South African Golfer

Golf increases the blood pressure, ruins the disposition, spoils the digestion, induces neurasthenia, hurts the eyes, callouses the hands, ties kinks in the nervous system, debauches the morals, drives men to drink or homicide, breaks up the family, turns ductless glands into internal warts, corrodes the pneumogastric nerve, breaks off the edges of the vertebrae, induces spinal meningitis and progressive mendacity, and starts angina pectoris. It's foolish, but it's fun!

BY DR. A. S. LAMB

FROM Golf Illustrated

THE UNOFFICIAL KING OF SCOTLAND

St. Andrews—The tumult and the shouting have died. Some of the captains and the kings may have departed. The long, slow twilight is gray over the Firth, and the turf of the Old Course shows gray in the foreground. The British Open Golf Championship of 1927 is over. And Bobby Jones is champion again. "The unofficial king of Scotland," an unusually unphlegmatic British golf writer has just called him, "for golf is the king of sports in Scotland, and Bobby Jones is king of golf."

Big Bob, his daddy, had just confessed to me that he could not follow Bobby in that last round. So I confessed to Big Bob that I did not intend to, myself. Bobby was starting with a lead of four strokes over the field. My idea was to go out and see him well started, and then drop back and see how his closest rivals were faring. But he did not start well. His par 4 at the first hole was followed by two distressing 5's then another 4 and then a 5 at the long fifth. And he was three above 4's—blowing a great lead; and I couldn't quit him.

He started the Loop badly enough, with a 4 at the short eighth; and if you're going to do any scoring at St. Andrews, you'll score in the Loop.

But that missed putt, of a scant yard at the eighth, was the spur that roweled the greatest competitor of them all into final action. Bobby arose in his might, and he took that Loop by its tail, and he jolly well twisted four consecutive 3's out of it, all but one of them birdies.

And that championship was settled as a champion should settle such matters. In a spin of six holes Bobby had gone from three strokes above 4's to two below. . . .

"That was what laid me low," Big Bob told me later. "I couldn't follow him, and the last news I had was from the fifth green. Three over. Bad enough—worse than that. So I was hanging around the seventeenth green, waiting for the army to charge, and somebody poked me in the ribs."

This was Stewart Maiden, Bobby's teacher. I gather from Big Bob's ornate language that Stewart was profoundly affected.

"His features were still there," said Big Bob, "but the expression had departed."

Stewart said:

"It's all over. Let's go."

This sounded to Big Bob like the trump of doom.

He said:

"What's all over?"

"The show," said the Silent Scot. "He's in."

They made for the hotel, ahead of the thundering herd—twenty-five thousand golfing maniacs charging down the seventeenth fairway. Big Bob rallied by the home green. He felt he might endure to watch the finish—if Bobby really was half a dozen strokes in the lead, as reported.

It was there I found Big Bob. I had escaped the thundering herd without being gored or even much trampled. I assisted him to watch the finish. That is, being a good bit taller, I peered over thousands of bobbing heads and reported progress.

Bobby hit a huge drive from the last tee of the long grind; 250 yards at the least, the ball stopping precisely in the center of the paved road which crosses the fairway, 110 yards from the green.

An ugly peril popped up and danced like a little demon about the home green where old Andrew Kirkaldy stood in majestic pomp by the last flag. Struck the merest shade away from an infinitesimal point of precisions, the ball from that paved surface would go flying over the green and the crowd and into a welter of press tents and railings, whence almost anything in the way of precious strokes might be lost. And in front of the home green dipped that famous swale known as the Valley of Sin—damnation of so many scores and championship aspirations.

Bobby chose his niblick and considered the pitch carefully. He stood to the ball in a breathing silence over which swung the slow roll of the surf from the North Sea; and it seemed that somewhere, a long way off, I could hear a bell ringing.

Bobby swung, and the blade rang on the pavement. But the ball was gone. Up it came, the gallery racing in pursuit. Down it came lightly, at the front of the big green; balanced, hung for an instant, and rolled slowly back into the Valley of Sin.

I told Big Bob. He moaned feebly; a bit profanely.

"It's a hell of a putt from there," he said. "I've tried it!"

Bobby again took his time, over the trickiest putt on any golf course in the world. . . . Up came the call, rolling, rolling. . . . A long gasp from the gallery; then a roar. It was hanging on the edge—dead for the par 4, and the championship.

Bobby walked up out of the Valley of Sin, and his face was gray under the sunburn, and his eyes looked an inch deep in his head. But he had an oddly contented look. He holed the tiny putt, and the gallery charged in. . . . Under the roar I heard somebody saying that the eighteenth green would be in a hell of a shape for the other competitors. I think it was Big Bob. But I do not think he knew he said it.

Six strokes ahead of the field. The lowest score, by six strokes, ever returned in a British open championship. Bobby had won, at St. Andrews.

Six big Scottish policemen finally got him down from the shoulders of that Scottish crowd, and opened a sort of way to the door of the Grand Hotel, fifty yards from the last green. And every foot of the way men and women and boys and girls were fighting to get near enough to touch him—to give him an affectionate pat on the stained old sweat-shirt in which he had played the tournament. And they said, over and over, "Good boy, Bobby! Good boy, Bobby!"

At the entrance to the Grand Hotel stood Big Bob. When Bobby got that far, he looked up suddenly, as if waking, and said, "Hello, Dad!"

Big Bob said nothing. He held out his arms and took Bobby into them, and kissed him, just as he used to when a tired little boy in rompers came home at dusk from a long afternoon on the old course at East Lake.

Twenty thousand men and women and children were cheering Bobby, this time. But he was just a tired little boy, to his dad.

BY O. B. KEELER

FROM *The Atlanta Journal*

When I have a match to play I begin to relax as soon as I awaken. Everything I do slow and easy. That goes for stroking the razor, getting dressed and eating breakfast. I'm practically slow motion.

By the time I am ready to tee off I am so used to taking my time that it's impossible to hurry my swing.

BY WALTER HAGEN

A Golf Course is an out-door insane asylum peopled with madmen suffering from the delusion that they WILL finally master the Game.

BY ROBERT H. DAVIS

That little ball won't move until you hit it, and there's nothing you can do for it after it has gone.

BY BABE ZAHARIAS

FROM *Championship Golf*

The two easiest shots in golf are the fourth putt and the explosion shot off the tee.

BY RING LARDNER

There is no mystery about golf, on every tee there is a marker telling you how many strokes to take to the next hole.

ANONYMOUS

DORMIE ONE

It was five o'clock and rapidly shading into dusk. The September sun, which earlier had set the air to simmering in tremulous heat-waves, now moved reluctant to ambush behind the hills, and, as though sullen at the exigency of its time, gave warning by its bloodshot eye of pitiless heat to be renewed with tomorrow's dawn. From the curving line of trees—thin elms and maples, bordering upon the hard-packed road—long, soothing shadows edged out into the fresh green of the fairway, measuring with their deeper green the flight of hours and peaceful ebbing of the afternoon.

From the distant Sound, a transient breeze, shy as a maiden in the manner of its coming, ventured out from the protection of the ridge, hesitated, wavered, and passed across the sward so fleetingly that almost before it seemed assured a fact, it was a memory.

Then, from the trees at the roadside, and from the trees beyond, and from the little brook dawdling along from east to west, and from the reeded lake far over to the right, a breath of evening crept out upon the lawns, and there was silence.

In a squared clearing at the southern end of the sinuous line of maples there was a trim plateau, close-shorn of grass, and sharply defined by boundaries of sedge and stubble. From this spot forward an expansive belt of untrimmed land stretched northward for a hundred yards, to merge presently with the more aristocratic turf of the fairway. Thereafter, narrowing between the trees and along alignment of arid pits, the trail of adventure ran through rolling country, skirted a grove of locusts, dipped down to ford the brook, climbed past a pair of shallow trenches which glistened with coarse sand, and finally found refuge on a terraced green, protected by towering chestnuts and flanked by the arm of a colonial house which rested comfortably beneath the trees.

From clearing to terrace the crow, flying as crows are popularly supposed to fly, would have accomplished five hundred and twenty yards. It was the eighteenth hole at Kenilworth.

The trim plateau, which was the eighteenth tee, now marked the apex of a human letter, a V of which a thousand men and women formed each stroke. Converging sharply toward that rectangle in the sedge, two thousand men and women—twin lines of white, slashed here and there with vivid, burning color—restrained and held in check by twisted ropes, leaned out and gaped and wondered, breathless; now standing hushed by things already seen, now vibrant to the future, uneasy, murmuring. And as in recompense for toiling through the humid afternoon, two thousand men and women held this privilege: to stand, and wait, and watch until a boy—a sturdy, laughing boy—and then a man —a grayed and quiet man—played, stroke by stroke, the eighteenth hole at Kenilworth.

And silhouetted in the background, nervous on the tee, stood man and boy, paired finalists for the Amateur Championship; two wizards of the links whose faces had gone rigid, whose palms were suddenly wet and cold, whose souls were newly strung upon the natural laws which govern flying objects. Each of them had reason for his agitation; their mutual loss of equilibrium was mutual in its cause; for of these two, the man—Hargrave the present champion—was dormie one.

He was fifty-five; in commercial life he had known bankruptcy at forty. Golf, which had been heretofore diversion, he made the solace of his penury; it had then constituted itself his religion. Within a decade he had snatched the national title for his keepsake; subsequently he had lost it, struggled for it desperately, regained and twice defended it. The gold medal meant infinitely more to him than a mere visible token of success at golf; it was suggestive of success elsewhere; it was the embodiment of conquests he had never made, of victories he never might accomplish. In other years wealth had eluded him, power had been alien to him, social distinction was to be classed among the possibilities; but when he stepped morosely out upon the course, he vaunted in his heart that he was highborn to the purple.

Granted that he was poor indeed in purse, he knew no multimillionaire in all the world who could undertake to meet him on equal terms; he could concede six strokes, and still administer a beating, to the finest gentleman and the finest golfer in the Social Register. And so, while golf was his theology, and the arbitrary standard of par his creed, he played the Scottish game as though it symbolized the life he had proved incapable of mastering—and he mastered the game instead. It was his single virtue; it was the hyphen which allied him to the rest of civilization.

To win was the wine of his existence; to surmount obstacles was the evidence of his regeneration; to come from behind, to turn impeding downfall into disconcerting triumph, was his acrid compensation for the days and months and years when the man in him had cried out for recognition, and the weakling in him had earned his failure. And he was dormie one—and it was Stoddard's honor at the last hole.

The man stiffened perceptibly as Stoddard, nodding to the referee, took a pinch of sand from the box, and teed for the final drive. Then, in accordance with the grimmest of his grim theories of golf, he abruptly turned his back on his opponent, and stared fixedly at the ground. He had trained himself to this practice for two unrelated reasons: the moral effect upon his adversary, and the opportunity to detach himself from the mechanics of his surroundings and to visualize himself in the act of playing his next stroke.

Habitually he conjured up a vision of the ball, the club, himself in the address, the swing, the attack, the aftermath. He compelled his faculties to rivet upon a superb ideal. And it was largely by virtue of this preliminary concentration that he was enabled to bring off his shots with such startling absence of delay: the orders were transmitted to his muscles in advance; his swing was often started when, to the open-mouthed observer, he had hardly reached the ball. And it was by virtue of his utter disregard of his opponent that he was never discouraged, never unnerved, never disheartened. He was neither cheered by the disaster of the enemy, nor cast down by the enemy's good fortune. He was contemptuous not only of the personality of the opponent, but also of his entity. He played his own game, and his best game, ironically, ignoring the fact that it was competitive. To all intents and purposes, Hargrave in contest was the only man on the course; he even disregarded his caddy, and expected the proper club, as he demanded it, to be placed in his hand extended backwards.

But as he now formally prepared to shut Stoddard out of his consciousness, and as he exerted his stern determination to picture himself in yet another perfect illustration of golfing form, he discovered that his will, though resolute, was curiously languid. It missed of its usual persistence. The ideal came and went, as though reflected on a motion film at lowered speed. There was no continuity; there was no welding of motor impulses. According to his theory, Hargrave should have been purely mechanical. On the contrary, he was thinking.

He entertained no sense of actual antagonism toward Stoddard. Indeed, from the inception of the finals, at ten o'clock this morning, the boy had shown himself considerate and generous, quick of applause and slow of alibi, a dashing, brilliant, dangerous golfer with the fire of an adventurer and the grace of a cavalier. He was confident, yet modest, and he had performed a score of feats for which his modesty was none of that inverted conceit of mediocrity in luck, but literal modesty, sheer lack of self-aggrandizement. He was dogged while he smiled; he was still smiling with his lips when his eyes betrayed his chastened mood; and the smile faded and vanished only when he saw that Hargrave was in difficulty. The gallery, nine-tenths of it, was with him boisterously. The gallery was frankly on the side of youth and spontaneity. The mass, unresponsive to the neutral tints of Hargrave's character, thrilled to the juvenile star ascendant.

The gray-haired champion, introspective on the tee, frowned and grimaced, and toyed with his dreadnaught driver. Early in the morning he had confessed guiltily to himself that Stoddard was the sort of lad he should have liked to call his son. And yet he knew that if he had ever married, if he had ever glowed to the possession of an heir, the boy couldn't conceivably have been in the least like Stoddard. Too many generations forbade the miracle. The mold of ancestry would have stamped out another failure, another charge upon the good opinion of the world. The child would have been the father of the man. And Stoddard—witness his behavior and his generosity—was of no varnished metal. He was without alloy. He was a gentleman because his great-grandfathers had been gentlemen. He was rich because they had made him so. But Hargrave had allowed himself to experience an anomalous and paternal emotion toward Stoddard—Stoddard who at twenty was higher in rank, higher in quality, higher in the affection of the people than Hargrave at fifty-five. He had nourished this emotion by trying to imagine what he could have made of himself if, at his majority, he had been of the type of Stoddard.

And now, recalling this quondam sentiment, he shuddered in a spasm of self-pity; and simultaneously, in one of those racking bursts of humanity which come to men unloving and unloved, he longed to whirl about, to stride toward Stoddard, to grip his hand and say—well, one of the common platitudes. "May the best man win"—something of that sort; anything to show that he, too, was living rapidly in the crisis.

In another moment he might have yielded; he might have bridged the fearful chasm of self-imposed restraint. But he was slothful to the impulse. Behind him there was the sharp, pistol-like crack of a clean and powerful drive; and before him, brought clear by reflex and by the will that had been lagging, the ghostly mirage of a ball, and of himself swinging steadily and hard, and of the joy of impact, and a tremendous carry and run, true to the flag. The champion had remembered that he was dormie one. A voice, low but distinct, came to him through a volume of in-coherent sound: "Mr. Hargrave!"

The man turned slowly. He saw neither the referee, who had spoken to him, nor Stoddard, who had stepped aside; he saw no caddies; he saw no fairway. Both lines of the V were weaving, undulating; on the faces of the men and women nearest him he perceived beatific, partisan delight. The thousand-tongued shout which had gone up in praise of Stoddard was dwindling by de-grees to a pleasant hum. He knew, as he had known for hours, how earnestly the public hoped for his defeat. He knew that if he bettered Stoddard's drive his sole reward would be a trifling rip-ple of applause, smirched by a universal prayer that ineptly he might spoil his second shot.

He grinned sardonically at the throng. He rubbed his palms together, drying them. He teed a ball, and took his stance; glanced down the course, took back the club a dozen inches, carried it ahead, and rested for the fraction of a second; then, accurate, machine-like to the tiniest detail, swung up, hit down, and felt his body carried forward in the full, strong finish of a master drive.

"Good ball!" said Stoddard in a voice that trembled slightly. From the V—sporadic handclapping. Hargrave, the national champion, had driven two hundred and sixty yards.

Ahead of him, as he walked defiantly through the rough, the fairway bobbed with men and women who, as they chattered busily, stumbled over the irregularities of the turf. Now and then a straggler threw a look of admiration over his shoulder, and, meeting the expressionless mask of the amateur champion, insouciantly shrugged that shoulder and resumed his march.

Hargrave's caddy, dour and uncommunicative as the champion himself, stalked abreast, the clubs rattling synchronously to his stride. Hargrave was studying the contour of the land in front; he glowered at the marshals who had suffered the gallery to break formation and overflow the course; and he was tempted to ask his caddy how, when the entire middle distance was blocked by gabbling spectators, the Golf Association thought a finalist could judge the hole. But he denied himself the question; it was seven years since he had condescended to complain of, or to criticize, the conditions of any tournament. Nevertheless he was annoyed; he was certain that the ground sloped off just where his second shot should properly be placed; his memory was positive. Blindfold, he could have aimed correctly to a surveyor's minute.

Still, he was impatient, irritated. He wanted to verify his scheme of play. He wanted to do it instantly. The muscles of his neck twitched spasmodically; and without warning, even to himself, his canker flared into red hate. His eyes flashed venomously; and when it seemed that unless that crowd dispersed, and gave him room, his nerves would shatter in a burst of rage, he saw the marshals tautening their lines, the gallery billowing out into a wide and spacious funnel, and felt the caddy's timid touch upon his sleeve.

"Look out, Mr. Hargrave! Stoddard's away!"

The champion halted, and without a glance toward Stoddard, stared at his own ball. It was an excellent lie; he nodded imperceptibly and took a brassie which the caddy, without instructions, placed in his outstretched hand. His fingers closed around the smooth-worn grip; he tested the spring of the shaft, and focused his whole attention upon the ball. He strove to summon that mental cinema of Hargrave, cool, collected, playing a full brassie to the green. But Stoddard again intruded.

In the morning round, Hargrave had won the first three holes in a row, and he had held the advantage, and brought in his man three down. He had made a seventy-four, one over par, and Stoddard had scored a creditable seventy-eight—doubly creditable in view of his ragged getaway. And in the afternoon Hargrave had won the first two holes, and stood five up with sixteen more to play, when Stoddard had begun an unexpected spurt. Hargrave scowled at the toe of his brassie as he recounted errors which, if they could have been eliminated from his total, would have erased five needless strokes, and ended the match long since. Cruelly, three of those errors were on successive holes. On the fifteenth he had missed a simple putt for the win; on the sixteenth he had over-approached and thrown away a half; on the seventeenth he had topped an iron and still accomplished a par four—but Stoddard had made a three.

The champion felt his heart flutter and his knees yield a trifle as he reflected what havoc one more ineffectual shot would work upon his nerves. He was surely, steadily slipping, and he knew it. The bulk of his vitality was gone; and he was drawing heavily upon his light reserve. He realized, not in cowardice but in truth and in fact, that if the match should go to an extra hole, he, and not Stoddard would be the loser. His customary command of his muscles was satisfactory, but his control of his nerves was waning. He was overgolfed; overstrained, stale. He could bear the strain of this hole, but that was all. His stamina had touched its limit; his fortitude could stand no more. He could gage it to a nicety; he had a debilitating intuition which told him that if he had to drive again from the first tee, he should founder wretchedly; and he believed this message from his soul, because he had never before received it.

If Stoddard won the eighteenth, it would be the fourth consecutive godsend for Stoddard, and Stoddard's game was improving, not deteriorating; he had moral courage behind him, he had the savage exhilaration of metamorphosing a forlorn chance into a delirious certainty, he had the stimulus and the impetus of his grand onrush, he had the responsive gallery to cheer him on. It was inevitable that Stoddard, if he won the eighteenth, would win the next; so that the champion, who was dormie one, must have a half—he must divide this hole with Stoddard. He *must!*

The champion grew restive. It needed the supreme effort of his career to force himself to inertia, to refrain from wheeling swiftly, and shrieking aloud to Stoddard, to demand why he didn't *play!* Was the boy asleep? Dead? Dreaming? Had he succumbed to paralysis? Was he gloating over his triumph? Hargrave wet his lips, and swallowed dustily.

A tremor ran through his limbs, and his wrists tightened in palsied fear. His eyes pained him; they reminded him of a doll's eyes, turning inward; he was aware that his face was drawn. He wondered stupidly whether the spoon would be safer than the brassie. He liked the spoon—but was the cleek surer yet? He caught his breath in a gasp, and at the same moment his spine was chilled in a paroxysm of futile terror. He essayed once more to swallow and thought that he was strangling. His soul cried heart-breakingly out to Stoddard: "Shoot! For God's sake, *shoot!*"

The tension snapped. A roar of jubilance went up from twice a thousand throats, a roar which, dying momentarily, swelled up in glory, and hung, and splintered into a thousand reverberations against the hills. Hargrave shivered and cleared his throat. For the life of him he couldn't maintain his principles; his nature revolted; and jerking his head towards the north, he was gazing at a tiny fleck of white ten feet to the side of the terrace, which was the eighteenth green. Stoddard was hole high in two! A lucky ricochet from the stones of the brook! Five hundred and twenty yards in two! Hargrave went sickly white, and looked despairingly at his caddy.

He needed a half, and Stoddard was hole high. There was an outside possibility, then, that Stoddard could make a four—one under par. And Hargrave was nearly three hundred yards away. Could he, too, make a four—for the half?

The champion, with two alternatives looming bold before him, shuddered in exquisite incertitude. He could attempt a heroic stroke with the brassie, sacrificing accuracy for distance, or he could play his normal shot, which was practically sure to clear the brook, but still would leave him at a critical disadvantage. In the latter instance he could guarantee himself a five, but already Stoddard was assured of four. And that four, if he achieved it, meant a squared match for Stoddard, and a resultant victory. Hargrave could halve the hole, only if Stoddard blundered; and for an hour and more Stoddard's golf had been flawless. There was no blunder in him.

But if Hargrave should risk his own crown on a mighty endeavor to equal Stoddard's titanic brassie shot, he would have the odds of war alarmingly against him. The trajectory must be perfect to be a ruled, undeviating line. The ball must either fall short of the brook by ten yards, or clear it by ten, and bounding neither to the left, among the trees, nor to the right, among the sandpits, surmount the grade. An unfortunate angle of consequence, a mere rub of the green, would be doubly fatal. The ball might even be unplayable. There would yet be a hazardous last chance for a five; but again, there was no reason to expect that Stoddard would need so many. Stoddard had been deadly, uncannily deadly, on those short, running approaches. Stoddard would make his four, and Hargrave knew it. He closed and unclosed his fingers around the grip of his brassie. A rim of ice, pressing inward, surrounded his heart. His brain was delicately clouded, as though he had just awakened out of the slumber of exhaustion, and looked upon the world without comprehending it, sensed it without perceiving its physiology. He passed a hand over his forehead, and found it damp with perspiration.

A year ago he had promised himself that, as champion, he would withdraw from competition. It was his dream to retire at the height of his prowess, to go down in the history of games as one of that rare company who have known when to file their resignations. Indeed, as late as February he had vowed not to defend his title this year. But when he had once sniffed the intoxicant atmosphere of a club grill, and after he had proved his strength in a practice round or two, he had diffidently entered for the Atlantic City tournament, and won it. Infectiously, the old ardor had throbbed in his veins. He was keenly alive to his dominant tenure; his nostrils dilated, his jaws set.

He would add one consummating honor to those that had gone before; he would take his third successive championship with him into exile. And so at Deal, at Apawamis, at Sleepy Hollow and at Garden City, at Montclair and Wykagyl and Piping Rock, he had groomed himself, thoroughly and deliberately, for the fitting climax. The metropolitan supremacy was his for the fifth occasion; he had finished fourth in the Metropolitan Open, third in the National Open. In the handicap list of the great central association he stood proudly aloof at scratch. He was invincible.

And now, with six days of irreproachable golf behind him; with the greatest prize of a lifetime shining in his very eyes, he looked at a distant red flag, drooping on its staff, and looked at a ball lying in tempting prominence on the fairway, and felt his chin quiver in the excess of his passionate longing, and felt a white-hot band searing his forehead, and penetrating deep.

He kept the brassie. And as he took his stance, and struggled to centralize his wishes upon the problem of combining vast length with absolute precision, his mind became so acutely receptive to impression, so marvelously subjective, that he found himself repeating over and over to himself the series of simple maxims he had learned painfully by heart when he was a novice, striving to break through the dread barrier which divides those who play over and those who play under a hundred strokes for the single round.

He experienced, for the first time in years, a subtle premonition of ineptitude. He was again a tyro, whose margin of error was ninety-five per cent. Where was the ball going? It was incredibly small, that sphere in the fairway; it was incredible that he should smite it so truly and so forcibly that it would fly even so far as a welcome furlong. Suppose he, a champion, with a champion's record, should slice, or pull, or top—or miss the ball completely?

Hargrave's teeth came grindingly together. His eyes dulled and contracted. He took the club back for a scant foot, raised it, took it forward, past the ball in the line of the hole, brought it to its original position, pressed it gently into the velvet turf with infinitesimal exertion of the left wrist, and swung. Wrists, forearms, shoulders and hips—his whole anatomy coordinated in that terrible assault. The click of the wood against the ball hadn't yet reached his ears when he knew, with exultation so stupendous that it nauseated him, that the shot had come off. His eager eyes picked up the ball in flight; and as he paused momentarily at the finish of his terrific drive, he was filled with a soft and yet an incongruously fierce content. Again he had foiled the gallery, and

Stoddard! He saw the ball drop, across the brook; saw it leap prodigiously high in the air, and fall again, and bound, and roll, slower and slower, and cease to roll—a good club's length from the lower pit, twenty yards from the green.

The champion and the challenger were on even terms.

Unlike the average man of gregarious instincts, Hargrave never sought proximity to his opponent during a match. His procedure was exactly as though, instead of playing against a flesh-and-blood antagonist, he were going around alone. He went his independent way, kept his peace, and entertained no thought of conversation or courtesy. If fortuitously he had to walk a course parallel to that of his opponent, and even if the interval between them were a matter of a scant rod or so, the champion was invariably thin-lipped, reflective, incommunicative.

He observed with a little flicker of amusement, that Stoddard was eying him sidewise, and he felt that Stoddard was not a little affected by that enormous brassie, as well as by Hargrave's outward indifference toward it. Hargrave, however, appraised his own flinty exterior as one of his championship assets. He never praised the other man; and if the other man chose to burst into fervid eulogy, the champion's manner was so arctic, so repelling, that not infrequently he gained a point on the very next shot through the adversary's dazed inefficiency and even one stroke in match play is worth saving.

He knew that he was unpopular, he knew that he was affirmatively disliked; he knew that the public, the good-natured and friendly public, yearned for Stoddard's triumph rather as a vindication of gentility than as a proof of might. But as he observed that Stoddard showed premonitory symptoms of increased nervousness, and that Stoddard was impelled to speak, and yet held his tongue to save himself from sure rebuff, the champion's breast expanded with golden hope.

Stoddard, after all, was a mere boy: a veteran golfer—yes, but immature in the mentality of golf. And Hargrave sometimes won his matches, especially from younger men, in the locker-room before he put on his shoes. If Stoddard congratulated him now, he could send Stoddard into catastrophe with one glowing sentence. But Stoddard didn't speak.

In addition to his other reasons, he was anxious to beat Stoddard because of his very youth. It had galled Hargrave to be called, by the luck of the draw, to meet five of the youngest experts of the country in this tournament; it had galled him, not because he was loath to win from younger men, but because the public naturally discounted his victories over them.

On Tuesday he had overwhelmed a Western prodigy, a freckled schoolboy who had blushingly donned full-length trousers for this great event. On Wednesday he had won, three up and two to go, from a Harvard freshman, a clubbable youngster who had capitulated to Hargrave primarily because his optimism had slowly been destroyed by Hargrave's rude acerbity. On Thursday he had met, and easily defeated, the junior champion of Westchester—defeated him by the psychology of the locker-room, by knocking him off balance at the outset, much as the gladiator Corbett once shook the poise of the gladiator Sullivan. In the semi-finals yesterday he had beaten his man—brow-beaten him—by diligently creating an atmosphere of such electric stress that a too-little-hardened Southron, sensitive as a girl, had gone to pieces at the ninth, surrendered at the twenty-seventh hole.

And Hargrave, whose bitterness toward the golfing world had progressed arithmetically through these earlier rounds, had come up to the finals in a mood of acid which, in the true analysis, was a form of specious envy and regret. He realized that in comparison with any of the men he had removed from brackets, he was unattractive, aged, cynical, repugnant. He envied youth—but how could he regain his own? How could he crystallize at fifty-five the secret ambitions of a boy too young to vote? He couldn't stand before this fashionable gallery and, indicating Stoddard, cry out to them: "But I *want* to be like him! I *want* to be! And it's too late! It's too late!"

A great wave of self-glorification swept over him, and left him calmer, more pragmatical. After all, he was Hargrave, phenomenon of the links, the man who, beginning serious golf at the age of forty, unaided by professional tutoring, unschooled by previous experience in the realm of sport, had wrenched three amateur championships and unnumbered lesser prizes from keen fields. He was the unconquerable Hargrave; the man who had victoriously invaded France, England, Austria, Canada, Scotland. He had averaged below seventy-five for the previous years on all courses and at all seasons. He had been six down with nine to play in the finals of the English Amateur, and come romping home to triumph, four under par. It was said of him that he was never beaten until the last putt on the last hole. Better than that, it was true.

By this time the gallery was massed rows deep around the eighteenth green. Hargrave crossed the little footbridge over the brook and permitted the vestige of a smile to temper the severity of his face. They hoped to see him lose, did they? Well, he had often disappointed them in the past; he could disappoint them now! All he required was a half, and he was barely off the green in two.

But even in the vanity which somewhat relieved the strain upon him, he was conscious of a burdening weariness which wasn't solely physical. He was impatient, not only to end the hole, and the match, but also to end his tournament golf forever. He was sure now that, winner or loser, he should never enter an important contest again. His nerves were disintegrating. He was losing that essential balance without which no man, however skilful in the academics of the game, may be renowned for his examples.

Next year he should unquestionably play with less surety, less vigor. Some unknown duffer would catch him unawares and vanquish him; and after that the descent from scratch would be rapid —headlong. It had been so with the greatest golfers of old; it would be so with Hargrave. Great as he was, he wasn't immune to the calendar. But to retire as merely runner-up—that was unthinkable! To retire in favor of a slim boy whose Bachelorhood of Arts was yet a fond delusion—that was impossible! He *must* win —and on the eighteenth green, after he had holed out, he would break his putter over his knee, and he would say to the gallery— and it ought to be dramatic. . . .

He brought himself to a standstill. His heart pounded suffocatingly. A lump rose in his throat, and choked him, and his whole intellect seemed to melt into confusion and feeble horror; there was a crushing weight on his chest. A slow, insistent cacophony poured through his brain, and for an instant his universe went black. The ball, which had appeared to carry so magnificently, and roll so well, had found a bowl-shaped depression in the turf, a wicked concavity an inch and a half in depth, two in diameter; and there it lay, part in the sunlight, part nestling under the shelter of a dry leaf, a ball accursed and sinister.

Blindly, and apprehensive, the champion turned to look at Stoddard. The boy was struggling to conceal the manifestation of his hopes; the muscles of his lower face were flexed and unrelenting. Between him and the flag was level turf, untroubled by the slightest taint of trickery or unevenness. He knew, and Hargrave knew, that nothing short of superhuman skill could bring the like to Hargrave. He knew, and Hargrave knew, that at the play-off of a tie the champion was doomed. The champion had faltered on the last few holes; his game was destined to collapse as surely as Stoddard's game was destined to rise supreme. As Hargrave paused, aghast, there came a rustle and a murmur from the gallery. A clear voice—a woman's voice—said ecstatically, "Then Bobby'll *win*, won't he?"

Hargrave glared in the direction of that voice. The veil of horror had gradually dissolved, but Hargrave, as he weighed the enigma of the shot, was visited by a cold apathy which staggered him. It wasn't a phlegmatic calm which sat upon him; it was inappetency—as though he had just been roused to a sense of proportionate values.

The matter of coaxing a golf ball out of a casual depression— what significance had it? To-morrow would yet be to-morrow; with breakfast, and the newspapers, and all the immaterial details of living and breathing. Why all this pother and heartache about it? What was golf, that it should stir a man to the otherwise unprobed depths of his soul? Why should he care, why should he squander so much mental torture as could be computed by one tick of a clock, why should he tremble at this ridiculous experiment with a little white ball and a bit of iron on the end of a shaft of hickory?

For one elemental moment he was almost irresistibly impelled to pick that ball out of its lie, and dash it in the face of the gallery, hurl his clubs after it, and empty himself of the accumulated passion of fifty-five years. Sulphurous phrases crowded to his lips . . .

And then he realized that all this time he had been glaring in the direction of a woman's voice. He exhaled fully, and held his hand backwards to the caddy.

"Niblick!" said Hargrave thickly.

The distance to the hole was greater than he had fancied. The lie of the ball was worse than he had feared. His calculation intimated that he must strike hard, and stiffly, with a pronounced up-and-down swing to get at the back of the ball. The force of the extricating stroke must be considerable; the green, however, was too fast, too fine, to permit liberty in the manner of approaching it. The ball, if it were to carry the full thirty yards to the pin, couldn't possibly receive sufficient reverse power to fall dead. It must, therefore, be played to reach the nearer rim of the green, and to drift gently on to the hole.

Hargrave caught his breath. The knowledge that he distrusted himself was infinitely more demoralizing than any other factor in the personal equation; he was shocked and baffled by his own uncertainty. Through his brain ran unceasingly the first tenets of the kindergarten of golf. He didn't imagine himself playing this shot: he speculated as to how Braid, or Vardon, or Ray or Duncan would play it. He was strangely convinced that for anyone else on earth it would be the simplest of recoveries, the easiest of pitches to the green.

He glanced at his caddy, and in that glance there was hidden an appeal which bespoke genuine pathos. Hargrave wasn't merely disturbed and distressed: he was palpitatingly afraid. He was afraid to strike, and he was afraid not to strike. His mind had lost its jurisdictive functions; he felt that his thews and sinews were in process of revolt against his will. He was excruciatingly perceptive of people watching him; of Stoddard regarding him humorously.

The collective enmity of the gallery oppressed and befuddled him. He was crazily in dread that when he swung the niblick upright, some one might snatch at it and divert its orbit. His ears strained for a crashing sound from the void; his overloaded nerves expected thunder. He knew that the fall of an oak-leaf would reverberate through his aching head like an explosion of maximite and make him strike awry. His vitals seemed suddenly to slip away from his body, leaving merely a febrile husk of clammy skin to hold his heart-beats. The throbbing of the veins in his wrists was agony.

The niblick turned in his perspiring hands. He gripped more firmly, and as his wrists reacted to the weight of the club-head, he was automatic. The niblick rose, and descended, smashing down the hinder edge of the bowl-like cavity, and tearing the ball free. A spray of dust sprang up, and bits of sod and dirt. The ball shot forward, overrunning the hole by a dozen feet. Almost before it came to rest, Stoddard played carefully with a jigger, and landed ten inches from the hole.

Hargrave's sensation was that he was encompassed with walls which were closing in to stifle and crush him. That they were living walls was evident by the continuous whisper of respiration, and by the cross-motion of the sides. He was buried under the tremendous weight of thousands of personalities in conflict with his own. He tottered on the verge of hysteria. He was nervously exhausted, and yet he was upheld, and compelled to go on, to play, to putt, by nervous energy which by its very goad was unendurable. Hargrave looked at the green under his feet, and fought back a mad impulse to throw himself prone upon it, to scream at the top of his lungs, and writhe, to curse and blaspheme, and claw the grass with his nails. Each breath he drew was cousin to a sob.

He stood behind the ball to trace the line, and recognized that he was seeing neither the ball nor the hole. He couldn't see clearly the grass itself. He was stricken, as far as his environment was concerned, with utter ophthalmia. And although the boy Stoddard was outside the scope of Hargrave's vision, the champion saw Stoddard's face, as he had seen it just now, before Stoddard turned away. He despised Stoddard; unreasonably but implacably he despised him, because of the light he had seen in Stoddard's eyes. The boy wasn't a philosopher, like Hargrave: he

270

was a baby, a whining infant grasping for the moon. *He* had no sense of proportion. That expression in his eyes had convicted him. This tournament was to him the horizon of his life. It *was* his life!

Hargrave's mouth was parched and bitter. He tried to moisten his lips. Details of the green began to develop in his consciousness as in a photographic negative. He saw the zinc-lined hole twelve feet away. His eye traced an imaginary line, starting from his ball and leading, along the briefest of undulations, swerving past a tiny spot where the grass was sun-scorched, and so to the haven of the hole.

If he could sink that curling putt, nothing could deprive him of his victory. He would be down in four, and Stoddard now lay three. He would have a half—and the match by one up in thirty-six holes. He would be the Amateur Champion of the United States—and he could quit! He could quit as the only man who ever won in three successive years. And if he missed, and Stoddard took the hole in four to five, Hargrave knew that even if his legs would support him to the first tee, his arms would fall at the next trial. He doubted if sanity itself would stay with him for another hole.

The murmur of the gallery appalled him with its vehemence. The noise was as the rushing of the falls of Niagara. Hargrave stood wearily erect, and eyed that section of the crowd which was before him. He was puzzled by the excitement, the anxiety of that crowd. He was violently angered that no smile of encouragement, of good-fellowship, met his inquiring gaze. The misanthrope in him surged to the surface, and he was supercilious—just for a second!—and then that sense of impotence, of futility, of shaken poise fell upon him once more, and his throat filled.

He needed the half. He must hole this putt. He was thinking now not so much of the result of holing it as of the result of missing it. He could fancy the wretched spectacle he would make of himself on the play-off; he could fancy the explosive, tumultuous joy of the gallery; he could picture the dumb, stunned radiance of Stoddard. And Stoddard was so young. Hargrave wouldn't have minded defeat at the hands of an older man, he told himself fiercely—but at the hands of a boy! Hargrave, the man who had made more whirlwind finishes than any other two players of the game, beaten by a stripling who had come from behind!

On the sixteenth and seventeenth holes the champion had reviled himself, scourged himself, between shots. He had clenched his teeth and sworn to achieve perfection. He had persuaded himself that each of his mishaps had been due to carelessness; and he had known in his heart that each of them was due to a fault, a palpable fault of execution. On the eighteenth hole he had reverted to sincerity with himself. He was harrowed and upset, and in confessing his culpability he had removed at least the crime of over-confidence. But this was far worse! He was doubting his own judgment now: he had determined upon the line of his putt, and he was reconsidering it.

He peered again and, blinking, discovered that there were tears in his eyes. The hole seemed farther away than ever, the green less true, the bare spot more prominent, the cup smaller. He wondered dully if he hadn't better putt straight for the hole. He braced himself, and tremblingly addressed the ball with his putter. This was the shot that would take stomach! This was the end!

He had a vision of to-morrow, and the day after, and the day after that. If he missed this putt, and lost the match, how could he exonerate himself? He had no other pleasure in life, he had no other recreation, no other balm for his wasted years. If he tried again next season, he would lose in the first round. He knew it. And he might live to be seventy—or eighty—always with this gloomy pall of failure hanging over him. Another failure—another Waterloo! And this time he would be to himself the apotheosis of failure! Why—Hargrave's heart stopped beating—*he wouldn't be champion!*

With a final hum, which was somehow different from those that had preceded it, the gallery faded from his consciousness. Stoddard was as though he had never existed. Hargrave bent over the putter, and a curious echo rang not unpleasantly in his ears. He saw a white ball in the sunlight, a stretch of lawn, a zinc-lined hole in shadow. There was no longer an objective world in which

272

he lived; there were no longer men and women. He himself was not corporeal. His brain, his rationality, were lost in the abysmal gulf of nothingness. He was merely a part of geometric space; he was an atom of that hypothetical line between two points. His whole being was, for the moment, the essence of the linear standard.

In a blank detachment—for he had no recollection of having putted—he saw the ball spinning on a course to the left of the hole. A terrible agony seized him, and for the second time a black curtain shut him off from actuality. It lifted, leaving him on the brink of apoplexy, and he saw that the ball had curved correctly to the fraction of an inch, and was just dropping solidly and unerringly into the cup.

And from the morning paper:

Hargrave was dormie one. Both men drove two hundred and fifty yards straight down the course. Stoddard banged away with his brassie, and nearly got home when the ball caromed off a stone in the brook. Hargrave, playing with that marvelous rapidity which characterizes his game, wouldn't be downed, and promptly sent off a screaming brassie which found a bad lie just off the green, but after studying it fully ten seconds—twice his usual allowance—he chipped out prettily with a niblick. Stoddard ran up, dead. Hardly glancing at the line of his fifteen-footer, Hargrave confidently ran down the putt for a birdie four, and the match. Probably no man living would have played the hole under similar conditions, with such absence of nerves and such abnormal assurance. From tee to green, Hargrave barely addressed the ball at all. And certainly in the United States, if not in the world, there is no player who can compete with Hargrave when the champion happens to be in a fighting mood.

To our reporter Hargrave stated positively after the match that he will defend his title next year.

BY HOLWORTHY HALL

FROM *The Omnibus of Sport*

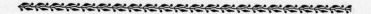

ONE DOWN

Weight distributed,
Free from strain,
Divots replaced,
Familiar terrain,
Straight left arm,
Unmoving head—
Here lies the golfer,
Cold and dead.

BY RICHARD ARMOUR

It doesn't much matter what kind of clubhead is on one end of that shiny metal shaft if a fat head is on the other.

BY ROBINSON MURRAY

FROM *Are Golfers Human?*

You can always recover from a bad drive, but there's no recovering from a bad putt. It's missing those 6-inchers that causes guys to break up their sticks.

BY JIMMY DEMARET

FROM *The Saturday Evening Post*

The three things I fear most in this game of golf are
Lightning.
Ben Hogan.
A downhill putt.

BY SAM SNEAD

A Decision by the Committee of a Golf Club in Southeast
England:

"Trousers may be worn by women golfers on the course, but
must be taken off on entering the club-house."

FROM *Golf Illustrated*

In a sense it was Li Hung-shang and not China that was fighting, and it may well have been that the majority of the Chinese
people knew nothing about the war. But in the north they knew,
of course, about it, and at Newchwang, the northernmost treaty
port of China, an old Major was considering the situation. He had
charge of the fort commanding the entrance to the Liao River.
The fort was old and dilapidated; it was only made of mud, and
its armament consisted of a few old cast-iron guns. But it was a
fort and there was war; so on his shoulders rested great responsi-
bilities; quite plainly he must pull up his socks, eschew opium

275

and keep his weather-eye lifting. Yet he hoped with earnestness that great issues would not fall on him for settlement. But luck was not his way; for on the wide mud flat which lay between his fortress and the sea, on which hitherto he had rarely seen a soul, there now appeared each evening a group of foreigners, whose actions were undoubtedly mysterious and suspicious. He watched them with his telescope, and in the morning when the place was clear, he scrutinized the little holes and larger banks which they had made and the flags that they had left behind. Then he sat down and wrote a formal letter to the Tao-tai, reporting what had happened.

He would have felt it his duty to report in any case, but doubly so in these crucial times. The foreigners had made small cylindrical holes in the ground and carefully and skilfully lined them with metal; they had dug short trenches here and there——a most suspicious fact. They were each armed with various shaped weapons, with which they propelled white projectiles for long distances. The whole proceeding was most mysterious and he could form no opinion as to what it meant. He could not say for certain that these operations were connected with the war, but he begged the Tao-tai to instruct him what to do.

On receipt of this letter, the Tao-tai sent it to the Senior Consul, with a covering despatch, referring to the war and the need for utmost caution. He concluded by saying that whatever might be the purpose of the operations on the mud flats, they must now be stopped. Would the Senior Consul please take note and the necessary action.

The Senior Consul was an Englishman. He would reply very formally and politely: . . . "What my co-nationals are doing is playing a well-known game which is played at every other port. It is usually done on grass, but as none exists here they are making the best they can of the deserted mud flat. They are merely amusing themselves; that is all."

The Senior Consul's letter was now sent to the Major with instructions from the Tao-tai for a further report by the light of the information given in it. So once more the old man took his brush in hand and wrote those upright columns of complicated characters: "I am an ignorant soldier, and this problem is beyond me. If these operations have no military significance, I have wondered whether they might not be connected with prospecting for minerals. It is the only suggestion I can make. As for the Senior Consul's so-called explanation, I have admitted that my ignorance disables me from saying what they are doing; but it is not so great as to disable me from saying, quite positively, and without a shadow of doubt about the matter, that they are not amusing themselves."

BY DANIELE VARÉ

FROM *The Last of the Empresses*

THE ORIGIN OF GOLF

Golf, besides being a royal game, is also a very ancient one. Although it cannot be determined when it was first played, there seems little doubt that it had its origin in the present geological period, golf links being, we are informed, of Pleistocene formation.

Confining ourselves to Scotland, no golfer can fail to be struck with the resemblance to a niblick of the so-called spectacle ornament of our sculptured stones.

Many antiquarians are of opinion that the game did not become popular till about the middle of the 15th century. This seems extremely probable, as in earlier and more lawless times a journey so far from home as the far-hole at St. Andrews would have been exceedingly dangerous for an unarmed man.

It is not likely that future research will unearth the discoverer of golf. Most probably a game so simple and natural in its essentials suggested itself gradually and spontaneously to the bucolic mind. A shepherd tending his sheep would often chance upon a round pebble, and, having his crook in his hand, he would strike it away; for it is as inevitable that a man with a stick in his hand should aim a blow at any loose object lying in his path as that he should breathe.

On pastures green this led to nothing: but once on a time (probably) a shepherd, feeding his sheep on a links—perhaps those of St. Andrews—rolled one of these stones into a rabbit scrape. "Marry," he quoth, "I could not do that if I tried"—a thought (so instinctive is ambition) which nerved him to the attempt. But man cannot long persevere alone in any arduous undertaking, so our shepherd hailed another, who was hard by, to witness his endeavour. "Forsooth, that is easy," said the friend, and trying failed. They now searched in the gorse for as round stones as possible, and, to their surprise, each found an old golf ball, which, as the reader knows, are to be found there in considerable quantity even to this day. Having deepened the rabbit scrape so that the balls might not jump out of it, they set themselves to practising putting. The stronger but less skilful shepherd, finding himself worsted at this amusement, protested that it was a fairer test of skill to play for the hole from a considerable distance. This being arranged, the game was found to be much more varied and interesting. They had at first called it "putty," because the immediate object was to putt or put the ball into the hole or scrape, but at the longer distance what we call driving was the chief interest, so the name was changed to "go off," or "golf." The sheep having meantime strayed, our shepherds had to go after them. This proving an exceedingly irksome interruption, they hit upon the ingenious device of making a circular course of holes, which enabled them to play and herd at the same time. The holes being now many and far apart, it became necessary to mark their whereabouts, which was easily done by means of a tag of wool from a sheep, attached to a stick, a primitive kind of flag still used on many greens almost in its original form.

Since these early days the essentials of the game have altered but little. Even the stymie must have been of early invention. It would naturally occur as a quibble to a golfer who was having the worst of the match, and the adversary, in the confidence of three or four up, would not strenuously oppose it.

That golf was taken up with keen interest by the Scottish people from an early day is evidenced by laws directed against those who preferred it to archery and church-going. This state of feeling has changed but little. Some historians are, however, of the opinion that during the seventeenth century golf lost some of its popularity. We know that the great Montrose was at one time devoted to it, and that he gave it up for what would now be considered the inferior sport of Covenanter-hunting. It is also an historical fact that Charles I. actually stopped in the middle of a game on Leith Links, because, forsooth, he learned that a rebellion had broken out in Ireland. Some, however, are of the opinion that he acted on this occasion with his usual cunning—that at the time the news arrived he was being beaten, and that he hurried away to save his half crown rather than his crown. Whatever the truth may be, it is certain that any one who in the present day abandoned a game because the stakes were not sufficiently high would be considered unworthy of the name of a golfer.

BY SIR W. G. SIMPSON

FROM *The Art of Golf*

SORRY, BABY, BUT—

Spring and the golfer go hand in hand
    And there's just no room for a wife;
Her place is at home, subduing the lawn,
    Or swinging a paring knife.
For golf is a man's game, my darling,
    And woman's a nuisance, no more;
She chirps like a sparrow from tee to green
    And smiles while forgetting her score.

Now spring awaits, and I must be gone;
　　I've a date made long months ago.
My clubs are polished, my swing is grooved,
　　This year I shoot par—or below!
I can only add that where'er you look,
　　From Kamchatka to Cardiff or Fife:
Spring and the golfer go hand in hand
　　And there's really no room for a wife.

(However, I shall take you dining when we finish and if you want any little thing like a new hat, coat or car, just speak up. I may be seasonable, but I'm not unreasonable.)

BY ROBERT CROMIE

FROM *The Saturday Evening Post*

A ST. ANDREWS CARD

Bobby was now in the finals of a championship he wanted to win more than any other. His opponent was Roger Wethered. Saturday was a holiday, and people came from all parts of Scotland to see the two great golfers play the final. It was estimated the gallery was somewhere between fifteen and twenty thousand. An interesting thing happened on the first tee. As the two golfers waited for the gallery to settle, an official of the Royal and Ancient Club, standing near Jones and Wethered, opened with the following: 'Golf has been played at St. Andrews for over a hundred years. During that time every one of the greatest golfers in the world has at some time or other played the Old Course. Wonderful scores have been made, but no one had been able to play a round without having at least one five on his card.' I was standing

280

very close to Bobby, and I saw his mouth tighten a bit, but he never said a word. The pair were called to the tee and they drove off.

Wethered and Jones were in great fettle as the fours were rattled off without a hitch. Bobby picked up a three on one of the early holes, which was offset by a four on the par three eighth, and at the end of nine holes the match, the final of the British amateur championship, was square, with each out in 35. Then Jones put on the pressure. With a string of fours, broken by a couple of threes, Bobby stood on the seventeenth tee five up, with two holes left of the morning round. The drives to the seventeenth were letter-perfect. Wethered had to take a chance and, playing a spoon, he hit a grand shot that landed and stayed on the narrow putting surface. Bobby also used a spoon, but he had a little too much draw on his shot, and it curled off toward the end of its flight and caught the tricky little trap on the edge of the green. There was nothing much the matter with the manner in which he played the stroke because, while trapped, Jones had the meanest sort of a shot to play. Just over the edge of the trap, the green sloped away sharply, and it was fast. He was approaching the hole at the narrowest point of the green and there was grave danger of overrunning it and going into the road. There was little sand, which made an explosion shot almost out of the question. I watched him take his swing, noticed he cut the legs from under the ball, saw it come up and barely clear the top of the bank. Then it hit on the down slope and suddenly began to twist and squirm. There was so much backswing on the ball that hit the down slope that it stopped almost instantly, and then trickled past the cup a scant two feet. What a shot! I was standing near an old St. Andrews player, and he said it was the finest shot he had ever seen. Wethered made a fine putt of eighteen feet that stopped on the edge. Bobby hurriedly took his stance and just as hurriedly hit his ball and—horrors! He missed. Missed the two-foot putt. He whaled his drive a mile up the eighteenth fairway. He was mad! The four he got won the hole, and he was five up again with eighteen holes remaining, the championship as good as won.

I crossed the street to the Grand Hotel and went to his room with him. He was wild. He looked at me with disgust, and I could not understand his attitude. 'What in the world has got into you, Bobby? You are five up,' I said. He answered, 'Did you hear what that official said on the first tee? I thought a moment. 'And I had to miss a two-foot putt to be the first man to play St. Andrews without taking a five.' I believe that incident on the first tee had whipped Bobby into an unbeatable frame of mind, and he was concentrating so intently on the fours he was making that it was responsible for the magnificent caliber of his golf.

After luncheon he went to work again. The crowd lined both sides of the fairway, and a tremendous crowd gathered in the back of the green. I have never seen anything to equal the size of that gallery, and it was possible only to see a shot now and then. I happened to be one of Bobby's marshals, along with George Von Elm, Tom Paine, and Sherwood Hirt from Atlanta, and it was all we could do to keep Jones from being stamped to death. Bobby kept adding a hole here and there, until the twelfth green was reached, and that is where the match ended. And such a demonstration! The gallery rushed madly onto the green and Bobby turned white as they surged forward. He is a great favorite, and in 1927, when he won the British open, also at St. Andrews, his victory met with such popular favor, that he was raised to the shoulders of a group and carried all over the place. He was fearful of a repetition, and he knew his limbs were in danger of being torn from his body.

As a further example of the crowd, let me say that Henry Lapham was standing on the edge of a trap not far from the green, and when the winning putt was made, Henry was rushed off his feet, and the next thing he knew he was in the bottom of the trap with many feet trampling over him. Please do not misunderstand me when I relate these incidents, as meaning the crowd was hostile. They were desirous only of paying tribute to Jones whom they admired so much. Bobby never forgot himself. He turned to me as the crowd rushed toward him, and said, 'Francis, please look after Roger.' I did the best I could under the conditions, and four mounted policemen—or maybe they were not mounted—escorted the winner back to the clubhouse.

That was the start of a record which I doubt will ever be

equaled, that of winning all four major championships in a single year, the British amateur and open and the United States open and amateur. I did not see Bobby play at Hoylake, so I know nothing of what took place there. Likewise, I did not see him win our open at Interlachen. However, when we started in to play at Merion for the amateur championship, every golfer and spectator hoped nothing would happen to spoil his record. Bobby took care of that incidental himself. The rest of us reminded me of a one-act show. We represented the chorus, or the scenery, or something, and the act was started.

BY FRANCIS OUIMET

FROM *A Game of Golf*

THE DEVIL'S ROUND

The following story, translated by Mrs. Anstruther Thomson from *Le Grand Choleur*, of M. Charles Deulin (*Contes du Roi Gambrinus*), gives a great deal of information about French and Flemish golf. As any reader will see, this ancient game represents a stage of evolution between golf and hockey. The object is to strike a ball, in as few strokes as possible, to a given point; but, after every three strokes, the opponent is allowed to *décholer*, or make one stroke back, or into a hazard. Here the element of hockey comes in. Get rid of this element, let each man hit his own ball, and, in place of striking to a point—say, the cemetery gate— let men "putt" into holes, and the Flemish game becomes golf. It is of great antiquity. Ducange, in his *Lexicon of Low Latin*, gives *Choulla*, French *choule*—"Globulus ligneus qui clava propellitur"—a wooden ball struck with a club. The head of the club was of iron (cf. *crossare*). This is borne out by a miniature in a missal of 1504, which represents peasants playing *choule* with clubs very like niblicks. Ducange quotes various MS. references of 1353, 1357, and other dates older by a century than our earliest Scotch references to golf. At present the game is played in Belgium with a strangely-shaped lofting iron and a ball of beechwood. M. Zola (*Germinal*, p. 310) represents his miners playing *chole*, or *choulle*, and says that they hit drives of more than 500 yards. Experiments made at Wimbledon with a Belgian club sent over by M. Charles Michel suggest that M. Zola has over-estimated the distance. But M. Zola and M. Deulin agree in making the players *run* after the ball. M. Henri Gaidoz adds that a similar game, called *soule*, is played in various departments of France. He refers to Laisnel de la Salle. The name *chole* may be connected with German *Kolbe*, and *golf* may be the form which this word would assume in a Celtic language. All this makes golf very old; but the question arises, Are the "holes" to which golfers play of Scotch or of Dutch origin? There are several old Flemish pictures of Golf; do any of them show players in the act of "holing out?" There is said to be such a picture at Neuchâtel.

ANDREW LANG

I

Once upon a time there lived at the hamlet of Coq, near Condé-sur-l'Escaut, a wheelwright called Roger. He was a good fellow, untiring both at his sport and at his toil, and as skilful in lofting a ball with a stroke of his club as in putting together a cartwheel. Everyone knows that the game of golf consists in driving towards a given point a ball of cherrywood with a club which has for head a sort of little iron shoe without a heel.

For my part, I do not know a more amusing game; and when the country is almost cleared of the harvest, men, women, children, everybody, drives his ball as you please, and there is nothing cheerier than to see them filing on a Sunday like a flight of starlings across potato-fields and ploughed lands.

II

Well, one Tuesday, it was a Shrove Tuesday, the wheelwright of Coq laid aside his plane, and was slipping on his blouse to go and drink his can of beer at Condé, when two strangers came in, club in hand.

"Would you put a new shaft to my club, master?" said one of them.

"What are you asking me, friends? A day like this! I wouldn't give the smallest stroke of the chisel for a brick of gold. Besides does any one play golf on Shrove Tuesday? You had much better go and see the mummers tumbling in the high street of Condé."

"We take no interest in the tumbling of mummers," replied the stranger. "We have challenged each other at golf, and we want to play it out. Come, you won't refuse to help us, you who are said to be one of the finest players of the country?"

"If it is a match, that is different," said Roger.

He turned up his sleeves, hooked on his apron, and in the twinkling of an eye had adjusted the shaft.

"How much do I owe you?" asked the unknown, drawing out his purse.

"Nothing at all, faith; it is not worth while."

The stranger insisted, but in vain.

III

"You are too honest, i' faith," said he to the wheelwright, "for me to be in your debt. I will grant you the fulfillment of three wishes."

"Don't forget to wish what is *best*," added his companion.

At these words the wheelwright smiled incredulously.

"Are you not a couple of the loafers of Capelette?" he asked, with a wink.

The idlers of the crossways of Capelette were considered the wildest wags in Condé.

"Whom do you take us for?" replied the unknown in a tone of severity, and with his club he touched an axle, made of iron, which instantly changed into one of pure silver.

"Who are you, then," cried Roger, "that your word is as good as ready money?"

"I am St. Peter, and my companion is St. Anthony, the patron of golfers."

"Take the trouble to walk in, gentlemen," said the wheelwright of Coq; and he ushered the two saints into the back parlor. He offered them chairs, and went to draw a jug of beer in the cellar. They clinked their glasses together, and after each had lit his pipe—

"Since you are so good, sir saints," said Roger, "as to grant me three wishes, know that for a long while I have desired three things. I wish, first of all, that whoever seats himself upon the elm-trunk at my door may not be able to rise without my permission. I like company, and it bores me to be always alone."

St. Peter shook his head, and St. Anthony nudged his client.

IV

"When I play a game of cards, on Sunday evening, at the 'Fighting Cock,'" continued the wheelwright, "it is no sooner nine o'clock than the garde-champêtre comes to chuck us out. I desire that whoever shall have his feet on my leathern apron cannot be driven from the place where I shall have spread it."

St. Peter shook his head, and St. Anthony, with a solemn air, repeated—

"Don't forget what is *best*."

"What is *best*," replied the wheelwright of Coq nobly, "is to be the first golfer in the world. Every time I find my master at golf it turns my blood as black as the inside of the chimney. So I want a club that will carry the ball as high as the belfry of Condé, and will infallibly win me my match."

"So be it," said St. Peter.

"You would have done better," said St. Anthony, "to have asked for your eternal salvation."

"Bah!" replied the other. "I have plenty of time to think of that; I am not yet greasing my boots for the long journey."

The two saints went out, and Roger followed them, curious to be present at such a rare game; but suddenly, near the Chapel of St. Anthony, they disappeared.

The wheelwright then went to see the mummers tumbling in the high street of Condé.

When he returned, towards midnight, he found at the corner of his door the desired club. To his great surprise it was only a bad little iron head attached to a wretched worn-out shaft. Nevertheless he took the gift of St. Peter and put it carefully away.

V

Next morning the Condéens scattered in crowds over the country, to play golf, eat red herrings, and drink beer, so as to scatter the fumes of wine from their heads, and to revive after the fatigues of the Carnival. The wheelwright of Coq came, too, with his miserable club, and made such fine strokes that all the players left their games to see him play. The following Sunday he proved still more expert; little by little his fame spread through the land. From ten leagues round the most skilful players hastened to come and be beaten, and it was then that he was named the Great Golfer.

He passed the whole Sunday in golfing, and in the evening he rested himself by playing a game of matrimony at the "Fighting Cock." He spread his apron under the feet of the players, and the devil himself could not have put them out of the tavern, much less the rural policeman. On Monday morning, he stopped the pilgrims who were going to worship at Notre Dame de Bon Secours; he induced them to rest themselves upon his *causeuse,* and did not let them go before he had confessed them well.

In short, he led the most agreeable life that a good Fleming can imagine, and only regretted one thing—namely, that he had not wished it might last forever.

VI

Well, it happened one day that the strongest player of Mons, who was called Paternostre, was found dead on the edge of a bunker. His head was broken, and near him was his niblick, red with blood.

They could not tell who had done this business, and as Paternostre often said that at golf he neither feared man nor devil, it occurred to them that he had challenged Mynheer van Belzébuth, and that as a punishment for this he had knocked him on the head. Mynheer van Belzébuth is, as every one knows, the greatest gamester that there is upon or under the earth, but the game he particularly affects is golf. When he goes his round in Flanders one always meets him, club in hand, like a true Fleming.

The wheelwright of Coq was very fond of Paternostre, who, next to himself, was the best golfer in the country. He went to his funeral with some golfers from the hamlets of Coq, La Cigogne, and La Queue de l'Ayache.

On returning from the cemetery they went to the tavern to drink, as they say, to the memory of the dead, and there they lost themselves in talk about the noble game of golf. When they separated, in the dusk of evening—

"A good journey to you," said the Belgian players, "and may St. Anthony, the patron of golfers, preserve you from meeting the devil on the way!"

"What do I care for the devil?" replied Roger. "If he challenged me I should soon beat him!"

The companions trotted from tavern to tavern without misadventure; but the wolf-bell had long tolled for retiring in the belfry of Condé when they returned each one to his own den.

VII

As he was putting the key into the lock the wheelwright though he heard a shout of mocking laughter. He turned, and saw in the darkness a man six feet high, who again burst out laughing.

"What are you laughing at?" said he crossly.

"At what? Why, at the *aplomb* with which you boasted a little while ago that you would dare measure yourself against the devil."

"Why not, if he challenged me?"

"Very well, my master, bring your clubs. I challenge you!" said Mynheer van Belzébuth, for it was himself. Roger recognized him by a certain odor of sulphur that always hangs about his majesty.

"What shall the stake be?" he asked resolutely.

288

"Your soul?"

"Against what?"

"Whatever you please."

The wheelwright reflected.

"What have you there in your sack?"

"My spoils of the week."

"Is the soul of Paternostre among them?"

"To be sure! and those of five other golfers; dead, like him, without confession."

"I play you my soul against that of Paternostre."

"Done!"

VIII

The two adversaries repaired to the adjoining field and chose for their goal the door of the cemetery of Condé.* Belzébuth teed a ball on a frozen heap, after which he said, according to custom—

"From here, as you lie, in how many turns of three strokes will you run in?"

"In two," replied the great golfer.

And his adversary was not a little surprised, for from there to the cemetery was nearly a quarter of a league.

"But how shall we see the ball?" continued the wheelwright.

"True!" said Belzébuth.

He touched the ball with his club, and it shone suddenly in the dark like an immense glow-worm.

"Fore!" cried Roger.

He hit the ball with the head of his club, and it rose to the sky like a star going to rejoin its sisters. In three strokes it crossed three-quarters of the distance.

"That is good!" said Belzébuth, whose astonishment redoubled. "My turn to play now!"**

With one stroke of the club he drove the ball over the roofs of Coq nearly to Maison Blanche, half a league away. The blow was so violent that the iron struck fire against a pebble.

"Good St. Anthony! I am lost, unless you come to my aid," murmured the wheelwright of Coq.

* They play to points, not holes.
** After each three strokes the opponent has one hit back, or into a hazard.

He struck tremblingly, but though his arm was uncertain, the club seemed to have acquired a new vigor. At the second stroke the ball went as if of itself and hit the door of the cemetery.

"By the horns of my grandfather!" cried Belzébuth, "it shall not be said that I have been beaten by a son of that fool Adam. Give me my revenge."

"What shall we play for?"

"Your soul and that of Paternostre against the souls of two golfers."

IX

The devil played up, "pressing" furiously; his club blazed at each stroke with showers of sparks. The ball flew from Condé to Bon Secours, to Pernwelz, to Leuze. Once it spun away to Tournai, six leagues from there.

It left behind a luminous tail like a comet, and the two golfers followed, so to speak, on its track. Roger was never able to understand how he ran, or rather flew, so fast, and without fatigue.

In short, he did not lose a single game, and won the souls of the six defunct golfers. Belzébuth rolled his eyes like an angry tomcat.

"Shall we go on?" said the wheelwright of Coq.

"No," replied the other; "they expect me at the Witches' Sabbath on the hill of Copiémont.

"That brigand," said he aside, "is capable of filching all my game."

And he vanished.

Returned home, the Great Golfer shut up his souls in a sack and went to bed, enchanted to have beaten Mynheer van Belzébuth.

X

Two years after, the wheelwright of Coq received a visit which he little expected. An old man, tall, thin, and yellow, came into his workshop carrying a scythe on his shoulder.

"Are you bringing me your scythe to haft anew, master?"

"No, faith, *my* scythe is never unhafted."

"Then how can I serve you?"

"By following me: your hour is come."

"The devil!" said the great golfer, "could you not wait a little till I have finished this wheel?"

"Be it so! I have done hard work to-day, and I have well earned a smoke."

"In that case, master, sit down there on the *causeuse*. I have at your service some famous tobacco at seven petards the pound."

"That's good, faith; make haste."

And Death lit his pipe and seated himself at the door on the elm-trunk.

Laughing in his sleeve, the wheelwright of Coq returned to his work. At the end of a quarter of an hour Death called to him—

"Ho! faith, will you soon have finished?"

The wheelwright turned a deaf ear and went on planing, singing—

> "*Attendez-moi sur l'orme;*
> *Vous m'attendrez longtemps.*"

"I don't think he hears me," said Death. "Ho! friend, are you ready?"

> "*Va-t-en-voir s'ils viennent, Jean,*
> *Va-t-en voir s'ils viennent,*"

replied the singer.

"Would the brute laugh at me?" said Death to himself.

And he tried to rise.

To his great surprise he could not detach himself from the *causeuse*. He then understood he was the sport of a superior power.

"Let me see," he said to Roger. "What will you take to let me go? Do you wish me to prolong your life ten years?"

> "*J'ai de bon tabac dans ma tabatière,*"

sang the great golfer.

"Will you take twenty years?"

> *"Il pleut, il pleut, bergère;*
> *Rentre tes blancs moutons."*

"Will you take fifty, wheelwright? —may the devil admire you!"

The wheelwright of Coq intoned—

> *"Bon voyage, cher Dumollet,*
> *A Saint-Malo débarquez sans naufrage."*

In the meanwhile the clock of Condé had just struck four, and the boys were coming out of school. The sight of this great dry heron of a creature who struggled on the *causeuse* like a devil in a holy water-pot, surprised and soon delighted them.

Never suspecting that when seated at the door of the old, Death watches the young, they thought it funny to put out their tongues at him, singing in chorus:—

> *"Bon voyage, cher Dumollet,*
> *A Saint-Malo débarquez sans naufrage."*

"Will you take a hundred years?" yelled Death.

"Hein? How? What? Were you not speaking of an extension of a hundred years? I accept with all my heart, master; but let us understand: I am not such a fool as to ask for the lengthening of my old age."

"Then what do you want?"

"From old age I only ask the experience which it gives by degrees. 'Si jeunesse savait, si vieillesse pouvait!' says the proverb. I wish to preserve for a hundred years the strength of a young man, and to acquire the experience of an old one."

"So be it," said Death; "I shall return this day a hundred years."

> *"Bon voyage, cher Dumollet,*
> *A Saint-Malo débarquez sans naufrage."*

XI

The great golfer began a new life. At first he enjoyed perfect happiness, which was increased by the certainty of its not ending for a hundred years. Thanks to his experience, he so well understood the management of his affairs that he could leave his mallet and shut up shop.

He experienced, nevertheless, an annoyance he had not foreseen. His wonderful skill at golf ended by frightening the players whom he had at first delighted, and was the cause of his never finding anyone who would play against him.

He therefore quitted the canton and set out on his travels over French Flanders, Belgium, and all the greens where the noble game is held in honor. At the end of twenty years he returned to Coq to be admired by a new generation of golfers, after which he departed to return twenty years later.

Alas! in spite of its apparent charm, this existence before long became a burden to him. Besides that, it bored him to win on every occasion; he was tired of passing like the Wandering Jew through generations, and of seeing the sons, grandsons, and great-grandsons of his friends grow old and die out. He was constantly reduced to making new friendships which were undone by the age or death of his fellows; all changed around him, he only did not change.

He grew impatient of this eternal youthfulness, which condemned him to taste the same pleasures forever, and he sometimes longed to know the calmer joys of old age. One day he caught himself at his looking-glass, examining whether his hair had not begun to grow white; nothing seemed so beautiful to him now as the snow on the forehead of the old.

XII

In addition to this, experience soon made him so wise that he was no longer amused at anything. If sometimes in the tavern he had a fancy for making use of his apron to pass the night at cards: "What is the good of this excess?" whispered experience; "it is not sufficient to be unable to shorten one's days, one must also avoid making one's self ill."

He reached the point of refusing himself the pleasure of drinking his pint and smoking his pipe. Why, indeed, plunge into dissipations which enervate the body and dull the brain?

The wretch went further, and gave up golf! Experience convinced him that the game is a dangerous one, which overheats one and is eminently adapted to produce colds, catarrhs, rheumatism, and inflammation of the lungs.

Besides, what is the use, and what great glory is it to be reputed the first golfer in the world?

Of what use is glory itself? A vain hope, vain as the smoke of a pipe.

When experience had thus bereft him one by one of his delusions, the unhappy golfer became mortally weary. He saw that he had deceived himself, that delusion has its price, and that the greatest charm of youth is perhaps its inexperience.

He thus arrived at the term agreed on in the contract, and as he had not had a paradise here below, he sought through his hardly-acquired wisdom a clever way of conquering one above.

XIII

Death found him at Coq at work in his shop. Experience had at least taught him that work is the most lasting of pleasures.

"Are you ready?" said Death.

"I am."

He took his club, put a score of balls in his pocket, threw his sack over his shoulder, and buckled his gaiters without taking off his apron.

"What do you want your club for?"

"Why, to golf in paradise with my patron St. Anthony."

"Do you fancy, then, that I am going to conduct you to paradise?"

"You must, as I have half a dozen souls to carry there that I once saved from the clutches of Belzébuth."

"Better have saved your own. *En route, cher Dumollet!*"

The great golfer saw that the old reaper bore him a grudge and that he was going to conduct him to the paradise of the lost.

Indeed, a quarter of an hour later the two travelers knocked at the gate of hell.

"Toc, toc!"

"Who is there?"

"The wheelwright of Coq," said the great golfer.

"Don't open the door," cried Belzébuth; "that rascal wins at every turn; he is capable of depopulating my empire."

Roger laughed in his sleeve.

"Oh! you are not saved," said Death. "I am going to take you where you won't be cold either."

Quicker than a beggar would have emptied a poor's box they were in purgatory.

"Toc, toc!"

"Who is there?"

"The wheelwright of Coq," said the great golfer.

"But he is in a state of mortal sin," cried the angel on duty. "Take him away from here—he can't come in."

"I cannot, all the same, let him linger between heaven and earth," said Death; "I shall shunt him back to Coq."

"Where they will take me for a ghost. Thank you! is there not still paradise?"

XIV

They were there at the end of a short hour.

"Toc, toc!"

"Who is there?"

"The wheelwright of Coq," said the great golfer.

"Ah! my lad," said St. Peter half opening the door, "I am really grieved. St. Anthony told you long ago you had better ask for the salvation of your soul."

"That is true, St. Peter," replied Roger with a sheepish air. "And how is he, that blessed St. Anthony? Could I not come in for one moment to return the visit he once paid me?"

"Why, here he comes," said St. Peter, throwing the door wide open.

In the twinkling of an eye the sly golfer had flung himself into paradise, unhooked his apron, let it fall to the ground, and seated himself down on it.

"Good morning, St. Anthony," said he with a fine salute. "You see I had plenty of time to think of paradise, for here we are!"

"What! *You* here!" cried St. Anthony.

"Yes, I and my company," replied Roger, opening his sack and scattering on the carpet the souls of six golfers.

"Will you have the goodness to pack right off, all of you?"

"Impossible!" said the great golfer, showing his apron.

"The rogue has made game of us," said St. Anthony. "Come, St. Peter, in memory of our game of golf, let him in with his souls. Besides, he has had his purgatory on earth."

"It is not a very good precedent," murmured St. Peter.

"Bah!" replied Roger, "if we have a few good golfers in paradise, where is the harm?"

XV

Thus, after having lived long, golfed much, and drunk many cans of beer, the wheelwright of Coq called the Great Golfer was admitted to paradise; but I advise no one to copy him, for it is not quite the right way to go, and St. Peter might not always be so compliant, though great allowances must be made for golfers.

BY CHARLES DEULIN
FROM ANDREW LANG's *A Batch of Golfing Papers*

ABOUT THE AUTHORS

Notes, mostly biographical, on some of the writers and the golfers mentioned in, or contributing to, this book.

ADE, GEORGE. George Ade (1886–1944) once said: "Many smart people come from Indiana, and the smarter they are the quicker they come." But he was jesting. Ade—newspaperman, humorist, and playwright—was born in Indiana and had his own golf course at his country home, Hazelden, near Brook, Indiana, where many famous golfers came to play. "The Fable of the Caddie Who Hurt His Head While Thinking" is from *Fables in Slang*, (Herbert S. Stone and Co., Chicago and New York, 1899).

ALLEN, MEL. "The Hawk They Couldn't Kill" is from *It Takes Heart*, written by Mel Allen and Frank Graham, Jr., and published by Harper and Brothers (now Harper & Row) in 1959. Allen, a native of Alabama and former teacher at his alma mater, the University of Alabama, has achieved fame as a broadcaster—particularly of New York Yankee games.

ANONYMOUS. The poem "The Reason" is from an anthology of poetry, *Lyrics of the Links*, by Henry Litchfield West, which contains many verses whose authorship is unknown. The book was published by The Macmillan Company in 1921.

BAILEY, C. W. Bailey, author of *The Brain and Golf* (Small, Maynard and Company, Boston, 1924) is an English writer. The excerpt is from that book, and the book itself, Bailey observes, "was written in the delightful golfing village of Machrihanish."

BARNETT, TED. "Slamming Suki Sukiyuki" originally appeared in *Golf Digest*. Barnett, a San Francisco advertising man and golfing enthusiast, specializes in the more exotic aspects of the game, and other

297

pieces by him include "The Strange Story of Pieter Van Schuyler," which concerns an ape who had only one shot—a wallop of 400 yards, since he lacked depth perception—and "The Lowest Round on Record," which tells of an impossible 47.

DALEY, ARTHUR. (1904–   ) This excellent sportswriter, a native New Yorker, has conducted the Sports of the Times column in *The New York Times* since 1952. "A Remarkable Woman" is from *Sports of the Times* (E. P. Dutton, New York, 1959). Daley won the Pulitzer Prize in 1956 for his sports coverage.

DARWIN, BERNARD. One of the greatest of all golf writers (and golfing writers), Darwin was born in Downe, Kent, England, in 1876 and wrote about his favorite sport for well over fifty years, until his recent death. He was golf correspondent for *The Times* and for *Country Life,* played in the first English-Scots match and the first Walker Cup match, was captain of the Royal and Ancient Golf Club in 1934, and chairman of the Rules of Golf committee in 1947. He is represented in this anthology by selections from *A Friendly Round* (Mills and Boon, Ltd., London, 1922) and *The World that Fred Made* (Chatto and Windus, London, 1955).

BAXTER, JOHN E. "The Perfect Golfer" is from *Locker Room Ballads* (D. Appleton and Company, New York and London, 1923), a book notable as much for the superb drawings by James Montgomery Flagg as for Baxter's verses.

BEACH, REX. (1887–1949) A native of Atwood, Michigan, Beach became famous for his novels about the frozen North (*The Spoilers* is perhaps his best-known work) and, as his introduction to Alex Morrison's *A New Way to Better Golf* would indicate, also liked golf. Morrison's work, incidentally, has gone into more than a score of printings since Simon and Schuster of New York first issued it in 1932.

CANDY, W. F. *Mr. Punch on the Links* (Methuen & Co., Ltd., London, 1929) consists of a number of sparkling pieces on golf, chosen by E. V. Knox (Evoe). None, however, is cleverer than W. F. Candy's title question, "Did Shakespeare Play Golf?" which he answers affirmatively.

CHATFIELD-TAYLOR, MRS. HOBART. One of the early feminine golfing enthusiasts in Chicago, Mrs. Chatfield-Taylor also wrote on the subject, as witness "The American Woman and Golf," which appeared in *Collier's* magazine for April 12, 1902.

COLLETT, GLENNA. (1903–   ) Glenna Collett was women's United States Open champion in 1922, 1923, 1924, and 1927. Her *Ladies in the Rough,* from which several excerpts have been taken, is made notable by a foreword in which Robert Tyre Jones pays high tribute to Miss Collett's accuracy with spoon and brassie (Nos. 3 and 2 woods to the younger generation of golfers.)

DAVIS, ROBERT H. (1869–1942) The author of the brief quotations comparing a golf course to an outdoor asylum (from what longer piece I do not know) came from Brownsville, Nebraska, to the New York *World* and the New York *Sun* as a columnist, writer, and editor, and also was for some time the editor of *Cosmopolitan* magazine.

DEMARET, JAMES. (1910–   ) This native Texan, once one of the most colorful adornments of the professional golfing tour, won the Masters' title at Augusta in 1940, 1947, and 1950, and also played on the Ryder Cup team. He is extremely articulate and very quotable, as this brief excerpt from a *Saturday Evening Post* article indicates.

DEULIN, CHARLES. *"Le Grand Choleur,"* by Deulin, was translated from the French by Mrs. Anstruther Thomson, and appears in *A Batch of Golfing Papers* by Andrew Lang (M. F. Mansfield, New York, 1897).

DUNNE, FINLEY PETER. (1867–1936) The creator of Mr. Dooley, a native of Chicago, made a name as a humorist some seventy years ago. "On Golf" comes from *Mr. Dooley in Peace and in War* (Small, Maynard and Company, Boston, 1898), and is one of the earliest of all American humorous pieces dealing with golf.

EATON, WALTER PRICHARD. (1878–1957) After working on newspapers in Boston and New York, and as drama critic for the *American Magazine,* Eaton taught playwriting at Yale University from 1933 to 1947. Like all sensible persons a golf enthusiast, he had a keen understanding of the game, as the excerpt from "On Giving Up Golf Forever" proves. It is from *Penguin Persons and Peppermints* (W. A. Wilde Co., Boston-Chicago, 1922).

EVANS, CHARLES (CHICK). (1890–   ) This famous Chicagoan, known wherever golf is played, won the National Open championship in 1916, was twice National Amateur champion, and has held the Western Amateur crown eight times. But he is proudest of the fact that he is the founder of the Evans' Scholars Fund, administered by the Western Golf Association, which has sent hundreds of former caddies through college. "The Mecca of Golf" is from *Ida Broke, the Humor and Philosophy of Golf* (Dutton, New York, 1929), written with Barrie Payne.

GRAHAM, FRANK, JR. (1925–   ) Son of a noted sportswriter, Graham—co-author with Mel Allen of *It Takes Heart,* from which came "The Hawk They Couldn't Kill"—has been publicity director of the Brooklyn (now Los Angeles) Dodgers, editor of *Sport* magazine, and a copyboy for the New York *Sun*, although not in that order. He also served in the Navy in the Pacific during World War II.

EVERARD, H. S. C. A British writer who was historian to the Royal and Ancient Golf Club, his advice on putting etiquette is from his *Golf in Theory and Practice* (George Bell and Sons, London, 1898).

GUEST, EDGAR. (1881–1959) For many years one of the most popular and widely syndicated versifiers in the United States, Guest was an enthusiastic golfer and a long-time member of the Detroit Golf Club, where the late Horton Smith, the Joplin Ghost, was professional. Guest was born in Birmingham, England, and began working for the Detroit *Free Press* in 1895. "The Lay of the Troubled Golfer" is from *The Passing Throng* (Reilly & Lee, Chicago, 1923).

HAGEN, WALTER. (1892–   ) Sir Walter (or The Haig), as this member of golfing royalty long has been known, won the United States Open in 1914 and 1919, the French Open in 1920, the British Open in 1922, 1924, 1928, and 1929, the United States P.G.A. title five times (in 1921 and four times in succession, 1924 through 1927), the Western Open five times, and some forty other major titles during thirty-odd years of tournament play. He was a master psychologist, a superb showman, a fashion plate, and the instrument for liberating the professional from second-class status by his refusal to go anything but first-class no matter where he was. Hagen was born in Rochester, New York, within walking distance of the Rochester Country Club, where he caddied. He now lives in Michigan. His friend Gene Sarazen has said of him: "All the professionals who have a chance to go after the big money today should say silent thanks to Walter Hagen each time they stretch a check between their fingers. It was Walter Hagen who made professional golf what it is."

HILTON, HAROLD. (1867–1942) Winner of the British Open in 1892 (the first time it was played at 72 holes) and again in 1897, four-time winner of the British Amateur, and winner—in 1911—of the U.S. Amateur, Hilton was regarded as a highly scientific golfer. Although only 5 feet 7 inches tall, he was a powerful hitter. He was the first editor of *Golf Monthly*, a post he held until 1914, and his remarks on the value of practice and the handicap of British-style sportswear are from *Modern Golf* (Macmillan, New York, 1922).

HUTCHINSON, HORACE. (1859–1932) A top-flight player for twenty years, Hutchinson won the British Amateur in 1886 and 1887 and was the first Englishman to captain the Royal and Ancient. He was a fine writer on golf, and "Advice to Beginners" is from *Hints on the Game of Golf* (William Blackwood and Sons, Edinburgh and London, 1886).

KEELER, O. B. An Atlanta newspaperman, Keeler was Robert Tyre Jones's Boswell and greatest fan, and covered virtually every major tournament Jones entered. The excerpts used are from *The Atlanta Journal* and *The Autobiography of an Average Golfer* (Greenberg, New York, 1925).

KIRKALDY, ANDRA. (1860–1934) As seems fitting for so estimable a golfer, Kirkaldy was born near St. Andrews and died in St. Andrews. The several pieces by him are from *My Fifty Years of Golf: Memories* (T. Fisher Unwin, Ltd., London, 1921). Kirkaldy served in the Black Watch in Egypt at the age of eighteen. He was a strong player, exceptionally skilled with the irons, and had a magnificent, if wry, sense of humor. Once during a match at St. Andrews a rival professional was out of sight in a bunker for so many minutes that Kirkaldy's partner remarked: "He is a long time in that bunker, what can he be doing?" Said Andra: "Ye can depend on it, he is making grand use of his time."

LARDNER, JOHN. (1912–1960) A son of the late Ring Lardner, John Lardner earned a name for himself as theater critic, sportswriter, and columnist on the New York *Herald Tribune* and *Newsweek* magazine, and served as a war correspondent for *The New Yorker*. He was the author of several books, among them *It Beats Working, White Hopes and Other Tigers, Strong Cigars and Lovely Women* and *The World of John Lardner*, from which comes the piece on Titanic Thompson.

LONGHURST, HENRY. (1909–) A British golf writer and excellent player, Longhurst captained the Cambridge University team during a golfing tour of the United States in 1930, and won the German amateur title. He is golf correspondent for the *Sunday Times*. Longhurst collaborated with Charles Graves in writing *Candid Caddies*. (Duckworth, London, 1936) from which comes the story of the Lady and the Caddie, and also wrote *Golf* (David McKay, Philadelphia, 1937), from which is taken some advice on concentration.

LEITCH, CECIL. Charlotte Cecilia Pitcairn Leitch, who wrote *Golf* (Butterworth, London, 1922), was four times British champion, five times the champion of France, and represented England in international play twelve times between 1910 and 1928. Her suggestions on self-deceiving golfers is from her book.

MANNING, REG. The author of *From Tee to Cup* (Reganson, Phoenix, 1954), from which several portions have been extracted, has been living near Phoenix since coming from Kansas City, Missouri, his birthplace, as a boy. He won the Pulitzer Prize for cartooning in 1951.

OUIMET, FRANCIS. (1893–   ) Ouimet is the man who gave the United States its golfing confidence by defeating two great British professionals, Ted Ray and Harry Vardon, in the 1913 National Open at Brookline in a playoff after a triple tie. Ouimet also won the U. S. Amateur in 1914 and 1931, was on the Walker Cup team as player or captain from 1922 through 1949, and in 1951 was named captain of the Royal and Ancient, the first non-British player to be so honored.

RICE, GRANTLAND. (1880–1954) The dean of American sports-writers and one of the most popular with his fellows, Rice was born in Murfreesboro, Tennessee, played and coached baseball at Vander-bilt, and started his long newspaper career in 1901 with the *Nashville News*. He was on the staff of the New York *Tribune* from 1914 to 1930, and wrote a syndicated column, The Sportlight, from 1930 until his death. The best known among his many books was *The Tumult and the Shouting* (1954). He is represented in *Par for the Course* by pieces from *Songs of the Stalwart* (D. Appleton & Co., New York and London, 1917), *Fifty Years of American Golf*, by H. B. Martin (Dodd, Mead, New York, 1936), *The American Golfer*, and the *Tribune*. Gene Fowler, in a memorial tribute, said: "Granny didn't preach the Sermon on the Mount. He lived it."

SARAZEN, GENE. (1902–   ) Sarazen began his golfing career as a caddie at the age of eight, still plays in Senior events, and is seen as one of the most articulate of commentators on televised golf shows. He won the United States Open title in 1922 and 1932, the P.G.A. championship in 1922, 1923, and 1933, and the Masters in 1935. His book, *Thirty Years of Championship Golf*, written in col-laboration with Herbert Warren Wind (Prentice-Hall, New York, 1950), is one of the most readable of all golf books, and from it comes his description of the 1935 Masters' triumph, complete with double eagle.

TAYLOR, JOSHUA. One of the fine English golfers of the early twentieth century, Taylor was runner-up for the British P.G.A. title in 1920 and represented England against the United States in 1921. He was a contributor to numerous golfing journals, and wrote several books, among them *The Art of Golf*, in which appears his suggestion that it is possible to carry too many clubs.

TOLLEY, CYRIL JAMES HASTINGS. (1896–   ) Winner of the Brit-ish Amateur title in 1920 and 1929, Tolley also won Welsh and French Open crowns, and has represented England in matches with the United

States, Ireland, Wales, South Africa, Sweden, and Denmark. The paragraph about prisoner golf is from *The Modern Golfer* (Knopf, New York, 1924).

TRAVERS, JEROME DUNSTAN. (1887–1951) Travers won the United States Open in 1915 and the National Amateur in 1907, 1908, 1912, and 1913. He wrote, with James R. Crowell, *The Fifth Estate* (Knopf, New York and London, 1926), and from it comes the story of Walter Travis's triumph in the 1904 British Amateur, and the tribute of the bravery of the early golfers in the days when golf was considered a "sissy" game.

VARDON, HARRY. (1870–1927) Vardon won the British Open in 1896, 1898, 1899, 1903, 1911, and 1914 and the United States Open in 1900, and lost in a play-off with Ted Ray and Francis Ouimet in 1913. "Of placid and serene disposition," says the *Golfer's Handbook*, "he endeared himself wherever he played. He was the supreme stylist, and no player ever equalled his skill in hitting full brassey shots to round about the pin. So great was his skill with this club that Vardon could depend upon hitting the ball within five yards on either side of the flag." He was buried in Totteridge Parish Churchyard in the presence of an assembly of his fellow golfers. "Concerning Caddies" is from his *The Complete Golfer* (Doubleday, Page, New York, 1914).

WODEHOUSE, PELHAM GRENVILLE. (1881–   ) Creator of the immortal Jeeves, the perfect valet, Wodehouse is still turning out the books which have made him one of the world's great funny writers. The story "Ordeal by Golf" comes from *Golf Without Tears* (Doubleday Doran, New York), one of several of his books of golfing stories.

WHITE, JACK. (1873–?). Famed as a putter, White won the British Open crown in 1904 and was among the first four finishers on three other occasions. His advice on putting is from his book, *Putting* (Country Life, London, 1921).

ZAHARIAS, MILDRED (BABE). (1915-1956) Considered by many experts the greatest woman golfer who ever lived, Mildred Didrikson won the first tournament she ever entered, and after turning professional in 1947 won two United States Open titles, four Western Open championships, and four consecutive World titles at Tam O'Shanter before being sidelined by illness. She died of cancer in Galveston. The Babe, who set three world records in the 1932 Olympic Games (the 80 meter hurdles, javelin throw, and high jump), was married to George Zaharias, the former wrestler. She was a native of Port Arthur, Texas, and the author of *Championship Golf* (A. S. Barnes, New York, 1948).

"The next best thing to playing golf is watching it played, and third on the list comes reading about it." With these words, veteran sportswriter Robert Cromie introduces this rich anthology of golfing lore— a one-of-its-kind harvest of fact and fancy, old and new, guaranteed to make even a rain-drenched June afternoon bearable.

Skillfully selected stories, firsthand reports, advice, humor, verse, and nineteenth-hole repartee are drawn from the cream of a thousand sources, American and British. These selections are designed to be savored slowly, with all the satisfaction reserved for a well-played round.

Here, for example, by the winner, is Francis Ouimet's own story, "The Open Championship of 1913," and Gene Sarazen's description of his historic double-eagle in the 1935 Masters at the Augusta National. Here, too, is Mrs. Chatfield Taylor on "The American Woman and Golf," as well as a grimmer distaff story about Mary Queen of Scots, who hooked and sliced "in the fields beside Seton" mere days after her royal consort had been blown to kingdom come.

Packed with treasures never before published in an anthology on the subject, PAR FOR THE COURSE is a delight for every golfer in your family, among your friends, and out at the clubhouse.